UNDERSTANDING THE EGYPTIAN GODS AND GODDESSES

UNDERSTANDING THE EGYPTIAN GODS AND GODDESSES

❖ MÉLUSINE DRACO ❖

PEN & SWORD
HISTORY

AN IMPRINT OF PEN & SWORD BOOKS LTD.
YORKSHIRE – PHILADELPHIA

First published in Great Britain in 2024 by
PEN AND SWORD HISTORY
An imprint of
Pen & Sword Books Ltd
Yorkshire – Philadelphia

Copyright © Mélusine Draco, 2024

ISBN 978 1 39905 538 3

The right of Mélusine Draco to be identified as Author of this work has been asserted by her in accordance with the Copyright, Designs and Patents Act 1988.

A CIP catalogue record for this book is available from the British Library.

All rights reserved. No part of this book may be reproduced or transmitted in any form or by any means, electronic or mechanical including photocopying, recording or by any information storage and retrieval system, without permission from the Publisher in writing.

Typeset in Times New Roman 10.5/13 by
SJmagic DESIGN SERVICES, India.
Printed and bound in the UK by CPI Group (UK) Ltd.

Pen & Sword Books Limited incorporates the imprints of Atlas, Archaeology, Aviation, Discovery, Family History, Fiction, History, Maritime, Military, After the Battle, Military Classics, Politics, Select, Transport, True Crime, Air World, Frontline Publishing, Leo Cooper, Remember When, Seaforth Publishing, The Praetorian Press, Wharncliffe Local History, Wharncliffe Transport, Wharncliffe True Crime and White Owl.

For a complete list of Pen & Sword titles please contact:
PEN & SWORD BOOKS LIMITED
George House, Units 12 & 13, Beevor Street, Off Pontefract Road,
Barnsley, South Yorkshire, S71 1HN, England
E-mail: enquiries@pen-and-sword.co.uk
Website: www.pen-and-sword.co.uk

or

PEN AND SWORD BOOKS
1950 Lawrence Rd, Havertown, PA 19083, USA
E-mail: uspen-and-sword@casematepublishers.com
Website: www.penandswordbooks.com

Contents

Chronology		vi
Introduction		vii
Chapter One	In the Beginning: Creation Myths	1
Chapter Two	A Magical Land	14
Chapter Three	The Imperishable Ones	32
Chapter Four	Early Cults and Divinities	43
Chapter Five	Old Kingdom Turmoil	56
Chapter Six	The Second Golden Age	67
Chapter Seven	The Unconquerable Sun	80
Chapter Eight	Thrice Great Thoth	89
Chapter Nine	Heka – Magic By Any Other Name	100
Chapter Ten	State Religion and Popular Magic	111
Chapter Eleven	Anthropomorphism and Zoomorphism	123
Chapter Twelve	Hieroglyphics – Language of the Gods	134
Chapter Thirteen	An Egyptian Bestiary	144
Chapter Fourteen	Power of the Bull and the Celestial Cow	153
Chapter Fifteen	Serpents and Scorpions	165
Chapter Sixteen	Gods of War	175
Chapter Seventeen	Offerings and Festivals	182
Chapter Eighteen	Major Celebrations	194
Sources and Bibliography		230
Acknowledgements		232

Chronology

Dates	Time Period
Pre-3100 BC	Archaic Period
3100–2600 BC	Early Dynastic Period 1st–3rd Dynasties
2600–2160 BC	Old Kingdom 4th–6th Dynasties
2160–2040 BC	First Intermediate Period 7th–10th Dynasties
2040–1700 BC	Middle Kingdom 11th–14th Dynasties
1700–1570 BC	Second Intermediate Period 15th–17th Dynasties
1570–1070 BC	New Kingdom 18th Dynasty 18th Dynasty Ramesside Period 19th–20th Dynasties
1070–600 BC	Third Intermediate Period 21st–25th Dynasties
600–332 BC	Late Period 25th–30th Dynasties 25th (Saitic) Dynasty Ptolemaic Period

Introduction

Contrary to popular belief, the modern Egyptian Mystery Tradition is not based solely on elaborate and complicated ritual. In strictly historical terms, these daily observances were carried out in the inner sanctum of the temple by the pharaoh, or the high priest acting on his behalf. Magic was used by all levels of society as a means of national and cultural preservation, but as far as the ordinary people were concerned, much of their religion was a blend of petitioning the *local* patron deity for help, and simple rites of protection or healing. Although Egyptian state magic was regarded as an exact science, with its secrets revealed only to the monarch and the highest orders of the priesthood, the homes of the common people contained small shrines dedicated to the more domestic deities, such as Hathor, Bes, and Tauret.

Using the resources at the British Museum and the Egypt Exploration Society, it was possible to put together basic introductory teaching that would be well within the grasp of any genuine seeker, whilst not compromising or trivialising authentic source material. Temple of Khem set itself apart from other modern systems of Egyptian magical traditions in that the bulk of its teaching was taken from early texts, rather than the later Greek works of the Hermetica and the dubious writings of Iamblichus. This pick-n-mix selection of multicultural deities was considered detrimental to the religious beliefs – diluting magical god-power, rather than enhancing it.

It was obvious from subsequent correspondence and conversations with a cross-section of practitioners that much of what passed for Egyptian Mysteries was a smattering of neo-Egyptian symbolism grafted onto contemporary Wiccan stock. Few were aware of the great social and religious upheavals within the 5,000-year span of its history, which gave Khem its unique pantheon of deities – or where they fitted into the scheme of things on both a mystical and magical level.

Temple of Khem explores the Egyptian Mystery Tradition from its primitive roots in Predynastic times, through the Heliopolitan and Hermopolitan cosmogonies – instead of attempting to condense a belief system that extended over five millennia. Whether drawn to the primordial forces of emerging civilisation, the mystery elements of a highly cultured people, or the 'dying god' concept of the cycle of life, the aim of the Temple of Khem was to help seekers find the path that is right for them.

> Ancient Egypt taps into the power of the mind's eye. With its soaring pyramids, sacred tombs, complex hieroglyphs, ancient temple walls, legends of exotic pharaohs, and colorful pantheon of gods, it is easy to be captivated by the landscape of a culture that richly and deeply stirs the imagination.
>
> (*Pacific Post*)

Taking a Jungian approach, here the Egyptian deities are archetypal ideas. Hence, Egyptian religion as a whole is looked at as the manifestation of various systems of the Enneads or 'companies of gods'. Myths and theological systems reveal psychic phenomena, i.e. collective and subjective ancient Egyptian perceptions of objective natural events, rather than observation of facts. Carl Jung pointed out that in all spiritual traditions, folklore, myths, and fairytales of humanity, *esoteric teachings are contents of the collective unconscious which have been perceived and changed into conscious formulae*. Archetypal ideas are the manifest, visible form of archetypes, defined as universal, primal symbols and images that derive from the collective unconscious, as proposed by Jung. They are the psychic counterpart of instinct.

But let's make no bones about it, today's Egyptian interpretation belongs to a revivalist tradition and should not claim to be anything else. Nevertheless, the system needs to be as close as it can be to the actual beliefs of ancient Egypt without falling into the trap of lumping all the gods together in one ageless pantheon... and expecting its *heka* to work!

This archetypal approach needs to be understood from the very beginning, but so too does the enormous time span of Egyptian history, which always tends to complicate matters when identifying with a particular deity or dynasty. For example, a Pre- or Early Dynastic Egyptian would probably not have a clue who Isis or Osiris were if they did not live in the particular province or *nome*, of which these were merely localised deities. Conversely, a New Kingdom priest would look upon Neith as simply a minor funerary goddess, whereas in her heyday she was the mighty hunter-warrior-creator goddess of the pre- and early eras.

A fundamental study is necessary because not everyone works magically or mystically, at the same level. Some take longer to realise that an intimate knowledge of Egyptian myth and its attendant politics *is* essential for the effective practice of magic/mysticism at a higher level of awareness. A knowledge that has to extend beyond the stereotypical deities of popular Egyptomania to embrace a wider and loftier range of supernatural beings; and to accept that the deities are *not* real 'gods' at the seeker's beck and call. This is why it becomes so important to successful magical belief to be able to differentiate between the different levels of magic, historical influence and religious emphasis that mark the subtle shifts of importance between the various paths. And to do so safely.

It may appear that this is merely massaging a system that purports to be all things to all men, but this is not the case. The original Egyptian religion *was* stellar based. Early texts refer to the stairway to heaven and the alignment of the mortuary temples situated toward the north; the direction of the circumpolar stars indicate the importance of the Imperishable Stars in the Mysteries. According to Egyptologists, the architectural changes in pyramid design reflect the shift from a stellar cult to one that was fully solar as the religious ideology changed and the newer priesthoods gained power. As each new centre became the focus of power, so the religion altered and a new set of myths were adapted to attest to the local gods' supremacy over the Older Ones.

These shifting influences on Egyptian history meant that reference texts fell roughly into two separate categories. Firstly, actual magical, religious, and mythological sources written by the early native priesthood for the Egyptian people and secondly, later accounts of magic, religion, and mythology translated by Greek and Roman historians and philosophers, who recorded information as told to them by latter-day Egyptian priests, since they were unable to read the ancient texts for themselves. And by the time of the Graeco-Roman invasions, the Egyptian priesthood were themselves extremely vague and uncertain about the Early Dynastic religion of their own country. Subsequent translations indicate that they did not really understand the rudimentary principles of the archaic religious system, the primitive stellar cult, or the nature of its symbolism.

Unfortunately, many present-day writings on the Egyptian Mystery Tradition make no attempt to unravel the tangled skeins of this magico-religious evolution. Rather, they impose some over-simplified form of eclectic order on the chaos created by the multitude of dual-purpose gods from different periods of history. There is, however, no way of simplifying this complicated tapestry because of the immense time span from Predynastic times to the Battle of Actium, which sealed the fate of the last ruling Great House of Egypt. Cleopatra, in terms of chronology, was nearer to man landing on the moon than to the building of the Great Pyramid at Giza during the Old Kingdom.

In the days of Egyptian antiquity, many of the gods were *abstract* concepts rather than the actual anthropomorphic god pictures familiar to us today. Many of the later fully morphed deities were originally theological concepts represented by a distinctive hieroglyph, very similar to the correspondences used in modern ritual magic. As the need for a controlling religion grew, so did the spiritual need for more tangible forms on which to focus the common people's devotions. The common man's mind dwelt on the concrete, not the abstract, and so the gods took on those strange but easily recognisable animal-human shapes to satisfy the religious-teaching-by-pictures demands of less scholarly folk. The images recorded in tomb paintings, bas-relief and statuary were intended to represent living forms of the gods themselves, or pharaoh as a god. There was a simple reason behind this. Egyptian life, magic and religion were inextricably intertwined; one simply could not – and did not – exist without the other. God, or a male/female/multiple concept of that god, was manifest in everything, animate and inanimate.

By the Middle Kingdom, the attributes of the major gods were subsequently extended to create a whole pantheon of relatives and helpers. For example, the concept of Ma'at as the symbolic terminology for cosmic order, and earthly truth and justice, was depicted in the *Pyramid Texts* by an ostrich feather. This concept later metamorphosed into a beautiful woman, who sat in judgement on those in the underworld; she was sometimes shown as the wife of Thoth, or the female embodiment of the god himself. In fact, the popular form of Egyptian religion, as most people know it today, is fundamentally a Greek interpretation.

The authentic Egyptian religion developed over thousands of years, with each deity assuming many forms under the influence of the many different religious movements and/or foreign invasions. Each form also developed its own positive and negative aspects, which responded in various ways to different people, and so it is now impossible to be dogmatic about how the gods of those different theologies relate and blend. It is also important to realise that the original religion was never an earth-bound concept since the priesthood explored mysticism on a *cosmic* scale: their spirituality extending to the stars and beyond. The Egyptian civilisation took over 3,000 years to fully evolve and a further 2,000 years to decay, which is why the Egyptian Mystery Tradition cannot be encapsulated into convenient modern packaging.

The study of Egyptian magic is a flexible science, in that rarely can any of the historical happenings be formally fixed with 100 per cent accuracy. On a religious, mystical and magical level, the authenticity of early translations is even more mercurial. Whichever theory one authority expounds, there will always be another who disagrees with the findings. Therefore, anyone who attempts to lay down the law over the Egyptian Mysteries can also expect howls of protest as others disagree with their teaching or working methods.

Therefore, Temple of Khem has chosen to augment its own teaching methods with a pre-determined belief system that is based on the genuine chronological history of Egypt. Neither does it make any attempt to sanitise the gods in the eyes of the seekers by offering up a squeaky-clean, holier-than-thou image of divinity. The Principal (and author of this book), Mélusine Draco, an Initiate of the Khemetic Mysteries, has been a magical and Temple of Khem spiritual

Introduction

instructor for over thirty years, and writer of several popular books on the Egyptian Mystery Tradition including *Liber Ægyptius: The Book of Egyptian Magic*; *The Egyptian Book of Days*; *The Egyptian Book of Nights*; *Thrice Great Thoth* and *Starchild* – a rediscovery of the ancient Egyptian stellar worship. Her highly individualistic teaching methods and writing draw on ancient sources, supported by academic texts and current archaeological findings.

Our approach to the Egyptian Mystery Tradition really is Egypt like you've never seen it before!

'May you enter favoured, and leave beloved.'
– Mélusine Draco, *Temple of Khem*

Chapter One

In the Beginning: Creation Myths

In the Beginning there was Nun, oldest of the ancient Egyptian gods and father of Re. His name meant 'primeval waters' and he represented the waters of chaos out of which Atum-Re began creation. Nun's qualities were boundlessness, darkness, and the turbulence of chaotic waters; these qualities were personified separately by pairs of deities. Nun, his female counterpart, Naunet, and three further pairs, together formed the Ogdoad (group of eight gods) of Hermopolis. Nevertheless, various classic creation myths also retained this image of the emergence of a Primeval Mound formed of mud churned from the chaotic waters of Nun. Since it was believed that the primeval ocean continued to surround the ordered cosmos, the creation myth was re-enacted each day as the sun god rose from the waters of chaos.

Rarely portrayed in art, Nun was also thought to continue to exist as the source of the annual flooding of the River Nile. As a curmudgeonly old chap, he was said to dwell in a cavern in the abyssal depths of the ocean. Although the Egyptians had many different creation myths, they all agreed that the universe came from the primordial waters of Nun, and many legends suggested that everything would slip back beneath these waters at the end of the world. Which may not be far from the reality... perhaps our present-day image of Nun should be those eerie pictures of the statuary lifted from the seabed at Thonis-Heracleion near Alexandria.

The Primordial Waters

Almost without exception, mythological and folkloric traditions around the ancient world were concerned with the matter of deep time and the earth's creation. While creation myths exhibited great variation and often echoed the prevailing psychology of their respective peoples, there is one critical motif that remains relatively common to a range of broadly dispersed ancient cultures from Mexico and Peru to Egypt and Sumeria: the primeval waters.

This surging, chaotic primordial 'Deep' features consistently among ancient traditions and is often referred to by contemporary folklorist beliefs as the 'cosmic ocean'. Rather than merely tabulating the widespread instances of this motif with the goal of highlighting their fundamental similarities, searching for shared meanings behind them may yield a more authentic understanding of the regular inclusion of the primeval waters within classic creation stories, twentieth-century anthropologist Walter Evans-Wentz advised students of mythology:

> To adduce parallels when studying a religion or a mythology is worth doing, in order to show the fundamental bond which unites all systems of belief in things called spiritual; but it is more important to try to understand why there should be such parallels and such a unifying principle behind them.

Where they appear in ancient creation myths, the primeval waters are often associated with chaos and disorder. In many of these myths, the act of creation becomes tantamount to setting order to chaos, or, in other words, to dividing the disordered, watery substance of pre-creation into its subsequent created forms. The Egyptians referred to this watery chaos of pre-creation as a state of unlimited potential out of which the first Primeval Mound of solid earth would eventually arise.

The primeval waters across creation myths often appear to have a twofold nature. On one hand, they signify a muddled state without the predictable patterns and cycles of the universe, the antithesis of creation and order. On the other, they represent limitless potential, the creator's blank slate for his impending creation. Researcher Michael Rappenglück, in his 2014 article in the *Mediterranean Archaeology and Archaeometry Journal*, describes the 'undifferentiated materia prima' of the waters as 'having the potentiality of creation and regeneration, but also of absorption and destruction of entities', suggesting a double nature to the watery, primeval state of the universe.

One Egyptian tradition, preserved in a papyrus from late antiquity in the Metropolitan Museum of Art (quoted by Meeks and Favard-Meeks in *Daily Life of the Egyptian Gods*), indicates that the ibis-headed god Thoth used the power of the spoken word to bring about creative processes:

> I am Thoth, master of the divine words ... I know what is concealed in the sky, inaccessible on earth, and hidden in the Primeval Ocean. I am the creator of the sky, he who is at the origin of the mountains ... I make the gods and men live.

The Primordial Mound

In Egyptian mythology of the Heliopolis theology, Heliopolis was the 'Primeval Mound', the first land to emerge at creation from the primeval waters. The primordial mound was that which arose from the primordial waters to become an important element in Egyptian religious thought and imagery – and would be the sacred space conceptualised in the practice of building the sanctuaries of temples over low mounds of pure sand. Similarly tombs and cenotaphs, such as the Osireion at Abydos, often incorporated a symbolic 'island' at their centre.

Egyptian temples were sacred places where priests served the gods... a house dedicated to one or more gods, who were believed to live within their statues in the temple's shrines. This was where cultural knowledge was stored and curated, and a major 'House of Life' was where such texts were compiled and copied. Temples were designed to reflect and maintain the universe; their decoration presenting a cross-section of the world as the Egyptians understood it. For example, the lower sections of the walls and columns were carved with plant motifs, the middle sections depict the king conducting rituals and worshipping the gods, and the ceilings covered in stars and constellations.

Without a doubt, temples were also powerful economic institutions. Their estates controlled huge amounts of land and wealth with many temple complexes resembling small towns, with the temple itself surrounded by workshops, storage areas, and living quarters for the staff. These temples continuously evolved throughout Egyptian history; developing from small structures built of organic materials to the large stone monuments that have endured to the present day, no two temples are the same but most surviving examples share a similar set of features.

The vast pylons were the monumental gates formed of two towers, joined by a central doorway symbolising the horizon, since it represents the horizon hieroglyph and often decorated with solar imagery. The outer face of the pylon was ornamented with huge flagpoles and images of the king smiting his enemies – which communicated the power of the king engaged in repelling chaotic forces away from the temple. Once through the gateway, the open court is where certain festivals and ritual activities took place and was often as far as non-priests were allowed to enter.

Between the open court and the inner sanctuary was the hypostyle hall, a roofed space filled with columns – often shaped like papyrus plants. These decorated columns were designed to resemble the mythological marshes that were said to surround the 'Mound of Creation', the first land to rise from the primordial waters at the beginning of time. The sanctuary was the darkest, most enclosed part of the temple featuring the highest floor level with the god's shrine. These architectural features protected the statue while also recreating the Mound on which the temple's deities now stood.

Some temples served primarily as houses of the gods, built and expanded over the millennia to serve their patron deities, while others were mortuary monuments built to serve the spirit of deceased kings. Within the walls of most of these sanctuaries and treasuries, offices, palaces, and schools might be found. Not only were many of the religious complexes centres of government, economy, and commerce, but also within these temples ancient science and scholarship thrived and the nature of existence itself was pondered by generations of learned priests.

In *The Complete Temples of Ancient Egypt*, we have it brought home to us that without a doubt, the temples of Egypt are among the most impressive monuments to have survived from the ancient world. As Richard H. Wilkinson observes, in these once shining cities, whose towers and gates 'pierced the sky' and whose gold and bronze-capped monuments shone 'like the sun in its rising', many of these structures still rank among the greatest architectural accomplishments of human history:

> But there is more than this. Beyond the physical stone of Egypt's temples we may still sense much of the symbolic nature of these structures, the deeper reasons for their construction. So well-fitted to their purpose were these buildings that even now, thousands of years since the chanting processions of priests were halted and the music of singers stilled, it is difficult to walk through the great courts, pillared halls and porticos of some of these structures and not sense once more something of their original life and presence.

An archaeologist in the field of Egyptology, Professor Wilkinson explains that as the interface between the divine and human spheres, the temple served as a theatre in which symbolic ritual dramas were enacted. The gods and goddesses of ancient Egypt were an integral part of the people's everyday lives and it is not surprising that there were over 1,500 of them known by name in the Egyptian pantheon according to the *World History Encyclopedia*. In these temples, the deities

> were fed, clothed and reassured that justice, order and balance were being preserved through the ritual services being performed by the pharaoh and the priests who functioned as his appointed agents. In return, the gods gave life to the land and upheld Egypt's ordained place in the cosmos. In one sense, the Egyptian temple was the source of power by which all of Egyptian society ran.

Lords of Creation

With the manifestation of the *prime* gods often came order, suggesting that the natural patterns and cycles of creation were believed to have been apportioned or maintained by a divine, creative hand. The *Pyramid Texts*, the religious texts inscribed within the 5th–8th Dynasty pyramids at Saqqara, relate that Re, by descending upon and calming the waters, 'put order in the place of chaos'.

If belief was to be accorded unity by the state, it became necessary to adopt abstract definitive terms to encompass the diversity of religious phenomena. For example, Nun, as the primordial embodiment of chaos, void, and of the cosmic ocean, was a swirling mass of energy, all primordials came from him in Egyptian mythology – he was the father of the entire Egyptian mythological family and represented the dwelling place of all that lay outside the bounds of the universe. Since he also symbolised the depths of the netherworld, he was sometimes portrayed as an austere bearded figure.

In the early days of Egyptian antiquity, many of the gods were abstract concepts rather than the actual 'god pictures' and prior to the Heliopolitan, Memphian, Hermopolitan, and Theban cosmogonies, many of the later deities were merely theological concepts represented by a distinctive hieroglyph. As the need for visualisation grew, so did the spiritual need for more tangible forms on which to focus the people's devotions. The common man's mind dwelt on the concrete, not the abstract and so the gods took on animal-human shape to satisfy the religious-teaching-by-pictures demands of less scholarly folk.

Such a use of abstract language, which could be regarded as 'clinical' in the sense of not being contaminated by the particular traditions and preconceptions of any one path, will necessarily fail to capture all the intrinsic qualities of any specific belief. It will exhaust neither the cognitive nor the emotional aspects of belief, ritual, symbolism, and institutions. This social-scientific approach enables objective comparison, analysis, and explanation, but it does not, and does not pretend to, convey the whole substance of the inner meaning or emotional appeal that a belief has for its own adherents.

Following the 'anthropomorphic evolution', the individual deities were distinguished and immediately identifiable by their different headdresses and by various attributes inherited from the original primitive animal-forms, which in many cases still surmount their heads. Paul Hamlyn writes that the divine types seem to be fixed as far as artistic representation is concerned, from the 2nd Dynasty. 'Thus art provides an element of continuity throughout three millennia, whatever the significance attributed to the gods at different periods may have been.' Many of these regionalised deities survived and found their way into the vast pictorial wealth of temple carving.

Egyptian creation myths are the ancient accounts of the creation of the world. The *Pyramid Texts*, tomb wall decorations, and writings dating back to the Old Kingdom have provided the majority of information regarding these creation myths – which also form the earliest religious compilations in history. The Egyptians had many creator gods and associated legends, and the world – or more specifically *Egypt* – was created in diverse ways according to different parts of the country. Some versions of the myth indicate spitting, others masturbation, as the act of creation. The earliest god, Re and/or Atum (both being creator/sun gods), emerged from a chaotic state of the world and gave rise to Shu (air) and Tefnut (moisture), from whose union came Geb (earth) and Nut (sky), who in turn created Osiris, Isis, Set, and Nephthys.

In all of these myths, the world was said to have emerged from an infinite, lifeless sea (Nun) when the sun rose for the first time, in a distant period known as *zp tpj* (sometimes transcribed as *zep tepi*), 'the first occasion'. Different myths attributed the creation to different gods: the set of eight primordial deities called the Ogdoad, the contemplative deity Ptah, and the mysterious, transcendent god Amun. While these differing cosmogonies competed to some extent, in other ways they were complementary, as different aspects of the Egyptian understanding of creation.

The different creation accounts were each associated with the cult of a particular god in one of the major cities of Egypt: Hermopolis, Heliopolis, Memphis, and Thebes. To some degree, these myths represent competing cosmogonies, but they also represented different aspects of the process of creation. Already these multi-faceted deities were beginning to emerge as *individuals* from behind the veil of misinformation drawn by the later Graeco-Roman historians.

Hermopolitan Cosmogony

At Hermopolis in Upper Egypt, the priesthood claimed even older antecedents for their cosmogony having the Ogdoad, or group of eight gods who created the world and ruled over what was considered to be the Golden Age. The Ogdoad comprised four frog gods and four snake goddesses, each frog being paired with one of the serpents – each pair symbolising different aspects of chaos before the creation.

Two of the gods, Amun (air) and Nun (water), originated the vision of the cosmic egg, laid by an ibis – the bird sacred to Thoth. Although the cult of Thoth was introduced later than that of the Ogdoad, it has been suggested that this was a priestly attempt to graft their own Thoth-legend onto the older version. As the waters of creation receded, the lotus blossom opened to reveal a divine child – Re, or in another account, the scarab beetle Khepri, the symbol of the sun.

It was at the end of 'The Pyramid Age' – 5th Dynasty or the beginning of the 6th Dynasty – that the old order – which had lasted so long – was finally shattered by social catastrophe. This affected the whole governing system as the different classes threw off the burden of obligations and resorted to violence, bringing about a revolutionary upheaval which destroyed customs and traditional religious practice forever. Archaeological evidence indicates that the fury of the mob spared neither temple nor royal monuments; even the archives of government buildings, and tombs were not respected. 'From the cemeteries of the great, blocks of stone were removed and used for the tombs of little men. As a result, a whole world was rent asunder...' (*Egypt*). For more than a century, social and religious values declined until they reverted to a primitive stage not seen in the Nile Valley since Predynastic times. Those remnants of the old tradition which remained after the radical upheaval were combined and modified to form a new mode of social existence in the new order but 'the soul of ancient Egypt never recovered completely from the shock of this decisive change...'

And Hermopolis never recovered its former grandeur.

Heliopolitan Cosmogony

The Theban Egyptians (and later the Greeks) were 'past masters at matching or marrying up their gods. It simply wasn't decent, they felt, for a highly respected deity to be without a mate, consort or whatever and, if progeny could be added, so much the better', wrote Murray Hope in *Practical Egyptian Magic*. This form of 'marrying up' distorted many aspects of the earlier pantheon as the power of the individual gods waxed and waned during the shifts in religious order.

According to an extract from *Egyptian Mythology*, the greatest surviving religious records at Heliopolis, the *Pyramid Texts*, only make passing references to the creation myth, indicating that basic knowledge of the origins of the Heliopolitan doctrine was assumed. Atum-Re, having made his first appearance on the Mound, which was later to be surmounted by the temple of Heliopolis, was without a mate and so he produced his son and daughter, Shu and Tefnut, by means of masturbation according to the earliest texts. Shu was god of air and giver of life, while Tefnut was goddess of moisture and the principle of world order – the original concept of *Ma'at*.

Later Atum was personified as the setting sun.

Their children, Geb and Nut, produced four (or five depending on the date of the source material) children: Osiris and Isis, Set and Nephthys, who were paired off in incestuous (but time-honoured) Egyptian fashion, and Horus the Elder. The so-called Ennead of Heliopolis became the well-established tradition in the Egyptian religious system with the same family associations being described 'in the literature of the other cult centres'. These inconsistencies may possibly be explained by the massaging of doctrine by the regional priesthoods to ensure their own localised gods fitted comfortably into the scheme of things.

In between times, however, we must take into account Anhur (Greek: Onuris), the god associated with war and hunting, whose cult was first attested in the Thinite region surrounding Abydos in Middle Egypt. Having been sent to recover the Eye of Re, which had gone off on its wanderings, Anhur was forced to intercede when the Eye became enraged at another Eye having taken its place; as a result, Re pacified it by placing it – in the shape of the *uraeus* serpent – on his forehead. According to the author, the *uraeus* was to become the effective ruler of the world, and as such was to be worn by the kings of Egypt as a symbol of their majesty and of their descent from the sun god.

Memphite Cosmogony

The original version of the Memphite cosmogony is recorded on the Shabaka Stone, now in the British Museum, which tells how Geb, the earth god and Set's father, intercedes in the great quarrel between Horus and Set. At a council of Nine Elder Gods, Set was created king of Upper Egypt and Horus the Elder, king of Lower Egypt, which was the 'Division-of-the-Two-Lands' and suggests a power-struggle between two individuals who had equal claim to the throne. The Memphite doctrine probably dates from around 3100 BC, when Menes made Memphis the capital of the newly united kingdom and the city became the religious and political centre of Egypt.

Here, it was declared that Ptah, the high god of Memphis and the master of destiny, was the creator of the world to rival the earlier Heliopolitan pantheon of Atum-Re. As Hamlyn had discovered:

> The tone of the Shabaka Stone text is polemical: it seems to take each point of the Heliopolitan beliefs in order almost to turn it upside down. This reinforces our belief that the priests of Memphis were concerned, for the glory of their own city, to deny a more widely held view of creation.

The Memphites believed him to be of greater antiquity than Atum since he had existed before both Nun and the Primeval Mound. Barbara Watterson records her view, in *Gods of Ancient Egypt*, that the Memphite version of creation is remarkable in that 'its concept of the theogony of Ptah is a highly spiritual one, unlike the grosser acts of creation' attributed to his contemporary, Atum. A point echoed by Professor W. B. Emery in *Archaic Egypt*:

> The cult of Ptah remained powerful throughout Egyptian history, particularly with the educated classes, for unlike those of other gods it was predominantly spiritual, and attained a higher level of religious thinking than that of the other more materialistic Egyptian faiths.

In the Memphite system, Atum was a subordinate of Ptah's and, under instruction from the 'cosmic architect', spat forth Shu and vomited out Tefnut.

In some references, Atum was declared to be merely the name of the Primeval Mound, not a deity created on it as the Heliopolitan father of the gods. Ptah is not only the universal and only creator of the physical world but the Divine Artificer of ethical order.

Although later considered to be divine, Imhotep was originally an earthly vizier and architect (designer of the great Step Pyramid at Sakkara) during the 3rd Dynasty; he has the unique distinction of being transformed into a god of healing some 2,000 years after his death. In classical texts he was described as 'the chief Kheri-heb priest ... the son of Ptah', although the true name of his earthly, i.e. natural father, is also recorded. Unlike the Greeks and Romans, who deified anything that moved, the Egyptians did not make a habit of elevating humans to divinity – their pharaoh already *was* the divine manifestation of the sun god.

The office of Kheri-heb involved the reading of magical texts during the performance of rituals believed to achieve supernatural results; hence the holder of the office was associated with magical knowledge and ability. Imhotep fits well with the Memphite concept of spirituality over materialism and can probably be compared with the later semi-divine prophets such as Jesus, Buddha, and Mohammed.

Theban Cosmogony

Thebes in Upper Egypt became the seat of centralised government in the New Kingdom and although its principal god was Amun, the priesthood quickly established the city as the birthplace of Osiris. Originally Osiris was a localised nature god who embodied the spirit of vegetation along similar lines to the classical representations of his father, Geb. He was 'handsome of countenance, dark-skinned and taller than all other men' and, having inherited the kingdom from his father, abolished cannibalism and teaching agricultural skills instead. He also taught his people how to produce grain and grapes for bread, wine, and beer, while introducing the justice system.

Having civilised Egypt, he travelled abroad to spread this knowledge throughout the world. As Hamlyn points out, however, the 'story bears a strong resemblance to the stories of Dionysus and Orpheus, that we may be entitled to wonder whether this is not an interpolation by Plutarch rather than the true Egyptian myth'. On his return, his brother Set, jealous of his powers, murders him; in order for her to bear a child, Isis and Thoth resurrect the body and Horus is conceived. Nevertheless, it is as the god of the dead that Osiris enjoys his greatest popularity and is usually depicted with his wife and son to form the Osirian Triad.

The popularity of Isis was so great that she finally absorbed the qualities of all the other goddesses; but originally she appears to have been a lesser divinity of the Delta, the protective goddess of Perehbet, north of Busiris, where she always 'retained a renowned temple', according to Hamlyn. Historically speaking and human nature being what it is, the Osirian family appealed to the populace at large since a guaranteed afterlife was now available to all from the Middle Kingdom onwards.

The priesthood of ancient Egypt was probably no more or less scrupulous than later cults when it came to attracting worshippers and donations to their temples. The social upheaval, which had destroyed the order and elitism of the Old Kingdom, needed to be brought back under control – and religion for the masses has always proved to have a uniting or calming effect on social unrest. The Theban priesthood had cornered the market with their own particular brand of evangelism; the propaganda machine geared into action and produced the Cult of Osiris, which Greek historians faithfully recorded for posterity as if nothing else had ever existed.

The fourth part of this family group is the sister of Isis, Osiris, and Set – Nephthys, the protectoress. According to the legend, she was married to Set but abandoned him when he murdered their brother; the parentage of Anubis is accredited to both Set and Osiris depending on the source of the text. Nephthys represents the land between desert and arable land; sometimes barren but fruitful when the Nile floods are especially high. She is an enigmatic deity and often seen as the other face of her sister, Isis.

The Thebes of Akhenaten's youth was dominated by the city god Amun and, linked with the royal sun god Re, he stood for the unseen, creative solar force. It has often been suggested that the development of Akhenaten's solar religion during the 18th Dynasty may have been an attempt to return to the idealism of the Old Kingdom, when the solar cult of Heliopolis gave pharaoh unique power. It is also a popular theory that the emergence of this new form of the solar cult – that of the visible sun disc or Aten – represented a modernised compromise that could win new adherents. Despite the more modern approach, the monotheistic pharaoh appears to have demanded a deep obeisance from those approaching him and this intensified reverence indicates that he was no longer 'one among the gods' but *the living solar divinity*. When Tutankhamen came to the throne, he restored the supremacy of Amun, together with the temples and statues of the old gods.

During the Second Intermediate Period under Hyksos rule, and again during the New Kingdom, the ancient cult of Set briefly re-emerged when Ramesses II's father, Seti I, 'the Setian', did not hesitate to proclaim himself 'the Beloved of Set'. Despite the patronage of the pharaoh, the newly resurrected cult was not strong enough to withstand the protests from the Osirian priesthood and by the 12th Dynasty, the god's statues were broken and the bas-reliefs smashed with hammers. 'Finally he was driven from the Egyptian pantheon and made a god of the unclean. Set, the ancient Lord of Upper Egypt, ended by becoming a kind of devil, enemy of all the gods' (*Egyptian Mythology*).

Following the spread of the Osirian cult across the land, Thebes remained the power centre for the Theban Triad of Amun ('the hidden one'), Mut and their son, Khons. In old Egyptian thought, he was perceived as the moving agent in the invisible breeze; as Theban influence increased, he became king of the gods and tutelary god of the empire.

The different myths have some elements in common. They all held that the world had arisen out of the lifeless waters of chaotic Nun. They also included a pyramid-shaped mound, called the *benben*, which was the first thing to emerge from these waters. These elements were likely inspired by the flooding of the Nile each year, the receding floodwaters leaving fertile soil in their wake, and the Egyptians may have equated this with the emergence of life from the primeval chaos. The imagery of the pyramidal mound derived from the highest mounds of earth emerging as the river receded.

In the ancient religion, Hapi was the personification of the annual inundation of the Nile and was the most important among numerous personifications of aspects of natural fertility. The flood deposited rich silt (fertile soil) on the river's banks, allowing the people to grow crops; he was not regarded as the god of the Nile itself but of the inundation event. His dominance increased during Egyptian history; hymns were composed in his honour, but he had no temples or formal cult except at the narrows of Jabal al-Silsila in the south, where shrines were built and offerings were cast annually into the river's rising waters. Hapi was represented as a fat man with swelling, pendulous breasts (as an indication of prosperity), dressed in a belt suitable to a marsh dweller or servant. This form, which was originally common to many personifications, became identified increasingly closely with Hapi (*Britannica*).

In the beginning, the universe only consisted of a great chaotic cosmic ocean, and the ocean itself was referred to as Nun, where in some myths, Mehet-Weret, portrayed as a cow with a sun disc between her horns, gave birth to the sun: said to have risen from the waters of creation and to have given birth to the sun god, Re. The universe was encircled by a vast mass of primordial waters, and the Benben, a pyramidal mound, emerged amid all this primal chaos. Beginning with the Middle Kingdom, Nun is described as 'the father of the gods' and depicted on temple walls throughout the duration of Egypt's long and ancient history.

Nun (or Nu) is the personification of the primordial watery abyss which existed at the time of creation and from which the creator sun god Re arose. Nu is also one of the eight deities of the Ogdoad representing ancient Chaos from which the primordial mound appeared. Nun can be seen as the first of all the gods and the creator of reality and personification of the cosmos; he is also considered the god that will destroy existence and return everything to the abyss from whence it came. The Ogdoad includes, along with Naunet and Nun, Amaunet and Amun, Hauhet and Heh, and Kauket and Kek. Like the other

Ogdoad deities, Nun did not have temples or any central focus of worship; even so, he was sometimes represented by a sacred lake, or, as at Abydos, by an underground stream.

The ancient Egyptians also envisaged the oceanic abyss of Nun as surrounding a bubble in which the sphere of life is encapsulated, representing the deepest mystery of their cosmogony.

In these ancient creation accounts, the original mound of land comes forth from the waters of Nun, the source of all that appears in a differentiated world, encompassing all aspects of divine and earthly existence. In the Ennead cosmogony, he is perceived as transcendent at the point of creation alongside Atum the creator god.

The sun was also closely associated with creation, and it was said to have first risen from the mound, as the general sun god Re, or as the god Khepri, who represented the newly risen sun. There were many versions of the sun's emergence, and it was said to have emerged directly from the mound or from a lotus flower that grew from the mound, in the form of a heron, falcon, scarab beetle, or human child. For the Egyptians, order was synonymous with Ma'at, the highly regarded concept of truth and justice, and by subduing the waters, Re established the supremacy of Ma'at. The primeval waters of chaos, although defeated, stood in opposition to Ma'at, and myths of their chaotic churnings served as a reminder of the constant threat of disorder against the established order guarded by the pharaoh.

The pantheon of Egyptian gods is a highly visual one but, as Wallis Budge pointed out, no attempt has been made in any text to describe the form and likeness of the Being, who was regarded as invisible, and no artist or sculpture ever made any representation of Him. His inscrutability, omnipresence, and omniscience are assumed, as is demonstrated by the following extract quoted in *Osiris and the Egyptian Resurrection*, Vol. I, and directed to Atum-Re.

> *Alone, without a second.*
> *One, the maker of all things,*
> *the Spirit, the hidden spirit, the make of spirits.*
> *He existed in the beginning, when nothing else was.*
> *What is he created after he came into being.*
> *Father of beginnings, eternal, infinite, ever-lasting.*
> *Hidden one, no man knoweth his form,*
> *or can search out his likeness;*
> *he is hidden to gods and men, and is a mystery to his creatures.*
> *No man knoweth how to know him;*
> *his name is a mystery and is hidden.*
> *His names are innumerable.*
> *He is the truth, he liveth on truth, he is the king of truth.*

He is life, through him man liveth; he gave life to man,
he breathed life into his nostrils.
He is the father and mother,
the fathers of fathers,
the mothers of mothers.
He begetteth, but was not begotten;
he bringeth forth, but was not brought forth;
he begat himself and gave birth to himself.
He created, but was not created, he made his own form and body.
He himself is existence; he neither increaseth nor diminished.
He made the universe,
the world, what was, what is, and what shall be.

Having taken Egyptian belief back to its creation, the board is now set for the main players of the mighty pantheon to take their places on the divine stage as they were in the beginning of our story.

Chapter Two

A Magical Land

At the start of the Predynastic Period, when our story began, Egypt was divided into provinces.

In the later Ptolemaic Period, the Greek term *nome* began to be used to refer to the forty-two traditional provinces of Egypt, which the ancient people called *sepat*. A system of division into provinces had been in existence since at least the beginning of pharaonic times. In the late 3rd Dynasty, a set of seven non-sepulchral step pyramids was erected at certain sites perhaps corresponding to proto-capitals of nomes: Zawiyet el-Mayitim, Abydos, Naqada, el-Kula, Edfu, Seila, and the island of Elephantine. The capitals of some nomes shifted over time, while the location of others remain uncertain.

For most of the Dynastic Period, there were twenty-two Upper Egyptian nomes, each governed by a nomarch and having its own symbol, usually represented in the form of a standard, which led to the provinces being described by such names as the 'hare nome' or the 'ibis nome'. The twenty Lower Egyptian nome signs are much later in date and did not incorporate standards. The reliefs in many temples and shrines include a lower register along which groups of personifications of estates or nomes processed around the temple, bearing food offerings to the cult. According to the *British Museum Dictionary of Ancient Egypt*:

> The Egyptians themselves made a clear geographical distinction between Upper Egypt, consisting of the Nile Valley from Memphis to Aswan, and Lower Egypt (or the Delta), where the Nile fans out into several tributaries in its final descent to the Mediterranean. The twenty-two *nomes*, or provinces, of Upper Egypt and the twenty *nomes* of Lower Egypt are clearly indicated, and the *nome* capitals, where known, are underlined. Each *nome* has its own symbol or standard, often incorporated animals, birds or fetishes sacred to the local deities.

The forty-two nomes with their corresponding deities have been compiled from the *British Museum Dictionary of Ancient Egypt*, *Liber Ægptius*, *Hieroglyphics: The Writings of Ancient Egypt*, Henadology, Wikipedia, and Tour Egypt.

The details of the Egyptian nomes were preserved on the exterior walls of the White Chapel of Senusret I originally built during the 12th Dynasty.

The twin-towered pylon gateways of the developed temple design are without doubt the most distinctive architectural feature of these ancient religious structures. This type of pylon seems to have developed in Old Kingdom pyramid temples and many later pylons were built with a casing around an inner core of re-used stones. Ironically, a number of temple structures that were consigned to oblivion in this manner were in fact preserved and protected from damage, the so-called White Chapel at Karnak being one of the most famous examples.

The White Chapel of Senusret I is a small, simple, but eloquent structure, built of Egyptian alabaster (calcite), most notable for its many inscriptions. Senusret I was the second king of Egypt's 12th Dynasty, and was the first monarch of the Middle Kingdom to invest in an extensive building programme. He constructed a number of temples from the Delta to as far south as Elephantine at modern Aswan, including structures at Thebes (modern Luxor).

This building project that was lost to us, but now is now found, is that little pavilion built for Senusret I's first jubilee (Sed) festival, which according to custom occurred during the king's thirtieth year as ruler. It was probably built to house the royal barque, since it is sometimes referred to as a 'barque shrine'. Popularly known as the White Chapel, it had been disassembled and used as filler in Amenhotep III's Third Pylon at Karnak during the 18th Dynasty. In 1924, the director general of the Egyptian Antiquities Service, Pierre Lacau, ordered his director of works at Karnak, Henri Chevrier, to repair this pylon, but in order to do so, the pylon had to be dismantled.

It took years to do so, because work could only be carried out when the Nile was in a low phase, due to invasive ground water. During this work, Chevrier discovered some 951 blocks that belonged to a total of eleven different structures that had been used as filler within the pylon. While many of the blocks were damaged, their reliefs were often in outstanding condition, due to the layers of mortar which had both bound them together and protected the blocks. This work progressed slowly, but methodically, and after determining the proper block orientation and placement, Chevrier was able to reconstruct almost completely the so-called 'White Chapel' of Senusret I in the Open Air Museum at Karnak, where it is considered by many to be the most elegant, as well as the oldest structure in Karnak today. Chevrier thought that the structure may have once been covered in gold foil, so it could have been all the more glorious where it first stood.

The reconstructed White Chapel also provides the earliest recorded details of the spheres of influence of the numerous deities and the symbols or standards sacred to them from the earliest times:

UPPER EGYPT (South)

Nome Name	Nome 1: Land of the arch or To Khentit: the frontier (Ta-Seti) from the first cataract of the Nile to Geel el-Silsila
Nome Symbol	Bow
White Chapel Deity	Horus
Major Deities	Khnum, Satis, Anukis, Isis, Horus the Elder, Sobek
City(s)/Temples	Abu (Greek Elephantine) (Khnum – Satet), Sunet (Greek Syene, Arabic Aswan), Isis Nubyt (Arabic Kom Ombo), Sobek with Horus
Notes	In ancient times, Upper Egypt extended from the Nile Delta (Memphis) to the first cataract. Further upstream, in what is modern Sudan, the land was later controlled by the Kingdom of Kush

Nome Name	Nome 2: Throne of Horus at Edfu
Nome Symbol	Falcon
White Chapel Deity	Horus of Behedet
Major Deities	Horus
City(s)/Temples	Djeba (Greek Apollonopolis, Arabic Edfu) – Horus
Notes	The earliest securely dated historical evidence in the region of Edfu is a rock-carving of the name of the 1st Dynasty king, Djet, in the desert to the east of the main site, as well as a necropolis of the Early Dynastic Period

Nome Name	Nome 3: The rural (Shrine) Hierakonpolis to the north of Esna
Nome Symbol	Fetish
White Chapel Deity	Nekhbet, Horus of Nekhen, Wenu (a prehistoric snake goddess)
Major Deities	Horus, Nekhbet, Khnum, Neith
City(s)/Temples	Nekheb desert valley – Hathor Shesmetet Nekheb (Greek Eleithyiaspolis, Arabic Elkab)/Nekhbet and Sobek
Notes	Important late Palaeolithic remains have also been found in the vicinity of Esna

A Magical Land

Nome Name	Nome 4: The sceptre – the Theban area
Nome Symbol	Sceptre
White Chapel Deity	Montu
Major Deities	Amun, Mut, Khons, Montu, Buchis (a sacred bull of Montu), Sobek
City(s)/Temples	Perhathor (Greek Pathyris, Arabic Gebelein) Hathor Imiotru (Arabic Rizeiqat)/Montu Djerty (Arabic Tod)/Montu Waset (Greek Thebes, Arabic Qurneh for West Bank, Luxor and Karnak for East Bank) Amun, Mut, Khons and Various Madu (Arabic Medamud) Montu
Notes	Four bull-headed statues of Montu were found at Medamud representing Montu as incarnate in the Buchis bull, conceived as ideally present simultaneously at the four cities of Thebes, Armant, Medamud, and Tod and constituting the magical defence of Thebes

Nome Name	Nome 5: The two falcons at Coptos
Nome Symbol	Two falcons
White Chapel Deity	Min of Coptos
Major Deities	Min, Seth
City(s)/Temples	Shenhur (retains name in Arabic) – Isis Gis (Greek Apollonopolis mikra, Arabic Qus)/Horus and Heqet, divine child Khons-Thoth Gebtyu (Greek Coptos, Arabic Qift)/Min and Isis Nubt (Greek Ombos, Arabic Naqada) – Seth
Notes	From the Predynastic Period onwards, Coptos has been one of the most favourable spots for human settlement in Upper Egypt

Nome Name	Nome 6: The crocodile – area of the east to west bend of the Nile
Nome Symbol	Crocodile
White Chapel Deity	Hathor of Iunet
Major Deities	Hathor
City(s)/Temples	Iunet (Greek Aphroditipolis, Arabic Dendera) – Hathor and Ihi
Notes	Ihi was the young son of Hathor and lord of the sistrum, the musical instrument which drives away evil powers

Understanding the Egyptian Gods and Goddesses

Nome Name	Nome 7: Sistrum – area around Nag Hammadi
Nome Symbol	Sistrum
White Chapel Deity	Bast
Major Deities	Bast
City(s)/Temples	Hut-Sekhem-Senusret (Arabic Hu) – Hathor and Sobek
Notes	The Gnostics were primarily an Egyptian movement, developing traditional religion in new directions and only later syncretised with the Judeo-Christian tradition; Egyptian material was already being incorporated into Judaism prior to the revolution that spawned Gnosticism

Nome Name	Nome 8: Great land – area around Abydos and Thinis
Nome Symbol	Fetish
White Chapel Deity	Khentamentiu
Major Deities	Khentamentiu, Osiris, Onuris
City(s)/Temples	Abdju (Greek Abydos, Arabic al-Arabah) – Osiris Khentamentiu
Notes	The earliest significant remains are the tombs of the named rulers of the Protodynastic and Early Dynastic periods. The earliest temple at the site is that of the canine god Osiris-Khentimentiu. The tutelary deity of the necropolis city in the Old Kingdom was the jackal god, called Khenti-Imentiu; in the 5th Dynasty his cult was gradually absorbed by that of Osiris, and the city soon became the focal point of the new cult (*Britannica*).

Nome Name	Nome 9: Minu (Min) – area around Akhmim
Nome Symbol	Fetish
White Chapel Deity	Min
Major Deities	Min
City(s)/Temples	Khentmin (Greek Panopolis, Arabic Akhmim), Min
Notes	Min, in ancient Egyptian religion, a god of fertility and harvest, embodiment of the masculine principle; he was also worshipped as the Lord of the Eastern Desert. His cult originated in Predynastic times (fourth millennium BC). Min was represented with phallus erect, a flail in his raised right hand. The lettuce was his sacred plant

Nome Name	**Nome 10: Cobra – of Qaw el-Kebir**
Nome Symbol	Cobra
White Chapel Deity	(Bau or Seru?) Unidentified
Major Deities	Seth, Mihos (a lion-headed god of war), Nemty – a falcon god (in older literature his name is written 'Anty – the wanderer')
City(s)/Temples	Tjebu (Greek Antaeopolis, Arabic Qau al-Kabir), Nemty
Notes	Mihos was seen as the son of the Creator god Ptah, as well as the feline goddess (Bast in Lower Egypt or Sekhmet in Upper Egypt), whose nature he shared. There is some evidence that he may have been identical with the lion god Apedemak worshipped in Nubia and Egypt's Western Desert

Nome Name	**Nome 11: The Set-animal (Seth) – area around Deir Rifa on the West Bank**
Nome Symbol	Set-animal
White Chapel Deity	Horus and Set
Major Deities	Horus and Set
City(s)/Temples	Shashotep (Greek Apotheke, Arabic Shutb), Set
Notes	The town site of ancient Nubt near Naqada; the town is the cult centre of the god of disorder, Set. In his favour, Set was a companion of Re, and his violent nature was put to good use in repelling the serpent Apophis

Nome Name	**Nome 12: Viper mountain – East Bank around Deir el-Gebrawi**
Nome Symbol	Snake with horizon
White Chapel Deity	Bast
Major Deities	Nemty
City(s)/Temples	Hut-Sekhem-Senusret (Arabic Hu)
Notes	Serpents appear widely in Egyptian symbolism from sources of evil and danger to images of powerful deities and the mystical ouroboros – a symbol of renewal and a manifestation of infinity

Nome Name	**Nome 13: Upper pomegranate tree – West Bank around Asyut**
Nome Symbol	Upper Sycamore and Viper

Understanding the Egyptian Gods and Goddesses

White Chapel Deity	Wepwawet
Major Deities	Wepwawet and Anubis
City(s)/Temples	Saut (Greek Lycopolis, Arabic Asyut) Wepwawet
Notes	This was an ancient wolf god whose worship originated in Upper Egypt. He was one of the earliest of the gods to be worshipped at Abydos, possibly predating (and absorbing) Khentyamentiu (another canine god of the Abydos necropolis). His image appears on the Narmer palette dating from the Protodynastic Period. His image differs from that of Anubis by having a blue/grey head

Nome Name	**Nome 14: Lower pomegranate tree – area of Meir and el-Qusiya**
Nome Symbol	Lower sycamore and viper
White Chapel Deity	Possibly Hathor
Major Deities	Hathor
City(s)/Temples	Qesy (Greek Cusae, Arabic al-Qusiya), Hathor
Notes	Meir is the necropolis of El Qusiya, which was ancient Cusae from the Old and Middle Kingdoms. Unusual and distinctive, scenes are very natural and realistic, particularly in the Chapels of Senbi and Ukhhotep. Tomb one and two, which adjoin each other, are inscribed with 720 pharaonic deities but during the early Christian era, the early Copts who used the tombs defaced many of these inscriptions

Nome Name	**Nome 15: Hare – area around el-Ashmunein and el-Amarna**
Nome Symbol	Hare
White Chapel Deity	Aha (early name for Bes), also Wenut, Thoth
Major Deities	Thoth, Ogdoad
City(s)/Temples	Khemenu (Greek Hermopolis, Arabic Ashmunein), Thoth
Notes	Briefly dedicated to Aten during the religious upheaval in 18th Dynasty

Nome Name	**Nome 16: Oryx – from Beni Hasan to north of el-Minya**
Nome Symbol	Oryx
White Chapel Deity	Horus of Hebenu

A Magical Land

Major Deities	Pakhet (lion goddess of war), Khnum
City(s)/Temples	Hebenu (Arabic Kom al-Ahmar), Horus, Tadehnet (Greek Akoris, Arabic Tehna), Amun, and Sobek
Notes	Note that Khnum is the deity of Herwer, named in the Beni Hasan tomb inscriptions, in this district

Nome Name	**Nome 17: The black dog (Jackal) – area around Samahut**
Nome Symbol	Anubis
White Chapel Deity	Anubis of Henu
Major Deities	Anubis
City(s)/Temples Notes	Saka (Arabic al-Qes)/Bata? Hardai/Anubis? Canine god of the dead, closely associated with embalming and mummification; he is usually represented as a black jackal, or a man with a jackal's head

Nome Name	**Nome 18: Falcon with spread wings – East Bank around el-Hiba**
Nome Symbol	Falcon with spread wings
White Chapel Deity	Nemty
Major Deities	Nemty
City(s)/Temples Notes	Hutnesut (Arabic Sharuna) – Horus-Dunanwy Dunanwy is mentioned several times along with Horus, Seth and Thoth, e.g. in PT utterances 25, 35, and 591, the four gods representing the cardinal points, with Dunanwy representing the east, Thoth the west, Seth the south, and Horus the north. The spells in question concern the offering of various substances – incense, natron, an unidentified plant in Spell 354 of the *Coffin Texts* – as well as the donning of the shesmet, a belt with an apron of beads and tassels (*Henadology*)

Nome Name	**Nome 19: The pure sceptre – West Bank around el-Bahnasa**
Nome Symbol	Two sceptres
White Chapel Deity	Unknown
Major Deities	Seth, Mormyrus fish

City(s)/Temples	Permedjed? (Greek Oxyrhynchus, Arabic Bahnasa)
Notes	Fish played an ambiguous position in ancient Egypt, sometimes sacred, sometimes scorned; eaten by some, forbidden to others

Nome Name	**Nome 20: Upper laurel – West Bank around Ben Suef**
Nome Symbol	Southern sycamore
White Chapel Deity	Empty
Major Deities	Heryshef (the ram god)
City(s)/Temples	Henennesut (Greek Heracleopolis, Arabic Ihnasya) – Heryshef
Notes	'The Goat of Mendes' caused a great deal of magical confusion down through the millennia as this was actually the ram god, lord of Djedet, which was mistaken for a goat by early travellers

Nome Name	**Nome 21: Lower laurel – West Bank around el-Wasta**
Nome Symbol	Northern sycamore
White Chapel Deity	Khnum
Major Deities	Khnum, Seneferu
City(s)/Temples	Shenakhen/Semenuhor (Greek Akanthon, perhaps near Arabic Kafr Ammar and Kafr Tarkhan)
Notes	Worshipped from the Early Dynastic Period in the form of the first rams domesticated in Egypt (*Ovis longipes*), which had corkscrew horns extending horizontally, as opposed to the later species (*Ovis platyra*) which had horns curving inwards towards the face

Nome Name	**Nome 22: Knife – northernmost nome of Upper Egypt stretching along the eastern desert towards Memphis**
Nome Symbol	Knife
White Chapel Deity	Neith, also Sobek of the Southern Lake
Major Deities	Hathor
City(s)/Temples	Tepihu (Greek Aphroditopolis, Arabic Atfih) – Hathor
Notes	The White Chapel entry implies that the Fayum region was considered part of this province

LOWER EGYPT (North)

Nome Name	Nome 1: White fortress (White Wall) – Memphis
Nome Symbol	Walled enclosure
White Chapel Deity	Horus before Inebhedj
Major Deities	Ptah, Sokar, Apis
City(s)/Temples	Inebhedj/Mennefer (Greek Memphis, Arabic Mit Rahina) – Ptah
Notes	Capital of Egypt for most of the Pharaonic Period and the ancient capital of Inebu-hedj, the first nome of Lower Egypt. Memphis was believed to be under the protection of the god Ptah, the patron of craftsmen. Its great temple, *Hut-ka-Ptah* (meaning 'Enclosure of the ka of Ptah'), was one of the most prominent structures in the city. The name of this temple, rendered in Greek as Αἴγυπτος (*Ai-gy-ptos*) by Manetho, is believed to be the etymological origin of the modern English name *Egypt*

Nome Name	Nome 2: Cow's Foreleg – the south-west Delta apex
Nome Symbol	Temple offering
White Chapel Deity	Khentykhem ('foremost of Khem')
Major Deities	Horus, Kherty
City(s)/Temples	Khem (Greek Letopolis, Arabic Ausim) – Horus-foremost-of-Khem
Notes	Letopolis was an ancient Egyptian city, the capital of the second nome of Lower Egypt. Its Egyptian name was Khem and the city was a centre of worship of the deity Khenty-irty or Khenty-khem, a form of the god Horus. The site and its deity are mentioned in texts from as far back as the Old Kingdom and a temple to the god probably stood there very early in Egyptian history

Nome Name	Nome 3: West – the north-west Delta flanked by the Libyan desert
Nome Symbol	Falcon standard
White Chapel Deity	Hepy of Hut-Ihyt
Major Deities	Hathor

City(s)/Temples	Imu (Arabic Komel-Hisn) – Hathor-Sekhmet
Notes	Capital of the Ptolemaic Period – founded by Alexander the Great in 331 BC. Lighthouse of Alexandria (Pharos) was the seventh wonder of the Ancient World; the Library was one of the largest in the world and was the intellectual and cultural centre of the ancient world

Nome Name	**Nome 4: Southern shield – the south-west Delta**
Nome Symbol	Shield and the *swt*-plant (symbolic plant of Upper Egypt)
White Chapel Deity	Neith and Sobek
Major Deities	Neith
City(s)/Temples	Sapi-Resy (Greek Prosopis, Arabic) – Sobek, Sau (Greek Sais, Arabic Sa el-Hagar) – Neith
Notes	Neith was a creator goddess of great antiquity, whose cult centre was at Sais in the Delta. Her most ancient symbol was a warlike motif consisting of a shield and crossed arrows which is attested as early as the 1st Dynasty

Nome Name	**Nome 5: Northern shield – Sais to the coastal area**
Nome Symbol	Shield and the lotus plant
White Chapel Deity	Sau ('of Sais')
Major Deities	Neith
City(s)/Temples	Sau (Greek Sais, Arabic Sa al-Hagar)/Neith
Notes	Sais was the capital of Egypt during the Late Dynastic Period and later a Greek commercial centre

Nome Name	**Nome 6: Khaset – mid-Delta to the coast**
Nome Symbol	Mountain bull against a mountain terrain
White Chapel Deity	(Entry unclear)
Major Deities	Re
City(s)/Temples	Khasu (Greek Xois, Arabic Sakha) – Re Pe and Dep (Greek Buto, Arabic Tell el-Farain)/Wadjyt
Notes	The hieroglyph shows the fighting bull, its head lowered, ready to gore, with each ideogram depicting the distinctive traits of the various bovine species that were to be found from the remotest times (*Hieroglyphics*)

Nome Name	Nome 7: Ament – the north-west Delta along the Rosetta tributary of the Nile
Nome Symbol	'Harpoon with cord' inscribed across provinces 7 and 8
White Chapel Deity	Hu
Major Deities	Hu, Sia
City(s)/Temples	Senti-nefert: Unexcavated
Notes	The Egyptian god Hu was one of the minor gods in some respects, but he was one of the most important gods for those serious about Egyptian deities. Hu is the power of the spoken word. He personifies the authority of utterance. Mortal men and women were created from the tears of Re. Re then drew blood from his own penis and created the gods Hu and Sia. These two gods represented the creative power of the gods. Hu and Sia were partners. Sia was the personification of Divine Knowledge/Omniscience, the mind of the gods. Hu was the personification of Divine Utterance, the voice of authority. During Ancient times, *heka*, the personification of Divine Power accompanied these two gods. Together, the three gods were very important to the rulers of ancient Egypt (*Tour Egypt*)

Nome Name	Nome 8: East harpoon – the east Delta along Wadi Tummilat to the Bitter Lakes
Nome Symbol	'Harpoon with cord' inscribed across provinces 7 and 8
White Chapel Deity	Atum
Major Deities	Atum
City(s)/Temples	Peratum (Biblical Pithom, Arabic Tell al-Maskhuta – Atum)
Notes	The reason why Bitter Lake is called by this name is due to its salt water, which is a quiet spot and far from the noise – and this is what distinguishes the city of Fayed in general, it is used as a place to wait for ships and ferries while travelling, surrounding the lake green lands and water everywhere

Nome Name	Nome 9: Anezti – the mid-Delta to Busiris
Nome Symbol	Andjety god image
White Chapel Deity	Osiris of Djedu
Major Deities	Osiris, Andjety (an early funerary god)

City(s)/Temples	Djedu (Greek Busiris, Arabic Abu Sir Bana) – Horus-Khentkhety
Notes	Andjety in his anthropomorphic form was originally worshipped in the mid-Delta in the Lower ninth nome. Andjety (meaning 'he of Andjet', i.e. the town of Busiris) was the precursor of Osiris at the cult centre of Busiris. The iconography of this god persuasively argues for his being the forerunner of Osiris. Andjety holds the two sceptres in the shape of a 'crook and flail', insignia which became Osiris's symbols of dominion. Also his high conical crown decorated with two feathers is clearly related to the 'atef' crown of Osiris (*Tour Egypt*)

Nome Name	**Nome 10: Black bull km-wr – the south-east Delta around Athribes**
Nome Symbol	Black ox
White Chapel Deity	(Block missing – no entry)
Major Deities	Horus
City(s)/Temples	Hutherib (Greek Athribis, Arabic Tell Atrib) – Osiris and Isis
Notes	Dating from Egypt's Late Period (664–332 BC), this granodiorite sacred bull is 'a gem of a piece', says Hannah Solomon, Christie's Specialist, Head of Sale for Antiquities. 'Wonderfully carved in delicate but powerful curves, he becomes the star of any room he inhabits.' The Late Period saw native Egyptian kings return to the throne after more than a century of foreign rule. They were keen to fortify their cultural traditions in the face of foreign powers, and a new era of patronage saw naturalistic modelling of flesh and features on both human and animal sculptures pushed to unprecedented heights. At the same time, traditional Egyptian cults flourished. While ancient Egyptians did not worship animals, zoomorphic representations exemplified qualities and characteristics that were important in society. The male bull in particular was an attractive symbol, as it had a cosmic association and generally represented strength and masculine virtue, which is why the animal had strong ties to kingship and monarchical ideology (Christie's)

Nome Name	Nome 11: Heb-Sed bull (Ox count) – the mid-Delta
Nome Symbol	Heb-Sed bull
White Chapel Deity	(Block missing – no entry)
Major Deities	She, Tefnut, Mihos
City(s)/Temples	Taremu (Greek Leontopolis, Arabic Tell al-Moqdam) – Mihos-Maihesa
Notes	Heb-Sed, also called Sed Festival, one of the oldest feasts of ancient Egypt, celebrated by the king after thirty years of rule and repeated every three years thereafter. There are many representations of this festival, which normally depict the king running alongside the Apis bull in order to prove his fitness to rule

Nome Name	Nome 12: Calf and Cow – the north-east Delta from Sebennytos to the coast
Nome Symbol	Cow with calf
White Chapel Deity	(Block missing – no entry)
Major Deities	Onuris (local warrior/hunter god)
City(s)/Temples	Tjebennetjer (Greek Sebennytus, Arabic Samanud) – Shu and Mehyt Perhebyt (Arabic Behbeit) – Isis of Hebyt From Tjebennetjer comes the monolithic sanctuary shrine Cairo CG 70015, set up by King Nakhthorhebyt for Shu and Bast
Notes	Mehyt was an ancient Egyptian goddess who, in the Early Dynastic Period, was depicted as a reclining lioness with three bent poles projecting from her back. In that era, she appears in numerous Early Dynastic sealings and ivory artefacts, usually together with a representation of any Upper Egyptian shrine

Nome Name	Nome 13: Prospering Sceptre – the south-east Delta apex
Nome Symbol	Sceptre
White Chapel Deity	Isis, Bast of Su
Major Deities	Atum, Iusaas, Mnevis
City(s)/Temples	Iunu (Greek Heliopolis, Arabic Matariya) – Re-Atum, Hathor Kheraha (Greek 'Babylon of Egypt', part of Old Cairo) – Atum

Notes	The crook and flail (*heka* and *nekhakha*) were symbols used in ancient Egyptian society. The shepherd's crook stood for kingship and became the insignia of pharaonic authority: the flail represented the fertility of the land

Nome Name	**Nome 14: East or anterior nome (jm.tj-xntj – foremost of the East) – the eastern frontier coastal Delta to Pelusium. This is the frontier zone of the 'ways of Horus' leading from Egypt across North Sinai**
Nome Symbol	Local standard
White Chapel Deity	Horus of Benu
Major Deities	Seth
City(s)/Temples	Tjaru (Greek Sile, Arabic Qantara) – Horus of Mesen? Tanis (Biblical Zoan, Arabic Tell Abu Sefa, modern Şān al-Ḥajar al-Qibliyyah)
Notes	An ancient city in the Nile River Delta, capital of the 14th nome (province) of Lower Egypt and, at one time, of the whole country. At the end of the New Kingdom, the royal residence of Pi-Ramesses was abandoned because the Pelusiac branch of the Nile in the Delta became silted up and its harbour consequently became unusable

Nome Name	**Nome 15: Ibis –the north-east Delta along the Damietta tributary of the Nile**
Nome Symbol	Ibis
White Chapel Deity	(Block missing – no entry)
Major Deities	Thoth
City(s)/Temples	Weprehwy (?) (Greek Hermopolis, Arabic Baqliya) – Thoth
Notes	In art, the god Thoth was often depicted as a man with the head of an ibis or a baboon, animals sacred to him. His feminine counterpart was Seshat, and his wife was Ma'at. He was the god of the moon, wisdom, writing, hieroglyphs, science, magic, art, and judgement. Thoth played many vital and prominent roles in Egyptian mythology, such as maintaining the universe, and being one of the two deities (the other being Ma'at) who stood on either side of Re's solar barque. In the later history, Thoth became heavily associated with the arbitration of godly disputes, the arts of magic, the system of writing, and the judgement of the dead

A Magical Land

Nome Name	Nome 16: Fish (or Floodwaters) – the north-east Delta from Mendes to the coast
Nome Symbol	Fish
White Chapel Deity	Banebdjedet 'of Djedet'
Major Deities	Banebdjedet, Hatmehyt
City(s)/Temples	Djedet (Greek Mendes) – Banebdjedet
Notes	The four sanctuary shrines at Djedet were set up by king Ahmose of the 26th Dynasty, with one for each of the four 'souls omnipresent within Banebdjedet'… Ra, Shu, Geb, Osiris

Nome Name	Nome 17: The throne (Behdet) – the north-east Delta coast to the west of the Damietta tributary of the Nile
Nome Symbol	The throne
White Chapel Deity	(Block missing – no entry)
Major Deities	Horus of Behdeti, Amun
City(s)/Temples	Semabehdet (Arabic Balamun) – Amun
Notes	Horus of Behdeti – the winged sun of Horus of Edfu and depicted on the top of pylons in the ancient temples throughout Egypt

Nome Name	Nome 18: Royal child upper nome – the north-east Delta around Bubastis
Nome Symbol	Prince of the South
White Chapel Deity	Bast
Major Deities	Bast
City(s)/Temples	Bast (Greek Bubastis, on edge of modern Zagazig)/Bast
Notes	Pharaoh Ramesses II had a large number of children: forty-eight to fifty sons, and forty to fifty-three daughters – whom he had depicted on several monuments. Ramesses apparently made no distinctions between the offspring of his first two principal wives, Nefertari and Isetnofret. Both queens' first-born sons and first few daughters had statues at the entrance of the Greater Abu Simbel temple, although only Nefertari's children were depicted in the smaller temple, dedicated to her. Ramesses's efforts to have his children depicted on several of his monuments are in contradiction with the earlier tradition of keeping royal children, especially boys, in the background unless they held important official titles

Nome Name	Nome 19: Royal child lower nome – the north-east Delta around Tanis
Nome Symbol	Prince of the North
White Chapel Deity	(Block missing – no entry)
Major Deities	Wadjyt
City(s)/Temples	Imet (ArabicNebesha) – Wadjyt, Djanet (Greek Tanis) – Amun, Mut, and Khonsu
Notes	Wadjet was the Predynastic cobra goddess of Lower Egypt, a goddess originally of a city who grew to become the goddess of Lower Egypt, took the title 'The Eye of Re', and one of the *nebty* (the 'two ladies') of the pharaoh. She rose from being the local goddess of Per-Wadjet (Buto) to become the patron goddess of all of Lower Egypt and twin in the guardianship of Egypt with the vulture goddess Nekhbet. These two were the *nebty* of the pharaoh and were an example of Egyptian duality – each of the two lands had to have its own patron goddess (*Tour Egypt*)

Nome Name	Nome 20: East – the north-east Delta above Wadi Tummilat
Nome Symbol	Plumed falcon
White Chapel Deity	(Block missing – no entry)
Major Deities	Sopdu
City(s)/Temples	Per-Sopdu (Arabic Saft al-Henna) – Sopdu
Notes	Sopdu (Soped, Sopedu) was a god of war associated with the eastern borders and the eastern desert, known as the 'lord of the east'. Sopdu was the son of Sopdet (Sirius) and Sahu (Orion) and according to the *Pyramid Texts*, the composite deity known as Sopdu-Horus was the child of the pharaoh (as Sahu) and Sopdet). As a war god, he was closely associated with the pharaoh (and Horus, the patron god of the kings) during the Middle Kingdom. His association with Horus also related to the fact that both were hawk gods, and Sopdu was given the epithet 'sharp of teeth' with reference to the bird of prey and to the hieroglyph used in his name

This classic listing of the forty-two nomes of Upper and Lower Egypt can serve as a compilation of magical correspondences from a people who were famous in the ancient world for their knowledge of magic. Religion, medicine, technology and what we would call magic co-existed without apparent conflict, and it was not unusual for magical and 'practical' remedies for illness, for example, to be used side by side. Magic was resorted to by everyone, from the pharaoh guarding his country with elaborate magical rituals to the expectant mother wearing amulets to safeguard her unborn child.

Geraldine Pinch, writing in *Magic in Ancient Egypt*, opens by telling us that the evidence for Egyptian magic spans about 4,500 years. Amulets go back as far as the early fourth millennium BC, while magical texts occur from the late third millennium BC until the fifth century AD. The Egyptians used the term *heka* to refer to magical power, in the sense of a divine force (sometimes personified as the god Heka) that could be invoked both by deities and humans to solve problems or crises. In modern times, a clear distinction is usually made between the use of prayers, medicine, or magic, but in ancient Egypt these three categories were regarded as overlapping and complementary. Thus a single problem, whether a disease or a hated rival, might be solved by a combination of magical rituals or treatments (*seshaw*), medicinal prescriptions (*pekhret*) and religious texts (*rw*).

According to the *British Museum Dictionary of Ancient Egypt*, a somewhat artificial distinction is usually made between the religious texts in tombs and temples and the 'magical' texts or 'spells' that were intended to solve the everyday problems of individuals. These texts range from the *Book of Gates* in New Kingdom royal tombs to curses inscribed on *ostraca*, or even spells to cure nasal catarrh, but all of them would have been regarded by the Egyptians as roughly comparable methods of gaining divine assistance. All employed *heka*, the primeval potency that empowered the creator god at the beginning of time.

There was another type of magic called *akhu* for enchantments, sorcery, or spells particularly associated with the dead that was the province of the goddess, Weret Hekau – 'Great of Magic' – who appeared in cobra-form and the snake-shaped wands carried by certain priests of the temple revealed those who followed her. 'The earth belongs to the serpents and scorpions. To understand the treasures of the earth, one must first gain the friendship of those who defend her. But that is impossible for one who is not a man of water, air and fire…'

Akhu is more closely aligned with the pure raw energy that comes from the bowels of the earth and the furthest reaches of the universe – this form of primordial power is normally associated with Western Ritual Magic and the gods of the Predynastic Period and the Old Kingdom. In Egypt, magic was regarded as an exact science, in its highest form; its secrets were revealed only to the highest orders of the priesthood who thus had the ability to control and regulate events and actions.

Chapter Three

The Imperishable Ones

Worship of the stars, which long predated astrology, was an underlying element in many ancient cults, more conspicuously in some than in others. The observable combination of change and variety with fixed and undeviating regularity (i.e. the motions of the sun, moon, and planets as contrasted with that of the 'fixed' stars and constellations) deeply impressed even the profoundest of thinkers. Some writers, both ancient and modern, have held that astral religion was the beginning of true worship as distinct from magic, and have often interpreted the Greek and Egyptian mythology as parables or allegories of the heavenly constellations. More probably, however, the constellations were interpreted from current mythology, and so received their names accordingly.

Often the sun was the chief god of the pantheon and the other heavenly bodies were his family or servants. This primeval cult not only influenced many others, both Semitic and Western as well as Egyptian, but even survived them. Astro-theology, astral mysticism, astral religion is the worship of the stars (individually or together as the night sky), the planets, and other heavenly bodies as deities, or the association of deities with heavenly bodies. In anthropological literature, these systems of practice may be referred to as astral cults.

For the Egyptians, however, those stars 'which grow not weary' have always had immense significance in their culture. The circumpolar stars that never set in the west were identified as 'the Imperishable Ones' and, according to the *Pyramid Texts*, the kings were raised up to heaven to join their company on death, to be free from change or decay. This association of the stars with the revered dead had a longstanding tradition in Egypt, which was revealed on the ceilings of the many tombs that were painted with stars, or the image of the arched sky goddess depicted on the lids of the coffins and sarcophagi. The hieroglyph of the five-pointed star represented the celestial 'world beyond the tomb' while the five-pointed star in a circle (an image so familiar in modern paganism) was the symbol for the place in the sky where the sun and the stars re-appeared after having been invisible, according to the *Pyramid Texts*. In later times, it came to represent Otherworld – celestial or subterranean, i.e. the Dwat and/or Amenti.

The constellation Ursa Major suggested a ritual object used ceremonially in 'the Opening of the Mouth' as part of the funerary rites. It also represented the thigh of a sacrificial animal and therefore connected to Set; while some sources have linked the constellation of Draco with Nut – the 'Mother of Set'. The distinctive constellation of Orion was first attributed to Sah, and later as 'the glorious soul of Osiris', holding a deep significance in Egyptian belief because of their continuing traditional connection between the stars and the dead. Sothis (or Sirius), the 'Dog Star', was originally identified with Sopdet, and later Isis, but more importantly, it was associated with the annual flooding of the Nile, the calendar having been based on the date of the heliacal rising of Sothis near the sun at the Summer Solstice, coinciding with the commencement of the Inundation. Ancient texts also assign other planets to the various gods – Jupiter with Horus 'who limits the two lands'; Mars with Horus of the Horizon; Mercury with Sebegu (a god associated with Set); Saturn with Horus, 'bull of the sky'; and Venus ('the one who crosses' or 'god of the morning') with Re or Osiris.

Although the Egyptians had both civic and astronomical calendars, it is almost impossible to fix precise dates in the chronology of the history of the Nile Valley. That said, as Raymond A. Wells points out in *Astronomy Before the Telescope*, more than six millennia ago, man's primal gleanings from the night sky crystallised into a variety of myths that formed the basis of Egyptian religion. 'Since its principal deities were heavenly bodies, the priesthood mastered the ability to predict the time and place of their gods' appearances ... Many of these achievements were already in place before the unification of Upper (Nile Valley) and Lower (Delta) Egypt.'

> Because the sun god Re was the pre-eminent god, the annual solar motion along the horizon at sunrise was keenly observed by the early Egyptians who noted its northernmost and southernmost turning points at the solstices. Almost all of Egyptian astronomy and religion are ultimately derived from this simple horizon movement.
>
> (*Astronomy in Egypt*)

During the Old Kingdom, the belief that mortals were reborn among the circumpolar stars led to the continued depiction of stars on the ceiling of the tombs as an important part of the funerary art of the day. As Wells also makes a point of explaining: 'The mythology of the sky goddess Nut giving birth to Re, catalysed both time-keeping and calendar development, endowed the concept of divine royalty, and instituted the matrilineal inheritance of the throne.' One of the utterances from the *Pyramid Texts* exhorts the sky goddess Nut to spread her protective body over the deceased so that he might ascend to join those already placed among the Imperishable Stars. The funerary rites with their attendant deities were regarded as microcosms of the universe itself, and just as Nut spread her star-spangled body over the earth, so she stretched herself over the dead. Even when the stellar beliefs of early Egypt were merged into the later solar beliefs, the practice of stellar decoration continued throughout the rest of the empire's history.

The Greeks credited the Egyptians with recognising the existence of the movement of the stars, and the earliest detailed records are the 'diagonal calendars' or star-clocks, also painted on the wooden coffin lids of the early Middle Kingdom. These calendars consisted of thirty-six columns, listing thirty-six groups of stars referred to as 'decans' into which the night sky was divided. Each decan rose above the horizon at dawn for a period of ten days every year. This system, however, was also flawed, since it did not take into account the fact that the Egyptian year was always around six hours short, adding up to a difference of ten days every forty years. Because of this 'slippage', it is doubtful whether these Middle Kingdom star-clocks were ever considered to be a practical measure of time; nevertheless this was another integral ingredient of tomb decoration, if only paying symbolic lip-service to the Old Ways.

The astronomical knowledge of the early priests and architects is further confirmed by examples of the ceremony of *pedj shes* ('stretching the cord'), first recorded on a granite block during the reign of the 2nd Dynasty ruler, Khasekhemwy. This method was reliant on the sighting of Ursa Major and Orion, using 'an instrument of knowing' (*merkhet*), which functioned on the same principle as the astrolabe, and a sighting tool constructed from a central rib of a palm leaf. Although many later texts described the *pedj shes*, it has been suggested that this, like all the old stellar religion's symbolism, had become mere ceremony and that in practice the temples were simply aligned in relation to the river.

Aligning of the Pyramids

As recent popular histories have revealed, the Great Pyramid was almost certainly aligned with the stars and, along with the Sphinx, are literally 'oriented' (that is, they faced due east, the direction of sunrise at the equinoxes). The shafts in the King's and Queen's Chambers in the Great Pyramid demonstrate the stellar alignments of all four shafts in the epoch of 2500 BC. The northern shaft in the Queen's Chamber is angled at 39 degrees and was aimed at Kochab (Beta Ursa Minor) in the constellation of Ursa Minor. The southern shaft, angled at 39 degrees 30, was directed at Sirius in the constellation of Alpha Canis Major. In the King's Chamber, the northern shaft, angled at 32 degrees 28, was directed at the ancient Pole Star, Thuban (Alpha Draconis) in the constellation of Draco. The southern shaft, angled at 45 degrees 14, focused on Al Nitak (Zeta Orionis), the brightest and lowest of the three stars in Orion's Belt.

In their book, *The Orion Mystery*, Bauval and Hancock also demonstrated that the three stars in Orion's Belt possibly correspond to the faulty diagonal line of the Great Pyramid (of Cheops) and the second pyramid (of Chephren), with the third pyramid (of Mycerinus) being offset slightly to the east. 'The first two stars (Al Nitak and Al Nilam) are in direct alignment, like the first and second Pyramids, and the third star (Mintaka) lies offset somewhat to the east of the axis formed by the other two.' The Egyptian word for pyramid (*mer*) means 'place of ascent' or more correctly 'what goes [straight] up from the *us*' (a word of uncertain meaning), the suggested ascending being done by the deceased pharaoh as he was transported into the sky to spend eternity among the Imperishable Ones. The development of the pyramids, of which there are some eighty (although many are now reduced to piles of rubble), began after 3000 BC and culminated in the colossal structures known as the Giza Group that were built between 2600 and 2500 BC.

After that, pyramid building went into decline, with ever-smaller structures being built. Some of the later (and grossly inferior) pyramids are nevertheless significant in that they contain fine examples of the *Pyramid Texts*: the set of magic spells dating from prehistoric times, giving a safe passage to the pharaoh into the sky. Many of the texts describe the journey of the king to the Other World, situated in the sky beyond the eastern horizon, and his activities upon arrival. Judging from the formation of the texts, it is significant that the king could not rely on any divine assistance from the gods during his journey but, armed with the magical power of the texts, he might overcome the hazards of his final trials before joining the sun god in his daily travels across the sky. According to Professor I. E. S. Edwards (*The Pyramids of Egypt*), for the most part, the *Pyramid Texts* were certainly not inventions of Dynasties 5 and 6, but had originated in much earlier times. 'It is hardly surprising, therefore, that they sometimes contain allusions to conditions which no longer prevailed at the time of Unas and his successors.'

In his academic paper, 'The King and the Star-Religion in the *Pyramid Texts*', R. O. Faulkner, acknowledged expert on ancient Egyptian writing, pointed out that the funerary art forms from the Middle Kingdom onwards were contemporary interpretations of 'a very ancient stratum of stellar religion, in which the stars were regarded as gods, or as the souls of the blessed dead'. Here we learn that there was a distinction between the sky (*pt*) as a natural element of daily life, and the 'Starry Sky' (*shdw*) where the king goes on death, as in: 'May you [the king] go to those northern gods the circumpolar stars...'

In his conclusion, Faulkner's analysis of the *Pyramid Texts* shows two distinct strata. One being concerned with the circumpolar stars and the northern sky, which appears as the abode of the gods and the illustrious royal dead, to which the king ascends on his journey from this world. The other is connected with the constellation of Orion and Sothis, the Morning Star and the Lone Star, with only three mentions of the moon. It is noticeable that these two strata overlap very little and, while one deals with the ultimate abode of the dead king in the northern sky, the other, the Lone Star apart, appears to be concerned with those celestial bodies which mark the passage of time in the course of the year...

Orion is a companion of the king, and is joined by him, making with Sothis a celestial trio; the king may thus be thought of as sharing in the responsibility for regulating times and seasons. The association of the Morning Star with the dead king and the entourage of Re often displays conflicting details, but without doubt it refers to Phosphorus-Venus as seen at dawn. The Lone Star is the king himself, and Faulkner suggests this is Hesperus-Venus as seen just after sunset, since the Lone Star is spoken of as 'ascending from the eastern sky' and as a 'hawk seen in the evening traversing the sky'. As fragmented as these details are, it shows that the power of this archaic stellar cult was still making itself felt, well into the Pyramid Age and beyond. But why, we may ask ourselves, did the Egyptians choose those pyramidal-shaped structures in the first place, and why the continuous references to the stars when everyone knows that the chief Egyptian god was the solar deity Atum-Re?

In *Rogue Asteroids and Doomsday Comets*, research astronomer at the Anglo-Australian Observatory, Duncan Steel, offered some further points to ponder which may alter the way we view the astronomer-priesthood of the Nile Valley. Apparently our earth moves through a permanent cloud called zodiacal dust. This name gets its name because it gives rise to the zodiacal light, a diffuse glow in a huge triangular shape that follows the path of the sun across the sky. This natural phenomenon is best seen an hour or two after sunset or before dawn, in near-tropical latitudes.

Few people are fortunate enough to observe zodiacal light today because it is necessary to be well away from any light pollution to be able to distinguish it, but it was known to the ancient people of the Middle East as the 'false dawn' because it stretched far above the horizon, more than halfway to the zenith. From an especially dark viewing site, it may even be possible to perceive a dim band reaching right across the sky along the ecliptic. 'This zodiacal band is due to dust that is exterior to the terrestrial orbit, while the zodiacal light proper (the pyramid in the sky) is due pre-dominantly to sunlight scattered from dust interior to our orbit.' Steel goes on to explain that when a large comet breaks up, an enormous amount of zodiacal dust will occur, making the zodiacal cloud and band much brighter than they appear today.

'In fact,' he writes, 'it would look like the river that Re navigates his boat along each day, followed also at night by the newly bright comets in low-inclination orbits. At each end of the "river" lies the triangular profile of the main zodiacal light, a pyramidal shape.' Could this be the 'ladder' the dead king needed to ascend in order to climb his stairway to heaven? Early written accounts of the sky speak of a phenomenon that historians, 'primed by astronomers who assumed in error that what was seen then was the same as what we see now, have interpreted as being the Milky Way'.

The same records state that this 'Milky Way' was the path formerly taken by the sun (that is, ecliptic) and that it was produced by comets. 'This is obviously not the Milky Way that we see now: what was being described was a super-intense zodiacal light and band.' Another important point is how the zodiacal light and band would appear as sunrise approached. According to Steel, the zodiacal band would come closer to being perpendicular to the horizon as the middle of the night passes and, as the pyramid of light begins to peek above the horizon hours before daybreak, it is still tilted far over. As time progresses, it straightens more and more, never quite reaching the perpendicular position. Then the whole sky would begin to brighten and redden in the north-east, until eventually the sun would rise from the middle of the zodiacal cloud. This would have created a very strong impression on the Egyptian people, especially if that zodiacal light was much brighter 5,000 years ago than it is now.

Before 'inviting anthropologists and antiquarians to have their paroxysms and apoplectic attacks', Steel presses home his theory that the ancient Egyptians would also have seen a much more pronounced 'brightness enhancement' due to the huge amount of dust released at that period into the Taurid stream. 'Is there anything to link the ancient Egyptians with such calamitous events occurring in the sky?' he asks. 'Well, one example is from the Egyptian hieroglyphics; the symbols for thunder and meteorite are the same, and contain a star. It seems that the Egyptians associated meteors and meteorites with explosions above their heads, which is certainly indicative of a tumult taking place in the sky of a type different to our experiences today.'

Nevertheless, although the stars played an integral part in Egyptian religion, we know that they did not adopt the astrological belief that the stars controlled human destiny until the much later Hellenistic Period. Absorbing these later influences from Mesopotamian astral beliefs and Chaldean astrologers, they quickly made up for lost time in immersing themselves in this new 'science'. According to S. G. F. Brandon (in *Man, Myth and Magic*), these 'new age' Egyptians adopted the idea with enthusiasm and developed a form of astral religion or mystical philosophy that became widely influential in the world of Graeco-Roman culture. 'Star charts were elaborated, comprising 56 deities who presided over the various time units of the year ... the importance of horoscopes became so great that they were inscribed on the roofs of [later] tombs.'

The first known book of astrological lore with its pseudo-scientific overtones, *Tetrabiblos*, was written by Ptolemy around the second century AD, in which he attributes all manner of influences to the planets in much the same way that modern astrology is consulted today. This star-lore was elaborated even further into the complex doctrine known as the *Corpus Hermetucum* (which also still exists), being attributed to Hermes Trismegistus, the Egyptian god

Thoth/Tahuti himself, although it is now accepted that they were compiled by an unknown Christian scholar. By the first century AD, the Babylonion zodiac at Dendera had been adopted and accepted as the 'Egyptian zodiac'.

Written in the Stars

But let's turn the clock right back to the beginning... to those archetypal figures known as the 'Imperishable Ones' who personified the ever-visible circumpolar stars in the northern sky. As we have discovered, archaeological evidence shows that for the Predynastic Egyptians, the religion of the time *was* stellar based. It was from this point in history that the observations made by those early people of the Nile Valley noted the northernmost and southernmost turning points of the sun at the solstices from which almost all of Egyptian astronomy and religion were ultimately derived.

In other words, even from the earliest period of history, the beliefs of Egypt were based on *scientific* observation, not primitive superstition and, as such, we can still identify with them today. All esoteric language is shot through with allegory and metaphor, sigils and correspondences, hieroglyphics and symbolism – and Egyptian magic is no exception – but we should not allow ourselves to forget that this astronomer-priesthood was at the scientific cutting-edge of their time. In fact, if we refer back to the quote from Carl Jung relating to the collective unconscious...

> In a pristine society such as Egypt's it should be possible to see it at work in quite a different way from the experience of later cultures. The collective unconscious is the fount from which all archetypes flow. The collective unconscious in Egypt would, in this view, be especially powerful and as pristine a phenomenon as the society itself.

... we see how the thread of scientific observation, influencing the magical symbology of religious and ritual magic archetypes, has endured for something like 6,000 years!

Here we have Nut, a beautiful and elegant sky goddess. A celestial mother, portrayed as a naked female stretched across the sky with the sun shown entering her mouth, passing through her star-speckled body, and emerging from her birth canal. The faint outer arm of the Milky Way was perceived as the goddess, whose legs are formed by a bifurcation at the cross-shape of the constellation Cygnus with its principal star Deneb marking the birth canal exit; while the face is situated in the 'swirling star clouds' in the vicinity of Gemini. About forty-five minutes after sunset at the Vernal Equinox, the head of Nut can be seen passing below the horizon face upwards with her mouth open at (or very close to) the position where the sun had set. Far-fetched ideas? Not at all...

Ronald Wells, contributor to the academic paper 'Astronomy in Egypt' (*Astronomy Before the Telescope*) describes the final act of the drama as occurring 272 days later on the morning of the Winter Solstice, when the lower half the goddess is visible above the horizon for only a few hours. As the rosy-hued dawn spreads across the sky, Deneb intersects the horizon at exactly the spot where the sun rises... a phenomenon only valid at the Winter Solstice, since the point of sunrise is further north on other dates. In other words, Re enters Nut at sunset on the Spring Equinox (at which time the goddess presumably conceives) and nine months later, she gives birth to him on the Winter Solstice.

'Perhaps the most remarkable aspect of these events, a convincing tie to actual astronomical observations, is that the number of days between the Spring Equinox and the Winter Solstice is the period of human gestation!' he concludes. The implied method of conception is oral, but that is not an unusual belief in a primitive society. By the Old Kingdom this stellar belief was confirmed by texts outlining the ruler's role in the afterlife; here pharaoh, represented by the Lone Star, devolves into the guide for the wise Imperishable Ones (the *ikhemu-sek*, literally 'the ones not knowing destruction') by the order of Atum.

From those Old Kingdom texts, we find one of the keys to the ancient stellar Mysteries. Here, it is revealed that the divinity of pharaoh is not diminished by physical death; it is also recorded that Egypt will descend back into the chaotic waters of Nun should he be prevented from becoming one with the star-gods in the afterlife. As if to emphasise this continuing of ancestral divinity, the deceased pharaoh is referred to by the title 'god older than the oldest' – in true Mystery Tradition meaning that he becomes One with the Creator until the Divine King is reborn in his successor.

In historical terms, this can be seen as an attempt to amalgamate firmly entrenched stellar beliefs with the now dominant solar theology, and throughout remaining Egyptian history the sun god travels across the celestial ocean with the Imperishable Ones (including pharaoh) in his *barque*. By the New Kingdom, however, the Imperishable Ones are reduced to merely twelve oar-carrying gods who are described 'as coming out of the primeval waters with Re'. The rapid growth of the Osirian death cult, however, saw them relegated to being merely referred to 'the followers of Osiris'. The subsequent Hellenisation of Egyptian culture introduced a much more elaborate conceptualisation of the night sky as it developed and expanded the concept of the 'decans' – the thirty-six star-gods (constellations), twenty-four moving by *barque* across the firmament in ten-day cycles. Tomb paintings depicting the star-gods travelling across the ceiling reveal the images of the constellations, but present-day archaeologists and astronomers remain uncertain about identifying the Egyptian star groupings by any equivalent 'modern' names.

The only major constellations that can be identified with any certainty are Orion with Sothis (Sirius), and Ursa Major (The Great Bear, or Plough) known as 'the four spirits of the north', who comprise the 'foreleg of Set'. Had we retained the Egyptian symbols for the constellations, we would today have a crocodile and the hippopotamus amongst the signs of the zodiac! Virginia Lee Davis, writing in *Archaeoastronomy*, admits that the identification of ancient Egyptian constellations is a tantalising field of study. On the one hand, there is the almost embarrassing abundance of constellation pictures produced in the course of more than two millennia and beautifully preserved right down to the present day. On the other hand, there is an almost complete dearth of *reliable* data on which to base attempts at identifying the pictured constellations.

Presumably the Egyptians felt no lack, each one having learned the constellations from the cradle by the simple expedient of having them pointed out to him. As an archaeologist, Davis is willing to trawl through the vast quantities of religious and mythological material in the hope of finding a few vague clues, but is no doubt hampered by an academic reluctance that prevents the cross-pollination of ideas between the applications of science, history, theology, philosophy, and magic. The old Egyptian stellar cult continued to form the basis of the ancient Mysteries, but just as every Egyptian child could have identified the stars themselves, only the higher levels of the astronomer-priesthood would have known the religio-magical significance of each of the constellations.

Neither child nor priest, however, would have required them to be written in stone on the walls of the funerary monuments in order to understand their symbolism, but even committed Egyptologists seem to demonstrate a marked reluctance to credit these people with even a fundamental grasp of astrophysics. Davis also cites the occasional reference in the *Pyramid Texts* of 'two skies', with frequent mention of a 'northern sky' and a 'southern sky' – but, she says, there is no mention of an eastern or western sky. 'There is also mention of "two horizons" and frequent mention of "eastern horizon" and "western horizon" (meaning the places of sunrise and sunset) but no mention of northern horizon or southern horizon.' When dealing with mystical, religious and philosophical matters, it is unwise to take the written word literally, since esoteric texts were never intended for the eyes or understanding of the layman.

We know that the Egyptians built the pyramids and aligned them with the stars... they were obviously descended from generations of star-gazers, so why shouldn't they be aware of the movement of certain stars between the northern and southern hemispheres, just as modern astronomers are today? They may not have been able to explain the phenomenon, but that doesn't mean they weren't aware of it, just as they were aware of the shifting position of the Milky Way in the heavens throughout the changing cycles of the year. The dual-headed god, Aker, was the guardian of the entrance and exit of the underworld, with one head facing east and the other west, and only places of mystical/magical significance would have been included in the *Pyramid Texts*.

Sir Norman Lockyer, one of the great Victorian astronomers, recorded his observations of this ancient science in *The Dawn of Astronomy*, first published in 1894. The various apparent movements of the heavenly bodies which are produced by the rotation and the revolution of the earth, and the effects of precession, *were* familiar to the ancient Egyptians, however ignorant they may have been of their actual causes; they carefully studied what they saw, and attempted to put their knowledge together in the most convenient fashion, associating it with their strange imaginings and their own system of worship. In her 'Introduction' to Christian Jacq's earlier edition of *Egyptian Magic*, Rosalie David stated that for the Egyptians, magic was regarded as an exact science in its highest form, its secrets revealed only to the highest orders of priesthood. This area of magic was used as a system of defence, and played an important role in the service of the State, protecting the country and its king.

In reality, however, by the end of the Old Kingdom, Egypt's 'Golden Age' was over as the land was plunged into anarchy and chaos as revolution overturned the old established order. From Predynastic times, right up until the collapse of the Old Kingdom, the king was considered personally responsible for the well-being and stability of the land and its people. He was the intermediary between gods and men, and his role in life was to ensure this equilibrium was maintained via the channels of daily prayers and offerings at the temple. If the king did not fulfil his daily obligations to the gods on behalf of his people, then there was the danger of plunging everything back into chaos and darkness from which it had originally sprung. We also know from historical evidence that around the end of the Old Kingdom, this system did, in fact, break down.

This ancient stellar knowledge would, of course, only be known to select members of the priesthood and probably not even understood by the king himself, despite holding the rank of the highest high priest. What is even more astounding is that this stellar knowledge may probably be the surviving remnants from *zep tepi* – the 'First Time' of the Nile civilisation whose origins are lost beneath the proverbial sands of time. This was also the time of the *Urshu*, that mysterious race of mystical beings that haunt the periphery of every culture, and all Adepts are familiar with the 'First Time' – the universal Golden Age during which the waters of the Abyss receded, the primordial darkness was banished, and humanity, emerging into the light, was brought the gifts of civilisation by these 'Watchers' or 'Light-bearers', who have acted as intermediaries between the gods and men.

Needless to say, many modern Egyptologists dismiss this 'First Time' as nothing more than myth, but the 'Building Texts' from the Temple of Edfu appear to refer to a 'mythical temple that came into existence at the beginning of the world' (*The Mythical Origin of the Egyptian Temple* – E. A. E. Reymond) and are synonymous with the First Time, or Early Primeval Age. The texts record that the 'Seven Sages', the 'Builder Gods', the 'Lords of Light', the 'Senior Ones' bringing light, i.e. *knowledge,* to the people – and the similarities between the Lords of Light of Edfu and the *shemsu hor* of the later Heliopolitan Period are so similar that they are probably all descriptions of the same shadowy brotherhood.

Chapter Four

Early Cults and Divinities

The beliefs and rituals surrounding these earliest of gods formed the core of ancient Egyptian religion, which emerged sometime in pre-history. Deities represented natural forces and phenomena, and the Egyptians supported and appeased them through offerings and rituals so that these forces would continue to function according to *Ma'at*, or divine order. After the founding of the Egyptian state around 3100 BC, the authority to perform these tasks was controlled by the pharaoh, who claimed to be the gods' representative and managed the temples where the rituals were carried out.

> The first written evidence of deities in Egypt comes from the Early Dynastic Period. Deities must have emerged sometime in the preceding Pre-dynastic Period (before 3100 BC) and grown out of pre-historic religious beliefs. Pre-dynastic artwork depicts a variety of animal and human figures. Some of these images, such as stars and cattle, are reminiscent of important features of Egyptian religion in later times, but in most cases, there is not enough evidence to say whether the images are connected with deities. In view of such a multiplicity of divine images it may seem strange to suggest that the early religion of Egypt is very imperfectly unknown to us. Such, however, is the case; though we know the names of these gods, and the temples in which they were worshipped, we understand little of their nature and seldom know even the original legends concerning them.
>
> (*Egyptian Mythology*)

We know of the *Urshu*, those ancient Lords of Light, the old Great Ones of *zep tepi* – Egypt's 'First Time' – who also have parallels in other esoteric cultures in the form of the Watchers or Light Bearers – great cosmic beings who acted as intermediaries between gods and men. That is, until they decamped following the destruction of the stellar priesthood; repulsed by the excesses of mankind when they witnessed first-hand its capacity for self-destruction. Their continued presence on the periphery of human vision contributed to the growing concept that appears to have originated in the Middle East surrounding these celestial beings.

> In their own histories, the ancient Egyptians attribute the greatness of their civilization to the inspiration and wisdom of a spiritual leadership stretching tens of thousands of years back in time. Several of the historical documents that have survived to this day – the Palermo Stone, the Turin Papyrus and Manetho's *History of Egypt* – refer to several stages of Egyptian civilization. The first era was the time of the *neteru* or *Urshu* (gods), who each ruled for thousands of years. This period ended with the last *neter*, Horus. Second was the era of the *Shemsu Hor* (followers of Horus). This period ended with Menes/Narmer and the era of the dynastic pharaohs. This is the period that Egyptologists study and which archaeological evidence has verified.
>
> (The Global Education Project)

As Otto Eberhard observed in his Introduction to *Gods and Temples in Egypt*:

> From an observation of the forms in which a deity could appear to an Egyptian one thing is clear: the human being was in no way the only, or even the preferred, form used by the deity. It was a pre-historic instinct to experience the deity in all natural forms: the list of divine beings included not only the firmament, the sun, moon and stars, but also the earth and the Nile, and so, too, the space between heaven and earth. The Egyptian invested animals, particularly those which were not domesticated, with divine powers, and made god appear in their forms.

As Egyptian society grew more sophisticated, clearer signs of religious activity appeared. The earliest known temples appeared in the last centuries of the Predynastic era, along with images that resemble the iconographies of known deities: the falcon that represents Horus and several other gods, the crossed arrows that were associated with Neith and the enigmatic 'Set animal' that represents Set/Sutekh.

The iconographic image of the falcon is probably the oldest cult-symbol. Horus, the falcon-headed god, is a familiar ancient figure who has become one of the most commonly used symbols of Egypt. Thus the pharaoh Horus became Horus on earth who was the ruler of both Upper and Lower Egypt, represented by the hawk as the god of the sky. It became a symbol of divine kingship and the protector of the one who is ruling. Horus represented the power and importance of the sun and sky in all aspects of ancient life and served as provider and protector of the Egyptian people, especially the pharaohs. One of the most important symbols associated with him is the 'Eye of Horus', a symbol meant to offer the protection of the gods.

Horus (Hor, Har, Her, or Heru, in ancient Egyptian) was a god in the form of a falcon whose right eye was the sun or morning star, representing power and quintessence; and whose left eye was the moon or evening star, representing healing. Falcon cults, which were in evidence from late Predynastic times, were widespread at this time. Horus also appeared as a local god in many places and under different names and epithets – for instance, as Harmakhis (Har-em-akhet, 'Horus in the Horizon'); Harpocrates (Har-pe-khrad, 'Horus the Child'); Harsiesis (Har-si-Ese, 'Horus, Son of Isis'); Harakhte ('Horus of the Horizon', closely associated with the sun god Re); and, at Kawm Umbū (Kom Ombo), as Haroeris (Harwer, 'Horus the Elder').

At Nekhen (Greek: Hierakonpolis), however, the conception arose that the reigning king was a manifestation of Horus, and, after Lower Egypt and Upper Egypt had been united by the kings from Nekhen, this notion became a generally accepted dogma. The most important of an Egyptian king's names (the number of which grew from three in Early Dynastic times to five later) was his Horus name – i.e. the name that identified him with Horus. This name appeared on monuments and tombs in a rectangular frame called a serekh. In addition to being characterised by a Horus name, the king was typically depicted with a hovering form of Horus above his head. Sometimes Horus is shown as a winged sun disc, representing the Horus of Behdet, a town in the Nile River Delta where the falcon god enjoyed a cult following.

If we go by the images of Horus (the Elder) on temple reliefs, we usually see a figure who is tall, with a physically attractive 'warrior physique'; exceptionally lean, toned, and wiry. Not surprisingly, from early times he was paired with Hathor, whose name means 'estate of Horus' or 'the House of Horus', and identified her as the wife of god and mother of the pharaohs. She was one of the most popular deities that had different characters, most importantly being the daughter of Re and recorded as being a bit of a 'flighty piece'.

Horus was also linked with Serket as the 'Seven Scorpion Goddess Wives of Horus'. Traces of them have been found in papyri, on ostraca, in graffiti, and on healing statues dating from the fourteenth century BC to the end of dynastic Egypt. There may even be an older allusion to them in the *Coffin Texts*, where Horus is said to 'belong to the Great Lady of the Desert, the Lady of Flame ... Who bites with Her mouth, Who strikes with Her tail'. So these goddesses were quite well known and remained so; the scorpion ideogram, one of the earliest known hieroglyphic signs, was depicted on wooden and ivory artefacts found in the late Pre-/Early Dynastic royal cemetery at Abydos, and also among a cache of cult equipment in the Early Dynastic temple at Hierakonpolis.

In one of the spells in the Turin papyrus, these goddesses are said to be daughters of Re and they bring drink and magical knots to heal Horus during one of his many mishaps. In one of the papyri collected by American mining magnate Chester Beatty, we find a long-ish spell against scorpion stings. In the spell, the scorpion's poison is called to flow out of the person. The poison is called forth seven times – in the names and by the power of each the seven wives of Horus. The most well-known source being the healing statue of Djed-Hor, which is quite damaged so we can't see all the names, though we know from the structure of the spell that seven were originally listed. Nevertheless, a list of all seven can be reconstructed from a variety of sources (*Britannica*).

There are two that are the most well known, appearing in a number of other surviving spells. They are Sepertuenes, and Ta-Bitchet; other scorpion goddesses identified as wives of Horus include Ifdet, Wepetsepu, and Sefedsepu... and finally, Metemet-nefertiyes (the first part of her name is not translatable), then Batcheh – defined in another text as 'the uraeus who bore the gods'. Some scholars think that all these scorpion goddesses may be manifestations of the one Great Scorpion Goddess, Serket. A classic goddess, Serket: note the stars on each of the scorpion's claws in tomb paintings, the cult of Serket is attested as early as the 1st Dynasty from Saqqara, although by the 18th Dynasty she had been relegated to the supporting quartet of the protective goddesses: Isis, Nephthys and Neith surrounding the golden shrine of Tutankhamun.

Despite his later unsavoury reputation, Set/Seth/Sutekh was the object of veneration; his cult had been centred at Naqada since Predynastic times, as well as in the north-eastern Delta. From the 1st Dynasty onward, Horus and Seth were presented as perpetual antagonists who were reconciled in the harmony of uniting Upper and Lower Egypt. The 2nd-Dynasty ruler Peribsen chose to write his principal name in a serekh surmounted by an image of Set rather than Horus in a radical change from traditional iconography, while his successor Khasekhemwy placed images of both gods above his name. Thereafter, however, the serekh remained uniquely associated with Horus.

It has been suggested (*British Museum Dictionary of Ancient Egypt*) that the struggle between the two gods may have served as a metaphor for the role of male sexuality in the cult of the Egyptian king. Eventually the gods were called upon to judge which of the two should be the earthly ruler. Set was favoured by Re on account of his seniority but eventually it was decreed that Horus should be the ruler of the living – hence his identification with the deceased king. As god of chaos and confusion, Set lay outside the ordered universe, thus serving as a necessary complement to the divine order, since everything within the Egyptian system needed and opposing force in order to maintain the necessary balance.

Set, part of whose violent nature probably derived from his sexual potency, found a better use for all his testosterone-fuelled machismo in remaining a 'companion of Re' to journey with the sun god in the solar barque through the twelve hours of the night. In this context, his violent nature was put to good use, defending Re from the coils of the serpent Apophis, whom he speared from the bow of the boat. Since the deceased king also journeyed with Re, he too enjoyed the protection of Set.

The reliefs of Set's image reveal a hunky warrior god with a human body but always featuring the head of a mysterious animal with its long nose and squared-off ears. The full animal form of the god was depicted with an erect forked tail and a canine body; the earliest known representation takes the form of a carved ivory artefact (perhaps a comb) from the Naqada Period; while the distinctive figure of the Set-animal is also portrayed on the mace-head of the Protodynastic ruler Scorpion.

Strangely, Set's images manifest as a not unattractive individual with high cheekbones and almond-shaped eyes that set him up in the masculinity stakes alongside his rival, Horus. From the late Third Intermediate Period (*c.*800 BC) onwards, there appears to have been a change in the way that Set was viewed. Whereas previously he has been regarded simply as an ambivalent force, avoided for most purposes but invoked for others, he began to be perceived as evil and undesirable to the extent that some of his statutes were re-carved with the attributes of Amun and he was transformed into the bad boy of Egyptian legend but no one could deny his impressive pedigree.

His grandparents, Shu and Tefnut, were the offspring of Atum-Re, a primeval cosmic solar god, progenitor of the elements of the universe. Shu symbolises dry air and the force of preservation. Tefnut symbolises moist or corrosive air that brings about change, creating the concept of time. As the air, Shu was considered to be a cooling, and thus calming, influence, and pacifier. Due to the association with dry air, calm, and thus *Ma'at* (truth, justice, order, and balance), Shu was depicted as the dry air/atmosphere between the earth and sky, separating the two realms after the event of the first occasion (*zep tepi*). Shu was also portrayed in art as wearing an ostrich feather – the symbolic of lightness and emptiness. Fog and clouds were also Shu's elements and they were often called his bones. Because of his position between the sky and earth, he was also identified as the wind.

The goddess Tefnut is portrayed as a woman with the head of a lioness and a sun disc resting on her head; she is the sister-consort of her brother Shu. According to the Heliopolitan cosmology, Shu and Tefnut are the first pair of cosmic elements, who created the sky goddess, Nut, and the earth god, Geb. Shu separated Nut from Geb as they were in the act of love, creating duality in the manifest world: above and below, light and dark, good and evil. The Egyptians believed that if Shu did not hold Nut (sky) and Geb (earth) apart, there would be no way for physically manifest life to exist. Shu is mostly represented as a man. Only in his function as a fighter and defender of the sun-god is he sometimes given a lion's head. He carries an ankh, the symbol of life.

The goddess Neith had one of the longest recorded spans in this ancient pantheon – she was worshipped from early in the Predynastic era through to the arrival of Roman rule. She was the goddess of creation, wisdom, weaving, and war, in addition to being worshipped as a funerary goddess. Neith was said to be there at the creation of the world, and some even called her the mother of Re, the sun god who went on to create everything else. She is also sometimes credited with being the mother of Sobek, the crocodile god. In this light, many worshipped her as the creator of birth.

As the goddess of wisdom, it was said that the other deities would come to her to help settle their disputes. Neith was also associated with weaving, which, in addition to her association with war, gave her several roles in the afterlife. She was said to shoot arrows at the enemies of the dead, in addition to dressing them with woven cloth. As the patroness of the city of Sais in the Nile River Delta, Neith was worshipped there as early as Predynastic times and several queens of the 1st Dynasty were named after her. The association between the goddess and the royal family is well attested.

She also became an important goddess in the capital city of Memphis. Her principal emblem was a pair of crossed arrows shown against the background of a leather shield. A further emblem was a bow case, which the goddess was sometimes depicted wearing on her head in place of a crown – but Neith was usually depicted as a woman wearing the Red Crown associated with Lower Egypt, holding crossed arrows and a bow. The shape of the crown is quite distinctive but its symbolic meaning with its curly protuberance at the front remains unclear. Neith was a warlike goddess whose name perhaps means 'the terrifying one' and personal names incorporating her name are also common amongst the retainers buried in the subsidiary graves surrounding the royal tombs at Abydos from the reign of Djer.

She was a part of the Triad of Latopolis at Esna along with Khnum ('The Great Potter' who fashioned human beings) and Heka (god of magic and medicine), replacing the goddess Menhet, who may have actually been only an aspect of Neith. She was also worshipped as the consort of Set, god of chaos, in another example of the importance of balance to the Egyptian religion. In the later Contendings of Horus and Set, Neith tells the gods of the tribunal that Horus should be declared king after his father Osiris's death and resurrection and that Set should rule the wild lands beyond Egypt's border and be given two goddesses, Anat and Astarte, as consorts to keep him company.

By the time of the Old Kingdom, she was considered a wise veteran and the dependable mediator of the gods and between the gods and humanity. Scholar Richard H. Wilkinson comments on this:

> Neith is one of the most ancient deities known from Egypt. There is ample evidence that she was one of the most important deities

of the prehistoric and Early Dynastic periods and, impressively, her veneration persisted to the very end of the pharaonic age. Her character was complex as her mythology continued to grow over this great span of time and, although many early myths of the goddess are undoubtedly lost to us, the picture we are able to recover is still one of a powerful deity whose roles encompassed aspects of this life and the beyond.

As with many, if not all, of the Egyptian deities, Neith was a part of a person's life from their birth through their death and on into the afterlife. One was never alone in the universe because the gods were constantly watching and protecting and guiding one on one's path and that path was eternal no matter how temporal it might seem to people on earth. Her annual festival was celebrated on the thirteenth day of the third month of summer and was known as the Festival of the Lamps. On this day, people arrived from all over Egypt to pay their respects to the goddess and offer her gifts. At night they would light lamps which, according to Herodotus, were 'saucers full of salt and oil, the wick floating thereon, and burning all night', and even those who did not attend the festival lighted such lamps in their homes, in other temples, and in the palaces so that the whole of Egypt would be illuminated all night long (Histories, II.62). These lamps were thought to mirror the stars in the night sky, which were claimed to be either deities or paths to those deities.

At Neith's festival, the veil between the earthly realm and the land of the dead was thought to part and people could see and speak with their departed friends and family members. The lights on earth mirroring the stars helped to part this veil because earth and the heavens would appear the same to both the living and the dead.

Amun/Amon was the most important aspect of both Re *and* Atum, later combined to establish an all-encompassing deity whose aspects were literally every facet of creation and who was the god of whom all the other gods, even Ptah and Re, were thought to be manifestations. Unlike most Egyptian creator gods, however, Ptah himself was *uncreated*, having existed before anyone or anything; he willed the world into existence with the power of his mind, like a great conjuror of celestial proportions. Not satisfied there, he used his speech (literally 'word') to give life to his creation. In Memphite texts, the present tense is used, indicating the ongoing act of sustaining life. As a deity of cosmic proportion, Set was also considered to be a fourth aspect of this powerful triad but few bother to talk about this!

Amun's role evolved over the centuries; during the Middle Kingdom he became the king of the deities and in the New Kingdom he became a nationally worshipped god. He eventually merged with Re, the ancient sun god, to become Amun-Re. It is thought that Amun created himself and then everything else in the universe, but distanced himself from it as 'the original inscrutable and indivisible creator'. When Amun and Re merged, he became a visible *and* invisible deity, which appealed to the ancient Egyptians' concept of *Ma'at* or balance. Amun is depicted as a goose, snake, or ram, and also as a man with the head of a ram, frog, royal cobra, crocodile, or ape.

Amun may have been originally one of the eight deities of the Hermopolite creation myth; his cult reached Thebes, where he became the patron of the pharaohs by the reign of Mentuhotep I. At that date, he was already identified with the sun-god Re of Heliopolis and, as Amon-Re, was received as a national god. Represented in human form, sometimes with a ram's head, or as a ram, Amun-Re was worshipped as part of the Theban triad, which included a goddess, Mut, and a youthful god, Khons. His temple at Karnak was among the largest and wealthiest in the land from the New Kingdom onward. Local forms of Amun were also worshipped at the Temple of Luxor on the east bank of Thebes and at Madīnat Habu (Medinet Habu) on the west bank.

His name meant the 'hidden one', and his image was painted blue to denote invisibility. And his influence was, in addition, closely linked to the political well-being of Egypt. During the Hyksos domination, the princes of Thebes sustained his worship. Following the Theban victory over the Hyksos and the creation of an empire, Amon's stature and the wealth of his temples grew (*Britannica*).

Predynastic Egypt originally consisted of small, independent settlements but because many deities in later times were strongly tied to particular settlements and regions, many scholars have suggested that the pantheon formed as disparate communities coalescing into larger states, spreading and intermingling the worship of the old local deities. Others have argued that the most important Predynastic gods were, like other elements of Egyptian culture, present all across the country despite its political divisions. Nevertheless, some important deities such as Isis and Amun (named) are not generally known to have appeared until the Old Kingdom.

At the beginning, each tribe or settlement probably had its own god – one related to the life of that particular group or location and so different cults were identified in specific areas of the Nile Valley; while differing religious beliefs grew up about the various cult centres. According to Paul Hamlyn, our knowledge of these comes from what appears to be the earliest representations of Egyptian deities.

> As we shall see, these symbols were to retain their significance for into the historical period, for later cults incorporated them into their own systems. Records of the religion practiced in Egypt extend over a longer span of time than for any other religion – and although the cult underwent some changes, basically the same

religion survived throughout all this period. If we accept that later accretions do not constitute an entirely new religion, then we must recognize that the Egyptian religion was in fact one with an unusually long life; its earliest manifestations date from the middle of the fourth millennium, and it was not finally eradicated in its later forms until the middle of the sixth century AD, when the cult of Isis was still carried on in the island of Philae.

(*Egyptian Mythology*)

Most Egyptian deities began by representing natural or social phenomena. The gods were generally said to be immanent in these phenomena – to be present within nature. The types of phenomena they represented include physical places and objects as well as abstract concepts and forces. Major gods were often involved in several types of phenomena. For instance, Khnum was the god of Elephantine Island in the midst of the Nile, the river that was essential to Egyptian civilisation. He was credited with producing the annual Nile flood that fertilised the country's farmland as part of a Triad with the goddesses Satet and Anuket. Perhaps as an outgrowth of this life-giving function, he was said to create all living things, fashioning their bodies on a potter's wheel. The best-preserved temple of Khnum is at Esna, where his consort was Menhyt, a relatively unknown lioness goddess. The so-called 'Famine Stele' at Sehel describes appeals to Khnum at a time of famine caused by low inundations.

Similarly, gods could share the same role in nature; Re, Atum, Khepri, Horus, and other deities acted as sun-gods. Despite their diverse functions, most gods had an overarching role in common: maintaining *Ma'at*, the universal order that was a central principle of Egyptian belief and was itself personified as a goddess. Yet some deities represented disruption to *Ma'at*. Most prominently, Apep was the force of chaos, constantly threatening to annihilate the order of the universe, and Set was an ambivalent member of divine society who could both fight disorder and foment it. Others had a more restricted role: like Shu was the deification of all the world's air; the goddess Meretsegar oversaw a limited region of the earth, i.e. the Theban Necropolis; and the god Sia personified the abstract notion of perception.

Likewise, Min was an ithyphallic fertility god of the harvest and the embodiment of the masculine principle, whose cult originated in Predynastic times. He was also worshipped as the Lord of the Eastern Desert and was represented with phallus erect, a flail in his raised right hand. Cult worship surrounding the fertility god was based upon the fetish of fossilised belemnite. Belemnite guards have been known since antiquity, and much folklore has evolved since. Before belemnites were identified as fossils, it was believed the amulets were some gemstone, namely lyngurium and amber. Later symbols widely used were the white bull, a barbed arrow, and a bed of lettuce that the

Egyptians believed to be an aphrodisiac. Egyptian lettuce was tall, straight, and released a milk-like sap when rubbed, characteristics superficially similar to the penis. Lettuce was sacrificially offered to the god, then eaten by men in an effort to achieve potency. Later pharaohs would offer the first fruits of harvest to the god to ensure plentiful harvest, with records of offerings of the first stems of sprouting wheat being offered during the Ptolemaic Period.

In Egyptian art, Min is depicted as an anthropomorphic male deity with a masculine body, covered in shrouds, wearing a crown with feathers, and often holding his erect penis in his left hand and a flail (referring to his authority) in his right. Around his forehead, the god wears a red ribbon that trails to the ground, claimed by some to represent sexual energy. The legs are bandaged because of his chthonic force, in the same manner as Ptah and Osiris. His skin was usually painted black, which symbolised the fertile soil of the Nile Valley. When he is represented as the constellation Orion, he can be distinguished from Osiris because the three bright stars of Orion's Belt are made to represent his erect penis.

His early images are the oldest examples of large-scale statuary found in Egypt so far. He was worshipped by King Scorpion of the Early Dynastic Period and his symbol appears on the El Amrah Palette (which is also known as the Min Palette). Because of his rather noticeable genitalia, images of Min were subject to a great deal of damage at the hands of more prudish visitors and during the Victorian period, Egyptologists regularly omitted the lower part of his body in photographs and drawings.

In a final insult to the god, nineteenth-century scholars mistranslated his name as Khem (meaning 'black' in Egyptian). This was in fact one of his epithets which related to his fertility aspect because black was associated with the fertile soil so central to the Egyptian way of life that the word also became a common term for the land of Egypt itself. Min's cult centre was Gebtu (Koptos), the capital of the fifth Nome of Upper Egypt, but in later times he was also associated with Khent-Min (Panopolis, Akhmim) the capital of the ninth Nome of Upper Egypt.

Nekhbet is an early Predynastic local goddess, who was the patron of the city of Nekheb (her name meaning 'of Nekheb'). Ultimately, she became the patron of Upper Egypt and one of the two patron deities for all of Egypt when it was unified. One of the oldest temples in Egypt is dedicated to her. The shrine was held in great esteem, as it housed one of Egypt's oldest oracles. Nekhbet's temple was supposedly so large and magnificent that the city of Nekheb was identified and known by it.

Her iconographic significance was firmly rooted in the duality of the 'Two Ladies' of Egyptian kingship from at least the 1st Dynasty. Most commonly she took the form of a vulture with wings outspread and talons holding *shen* signs (symbols of eternity) and it was in this form she usually appeared on royal pectorals and regalia. In paintings and reliefs, she was frequently depicted in a protective posture with one wing outstretched as she hovered over the scene below. In the *Pyramid Texts*, she is described as the 'White Crown' and associated with the principal shrine of Upper Egypt.

Of the several different species of vulture found in ancient Egypt, it was the 'griffon vulture' (*Gyps fulvus*) that was most frequently represented, whereas the hieroglyph with the phonetic value 'a' was the so-called Egyptian vulture (*Neophron percnopterus*). One of the earliest representations of Nekhbet as the griffon vulture is from a 2nd Dynasty stone vase of Khasekhemwy from Hierakonpolis.

Nekhbet was the patron of the Egyptian royal family. The queens of Egypt wore vulture headdresses. Due to her affiliation with the royal family, Nekhbet became one of the most renowned goddesses of Egypt, who preceded and guided the coronation festivities of a new king. Her symbols were etched onto the king's crown, as an emblem of guidance and protection; in art, Nekhbet was depicted as a vulture protecting the kings and their royal image. This role as protector of the king can be seen in the epic battle between Horus and Seth as Nekhbet protected Horus and guided him on his attempt to reclaim the throne.

Wadjet was the cobra goddess, whose name means 'the green one'. Her cult was particularly associated with the Lower Egyptian town of Buto, which dates back to the Predynastic Period. Usually portrayed as a rearing cobra, she was inextricably linked with the *uraeus* – the archetypal serpent-image of kingship that protruded just above the forehead on most royal crowns and headdresses.

The cobra served as the sacred image of Wadjet and as ruler of the Two Lands, the king included the cobra (*iaret*) and the vulture among his titles and insignia. The uraeus was sometimes described as the 'great enchantress' (*Weret hekaw*) and could be depicted as a cobra with a human head. Even before its identification with the king, the cobra's protective attributes were recognised and it was identified as the 'Eye of Re', sometimes shown protecting his solar images by spitting fire and venom. Pairs of cobras also guarded the gates that divided the individual hours of the underworld in the *Book of Gates*.

As the patron goddess, she was associated with the land and depicted as a snake-headed woman or a snake – usually an Egyptian cobra, a venomous snake common to the region; sometimes she was depicted as a woman with two snake heads and, at other times, a snake with a woman's head. Her oracle was in the renowned temple in Per-Wadjet that was dedicated to her worship and gave the city its name. This oracle may have been the source for the oracular tradition that spread to Greece from Egypt.

Another early depiction of Wadjet is as a cobra entwined around a papyrus stem, beginning in the Predynastic era (prior to 3100 BC) and it is thought to be the first image that shows a snake entwined around a staff symbol. This is a sacred image that appeared repeatedly in the later images and myths of cultures surrounding the Mediterranean, called the *caduceus*, which may have had separate origins.

The Memphite Cosmogony

The most important of the innumerable gods worshipped at Memphis was the sacred Apis bull, who served as the herald or go-between for the principal creator god, or demiurge – Ptah. Besides him stands Sekhmet – the lion goddess, whose name means 'the powerful one'. She is represented as a woman with a lioness-head and since the Egyptians thought that the desert was the source of all disease and pestilence – and since Sekhmet was considered as the ruler of the desert – doctors were referred to as the priests of Sekhmet. She is Ptah's consort, and called 'the one beloved of Ptah', who, along with Nefertum, were the divine family that made up the Memphite Triad.

The significance of the Triad held a marked importance within the religion which could take on the significance of a family grouping. Triads could be created to link local deities, or form an association of gods with similar aspects – the three gods representing divine power in its entirety; together creating a divine unity.

One Memphite god that should be mentioned is Imhotep, the chief architect of the king Zoser. After his death, he lived on in the memories of people for thousands of years until, in the Late Dynastic Period, he was defied. A cult of his own was developed, he was assigned special festival days, and was adopted into the divine world of the Memphite gods as the 'son of Ptah'.

> Imhotep's high standing in Djoser's court is affirmed by an inscription bearing his name on a statue of Djoser found at the site of the Ṣaqqārah pyramid. The inscription lists a variety of titles, including chief of the sculptors and chief of the seers. Although no contemporary account has been found that refers to Imhotep as a practicing physician, ancient documents illustrating Egyptian society and medicine during the Old Kingdom show that the chief magician of pharaoh's court also frequently served as the nation's chief physician. Imhotep's reputation as the reigning genius of the time, his position in the court, his training as a scribe, and his becoming known as a medical demigod only 100 years after his death are strong indications that he must have been a physician of considerable skill.
>
> (*Britannica*)

In the Cairo area, various cemeteries which date to the Early Dynastic Period have been excavated on both sides of the Nile, which has moved to the east since that time. David G. Jefferys of the Egypt Exploration Society has suggested that the settlement of Memphis was on the west bank of the Nile close to the escarpment where the elite tombs of north Saqqara are situated and that it was abandoned in the 3rd Dynasty when the river receded.

On the border between the Delta and the Nile Valley, Memphis was the royal residence and capital of Egypt during the Early Dynastic Period and Old Kingdom – and a city of major importance throughout the rest of its history. Many great temples must have been constructed there, including the sanctuary Hikuptah – 'the temple of the *ka* of Ptath'. Great as the city of Memphis was, it eventually declined and has long since disappeared under Nile-borne silt deposits. Only a few scant remains of one part of the sprawling site can be seen in the area of modern Mit Rahina. While hardly anything of the ancient capital of Memphis and its temples has survived, the vast burial grounds of the city proved to be more lasting and represent the greatest necropolis in the world.

Chapter Five

Old Kingdom Turmoil

In Egypt, the bridge between pre-history and history was a short but crucial period of transition when the main nation formed into a united state ruled by one king. These records show that before the beginning of the 1st Dynasty, the country was still divided into two kingdoms: the northern state with its capital in Buto (Pe and Dep) and the southern state, whose capital was Hierakonopolis (Nekken). According to the *Turin Canon* and the *King List* at Abydos, the unifier of the state and the first ruler of the 1st Dynasty bore the names of Menes, which some scholars identify with Narmer or Aha.

The emergence of this mighty civilisation in the Nile Valley at the end of the fourth millennium BC was to affect, in one way or another, not only the following 3,000 years of Egyptian history but also many of the subsequent civilisations of the ancient Near East. According to the *Chronicle of the Pharaohs*, these first kings came from This, an area somewhere near Abydos in Middle Egypt, and were called the Thinite rulers. As Peter A. Clayton records:

> Whatever their origins, they had the foresight, and power to match it, to mould the first two dynasties. Such is the gap in time, that we can only speculate, in many instances, on the political and economic situations and high level of technology, artistic achievement and religious awareness which, within about 500 years, laid down many of the concepts that were to govern later thought in ancient Egypt.

Nevertheless, as Toby A. H. Wilkinson observes in *Early Dynastic Egypt*:

> without central control of the economy, the royal court would not have had the resources to engage in monumental building projects. Without the ability to command the necessary manpower, the pyramids could not have been raised. Without the religious and ideological motivation, the construction of huge funerary monuments would, quite literally, never have got off the ground.

Religion plays an important role in most societies and early Egypt was no exception. The bewildering array of cults so characteristic of pharaonic Egypt was a feature of religious life in the Nile Valley from the beginning of history. Numerous deities are known from Early Dynastic times, together with religious festivals and other cultic observances. Academic writings have examined the way in which religion was manipulated by the royal court for its own ends; where the concerns of the individual and those of the state rarely coincided; where interaction with the divine sphere was involved. Nothing illustrates the divide between the early Egyptian state and its subjects better than its lavish temple-building programmes and the parsimonious attention given to local shrines. By analysing the religion in the first three Dynasties, Toby A. H. Wilkinson is able to highlight the tension that existed between rulers and ruled: a tension that Egypt's first kings sought to contain, but which led to the cataclysmic social upheaval at the end of the Pyramid Age.

According to *Encyclopaedia Britannica*, Egyptian religious beliefs and practices were closely integrated into the historical period. Although there were probably many survivals from pre-history, these may be relatively unimportant for understanding later times, because the transformation that established the beliefs of the Egyptian state created an entirely new context for religion.

Religious phenomena were pervasive, so much so that it is not meaningful to view religion as a single entity that cohered as a system. Nevertheless, religion must be seen against a background of potentially non-religious human activities and values. During its more than 3,000 years of development, Egyptian religion underwent significant changes of emphasis and practice, but in all periods religion had a clear consistency in character and style.

References to the Ogdoad, for example, date to the pre-history of Egypt, and even at the time of composition of the *Pyramid Texts* appear to have been antiquated and mostly forgotten by everyone except theologians. They are frequently mentioned in the *Coffin Texts* of the Middle Kingdom. The oldest known pictorial representations of the group do not pre-date the time of Seti I of the New Kingdom, when the group appears to be rediscovered by the priesthood of Hermopolis Magna for the purposes of creating a more elaborate creation-account.

These primal entities represented a stage of the cosmos prior to the appearance of the land and the light, and were: Nun and Nunet, 'the Abyss'; Heh and Hehet, 'Unlimitedness'; Kek and Keket, 'Darkness'; Amun and Amunet, 'Hiddenness'. Occasionally Tenem and Tenemet (Tenemuit) were later substituted for Amun and Amunet, the latter being increasingly distinguished from the rest of the Ogdoad as Amun rose to prominence as a god of national significance. Tenem, coming from a root meaning to go astray or become lost, is sometimes translated as 'Gloom' but is perhaps better understood, in accord with the generally privative character of the members of the Ogdoad, as 'the Nowhere'.

It may appear far-fetched to credit this ancient culture with such a sophisticated approach to beliefs in intuitive or reflective philosophical terms but the ancient Egyptians were extremely progressive in ways we find difficult to imagine. Many religious concepts are considered to be 'cross-culturally ubiquitous' as they are 'cognitively natural'. They are considered to be intuitive, meaning that they arise without much direction, instruction, or coaching in the early stages of intellectual development, and do not necessarily arise from cultural influence; such as religious concepts concerning 'afterlife', the five distinct parts of the individual: the physical body, the *ba*, the *ka*, the Name and the Shadow, together with certain supernatural agencies and miraculous events.

Other concepts required deliberate teaching to ensure transmission of these ideas and beliefs that are categorised as 'reflective', and are often stored in linguistic format that allows for ease of transmission within the House of Life. Reflective philosophies are thought to contribute significantly to the continuation of cultural and religious beliefs, such as fate, divine immanent justice, or providence, and also encompassing theological concepts such as the world emerging from an infinite, lifeless sea of chaos… to which all will return if the basic human obsequies – and other rites – are not observed.

The principal stages in the cosmogony involving the Ogdoad are typical of all Egyptian cosmogonies: the appearance of solidity amidst the watery abyss, in the form of a primeval mound of earth, followed by the coming forth of light. In the purest form of the Hermopolitan cosmogony, which may have existed at an early period or only developed later with the progress of speculative thought… 'They step upon the primeval mound and create light', as the 'fathers and mothers who came into being in the beginning, who gave birth to the sun, who created Atum'. Appropriations of the Hermopolitan cosmogony, however, generally treat the members of the Ogdoad as more akin to the material of cosmogenesis than its agents, in accord with their manifest attributes of indefiniteness and inertness. A catalyst of some kind is thus posited for whatever coagulation or reaction among the Ogdoad leads to the next stage in the creation, culminating in the advent of light at a mythical place known as the Isle of Flames, Iu-Neserser (*Henadology*).

According to *Britannica*, there were two essential foci of public religion: the king and the gods. Both are among the most characteristic features of Egyptian civilisation. The king had a unique status between humanity and the gods, straddled the world of the gods, and constructed great, religiously motivated funerary monuments for his afterlife. Egyptian gods were renowned for their wide variety of forms, including an animal head on a human body. The most important deities were the sun god, who had several names and aspects and was associated with many supernatural beings in a solar cycle modelled on the alternation of night and day, and Osiris, the god of the dead and ruler of the underworld. Later, with his consort, Isis, Osiris became dominant in many contexts during the first millennium BC, when solar worship was in relative decline.

The Egyptians conceived of the cosmos as including the gods and the present world – whose centre was, of course, Egypt – and as being surrounded by the realm of disorder, from which order had arisen and to which it would finally revert. *Disorder had to be kept at bay*. The task of the king as the protagonist of human society was to retain the benevolence of the gods in maintaining order against disorder. This ultimately pessimistic view of the cosmos was associated principally with the sun god and the solar cycle. It formed a powerful legitimation of king and elite in their task of preserving order.

Despite this pessimism, the official presentation of the cosmos on monuments was positive and optimistic, showing the king and the gods in perpetual reciprocity and harmony. This implied contrast reaffirming the fragile order. The restricted character of the monuments was also fundamental to a system of decorum that defined what could be shown, in what *way* it could be shown, and in what context. Decorum and the affirmation of order reinforced each other. These beliefs are known from monuments and documents created by and for the king and a small elite; the beliefs and practices of the rest of the people are poorly known. While there is no reason to believe that there was a radical opposition between the beliefs of the elite and those of others, this possibility cannot be ruled out.

In reality, however, by the end of the Old Kingdom, Egypt's 'Golden Age' was over as the land was plunged into anarchy and chaos, and revolution overturned the old established order. From Predynastic times, right up until the collapse of the Old Kingdom, the king was considered *personally* responsible for the well-being and stability of the land and its people. He was the intermediary between gods and men, and his role in life was to ensure this equilibrium was maintained via the channels of daily prayers and offerings at the temple. If the king did not fulfil his daily obligations to the gods on behalf of his people, then there *was* the danger of plunging everything back into Chaos and darkness from which it had originally sprung. We also know from historical evidence that around the end of the Old Kingdom, this system *did*, in fact, break down.

Archaeologists argue over whether the cause for such social catastrophe was due to several long years of famine, or civil unrest against the established system of a failing monarchy, but recent excavations suggest that it could have been a combination of both. During work at the temple site of Mendes, in Lower Egypt, during 1999–2000, Professor Donald B. Redford's team discovered, under the 18th Dynasty foundations, human remains dating to the second half of the 6th Dynasty.

> Found sprawled where they had fallen ... were the remains, in whole or in part, of 20 human individuals of all ages and sexes. Some lay in piles: an old woman over an old man who in turn lay

over a child; others lay singly: two adult males beside a slain pig. A young teen had fallen ... clutching a rodent of all things! Not a few had been dismembered as they lay. Following the slaughter (for such it surely was) came the destruction: parts of the mud-brick structure, which can only be the temple itself, had been demolished, and the debris allowed to fall on the bodies. Then someone had set fire to some combustibles and a conflagration had ensured, sending more fired and reddened brick cascading over the area.

(Susan Redford (ed.),
The Akhenaten Temple Project Newsletter)

The excavation revealed that a number of people had perished in the destruction – with many sprawled in groups, attempting to flee the temple, and in the aftermath no one returned to retrieve the corpses for burial. At other sites dating from the same period (6th Dynasty), excavations have uncovered mass graves, which indicate that people died, or were killed in large enough numbers that traditional burial was impossible. Whatever happened at the end of the 6th Dynasty, the Old Order that had lasted for so long was finally shattered by social revolution. This affected the whole governing system as the different classes threw off their burden of obligation and resorted to violence, bringing about a revolutionary upheaval that destroyed the ancient customs and traditional religious practice forever. Archaeological evidence indicates that the fury of the mob spared neither temples nor royal monuments; even the archives of government buildings and tombs were not respected.

From the cemeteries of the great, blocks of stone were removed and used for the tombs of little men. As a result a whole world was rent asunder ... For more than a century, social and religious values declined until the country reverted to a primitive state not seen in the Nile Valley since pre-dynastic times. Those remnants of the old traditions, which remained after the radical upheaval, were combined and modified to form a new mode of social existence in the new order, but the soul of ancient Egypt never recovered completely from the shock of this decisive change.

(K. Lange and M. Hirmer, *Egypt*)

This social upheaval, which destroyed the elitism of the Old Kingdom, needed to be brought back under control, and religion for the masses has always proved to have a uniting or calming effect on civic unrest. While the sun god remained the deity of the ruling family, the Theban priesthood had cornered the market with their own particular brand of evangelism; the propaganda machine geared into action, introducing the 'Cult of Osiris', which subsequent Greek historians faithfully recorded for posterity as if nothing else had ever existed...

What history *doesn't* tell us is what happened to the priesthood of the old stellar cult following this revolutionary uprising. *If* the discoveries at the Temple of the Divine Cult of *Ba-neb-djed* ('Ram-Lord of Djedet') at Mendes are anything to go by, it is possible that many of the stellar priesthood were butchered within the confines of their own temples. *If* the people believed the gods had deserted them, then someone would need to be held to account – and who more appropriate that the priests who had failed to serve them? *If* such massacres took place, then some of the priests (along with their families) would have been forced to flee the country, taking their vast stores of magico-religious knowledge with them.

Logic and historical precedence tell us that isolated pockets of Egyptian 'magi' would have survived, both inside and outside Egypt since it is impossible, either by legislation or genocide, to wipe a faith out of existence. There are subtle hints that the Mysteries still played an important part in Egyptian royal worship right up until 19th Dynasty, but this would have been a private affair, hidden from the scrutiny of the public and the lower echelons of the priesthood. Nevertheless, oral traditions can be incredibly tenacious, especially those that have been subjected to local variations and, in this manner, quite a considerable amount of stellar wisdom would have spread around the Mediterranean as the exiles moved further away from their native land – just as much later material would survive in the form of *Hermetic* texts.

Like many ancient deities, Anubis assumed different roles in various contexts at different times. Depicted as a protector of graves as early as the 1st Dynasty, Anubis was also an embalmer, or preserver. By the Middle Kingdom, he had been replaced by Osiris in his role as 'lord of the underworld'. One of Anubis's prominent and extant roles was that of a royal psychopomp, who ushers souls into the afterlife. He attended the weighing scale during the 'Weighing of the Heart', in which it was determined whether a soul would be allowed to enter the realm of the dead or face eternal destruction via the jaws of the demon, Ammut.

Despite the numerous depictions in horror movies as a 'baddie', this big black dog is one of the most popular of the Egyptian gods, and one of the most frequently depicted and mentioned gods in the pantheon, even though no relevant myths involved him. Anubis was depicted in black, a colour that symbolised regeneration, life, the soil of the Nile River, and the discoloration of the corpse after embalming. Associated with Wepwawet, another deity portrayed with a dog's head or in canine form, but with grey or blue fur, historians assume that the two figures were eventually combined. Both are depicted in art as a personable 'young dogs about town' and pleasing to the eye as a trusty companion.

The parentage of Anubis varied between myths, times, and sources. In early mythology, he was portrayed as a son of Re. In the *Coffin Texts*, which were compiled in the First Intermediate Period, Anubis is the son of either the cow goddess Hesat (associated with Hathor) or the cat-headed Bastet. Another tradition depicted him as the son of Set and Nephthys. The Greek Plutarch reported a tradition that Anubis was the illegitimate son of Nephthys and Osiris, but that he was adopted by Osiris's wife Isis. George Hart sees this story as an 'attempt to incorporate the independent deity Anubis into the Osirian pantheon'.

> For when Isis found out that Osiris loved her sister and had relations with her in mistaking her sister for herself, and when she saw a proof of it in the form of a garland of clover that he had left to Nephthys – she was looking for a baby, because Nephthys abandoned it at once after it had been born for fear of Seth; and when Isis found the baby helped by the dogs which with great difficulties led her there, she raised him and he became her guard and ally by the name of Anubis.

Anubis was one of the most frequently represented deities in ancient art and depicted in royal tombs as early as the 1st Dynasty. The god is typically treating a king's corpse, providing sovereignty to mummification rituals and funerals, or standing with fellow gods at the 'Weighing of the Heart of the Soul in the Hall of Two Truths'. One of his most popular representations is of him, with the body of a man and the head of a jackal with pointed ears, standing or kneeling, holding a gold scale while a heart of the soul is being weighed against *Ma'at*'s white feather.

The ancient Egyptians stood out for having numerous pets and for the particular affection they felt for them. The famous Greek historian Herodotus of Halicarnassus, who visited Egypt in the middle of the fifth century BC, stressed that 'domestic animals were abundant' and gave testimony of the great desolation that the death of a pet produced among the inhabitants of the house: 'They plucked their eyebrows in distress when their cat died, and they shaved the entire body, including the head, if it was a dog that died.'

It is not surprising, therefore, that since the Old Kingdom, the ancient Egyptians were represented with their pets on the walls of their tombs, on funerary stelae, and on sarcophagi.

The magical and religious power that was attributed to the image in Pharaonic Egypt (whether in the form of sculpture, relief, or painting) ensured that the owner and the animal he loved, thus represented, continued to enjoy each other's company in the Hereafter.

For the Egyptians, the dog was already man's best friend, the most faithful companion in the house and also the best companion in the hunt.

The domesticated dog entered the house and walked freely throughout it, accommodating itself under the chairs to eat, sleep, or rest near its caregivers. Ancient artists painted graceful dogs of different species and breeds on the walls of the tombs, sparing no details: some had a uniform coat, others were spotted; some had large, drooping ears, and others pointed and straight; there were sheepdogs and watchdogs; some were small, and others were energetic and fierce like the hound, a hunting dog that we recognise by its long snout, long, thin legs, and curly tail.

The cat, which the ancient Egyptians called *miu*, was domesticated from the Middle Kingdom. This feline was an effective hunter of mice, snakes, and other unwanted animals in homes and barns. For this he won the affection and sympathy of the peasants, and became one more guest of the house. Cats allowed a collar or a beautiful neckband to be put on them and often remained motionless under their masters' chairs while they enjoyed an appetising feast.

Starting in the New Kingdom, the cat is represented on the walls of the tombs of its owners with greater frequency. Judging by the images, this animal became the favourite pet of some royals, such as Queen Tiye, Princess Sitamun, and Prince Thutmose, the first-born of Amenhotep III – who had a magnificent stone sarcophagus made with beautiful reliefs and inscriptions for his beloved cat Tamit.

> Pets lived close to their masters, inside the houses. They received all kinds of care during their lives and when they died they were painstakingly mummified. The corpse of the animal was placed on a special embalming table to eviscerate it, that is, to extract its internal organs, which was done through an incision made in the side. Since the cost of embalming was considerable, the fact that a pet was mummified indicated that it had been extremely important to its owner. The attachment and affection that the Egyptians showed towards their domestic animals not only led them to represent them in a multitude of circumstances and places, but also to bury them in their own tombs. Some ancient Egyptian took this custom even further and introduced the mummy of his most beloved animal inside his own sarcophagus: Carefully mummified dogs have been found curled up at the feet of their masters. Perhaps in life the pet and its owner slept together and the owner wanted to continue to do so during his afterlife. The study of the mummies of the companion animals indicates that they received careful care during their earthly lives: shiny hair and strong bones reveal a continuous, healthy and balanced diet.
>
> (www.historicaleve.com)

Bastet, also called Bast, was worshipped in the form of a lioness and later a cat. The daughter of the sun god Re, Bastet was an ancient deity whose ferocious nature was tempered after the domestication of the cat around 1500 BC. She was native to Bubastis in the Nile Delta but also had an important cult at Memphis. In the Late and Ptolemaic Periods, large cemeteries of mummified cats were created at both sites, and thousands of bronze statuettes of the goddess were deposited as votive offerings. Small figures of cats were also worn as amulets; this too was probably related to the cult of Bastet.

According to *Early Dynastic Egypt*, Bastet assumed a degree of prominence in the early 2nd Dynasty, with inscriptions from the following reign naming the phyle of priests responsible for the provisioning and maintaining her cult. But the earliest attestations come from the galleries under the famous Step Pyramid of Djoser at Saqqara near Memphis. Thousands of sherds of stone vessels from burials of the 2nd Dynasty were discovered there. Some have short inscriptions mentioning deities, including a Bastet depicted as a female with the head of a lioness, plus priests and a possible cult place of Bastet in Memphis. It might be that Bastet was originally a deity of the royal residence.

Represented as a woman with a cat's head, Bastet carries an ancient percussion instrument, the *sistrum*, in her right hand; a so-called aegis, or breastplate (in Bastet's case, surmounted with the head of a lioness), in her left hand; and a small bag over her left arm. She wears an elaborately ornamented dress. Her cult was carried to Italy by the Romans, and traces have been found in Rome, Ostia, Nemi, and Pompeii (*Britannica*).

From her earliest attestations until the later New Kingdom, Bastet is exclusively shown as a lioness. Her famed symbolisation as a cat is a later development that reflects subtle changes in religious beliefs over many centuries of Egyptian history. In fact, a double nature of Bastet as lioness and cat is often expressed by her conflation with Sekhmet, another famous lioness goddess. This double nature of Bastet had been thematised in earlier textual sources. The so-called 'Loyalist teaching' of the 12th Dynasty describes the ideal character of the king as: 'He is Bastet who protects the two lands. He who worships him will be protected by his arm. He is Sekhmet against he who transgresses his order. The one he hates will be under distress.'

This ambivalent character of feline goddesses and especially Bastet developed further in subsequent periods. A cat symbolised the gentler, more accessible, more attractive nature of a feline goddess. This re-imagination of Bastet as a kinder form of lioness evidently led to her depiction as a cat, which did not pose the same threat to people as a real lioness. Interestingly, the Middle Kingdom is also the first time in which cats, although still close to their wild form *felis silvestris*, are shown as pets in tomb paintings. From the New Kingdom onward, the cult of Bastet enjoyed increasing popularity, especially in the first millennium BC when it spread outside Egypt into the Mediterranean world. The temples of Bastet at Saqqara and Alexandria were witness to this increasingly cosmopolitan cult.

The Old Gods of ancient Egypt underwent a startling metamorphosis as a result of the social upheaval of the 6th Dynasty. Nevertheless, the religion, as we have seen, was one whose creed was not laid down in a rigid formula, but was open to constant re-interpretation through cult and usage, and this is turn depended in part on external political or historical influences.

> As a religion embodied in the cult rather than in the doctrine, it could be kept alive only through the constant search of its adepts for new interpretations. It therefore adapted itself to the needs of the particular worshipper. The search for new symbols went on constantly; each one was considered to represent one facet of the truth and did not necessarily entail rejection of previously held concepts. Equally, as the symbols changed, so shifts of emphasis could occur over the centuries as to the interpretation of the myths.
>
> (*Egyptian Mythology*)

As scholarly work increases over the length and breadth of the Nile, we are made increasingly aware of the various milestones that mark the various important changes along the way. As Toby A. H. Wilkinson recorded in the Epilogue to his *Early Dynastic Egypt*, this period of history can no longer be regarded as an obscure transition, bridging the gap between the beguiling Predynastic Period and the spectacular Old Kingdom:

> The Early Dynastic period deserves to be treated in its own right as a major stage of ancient Egyptian civilisation; not just any stage, but the formative one. As we can see, most of the key features which, for us, define the ancient Egyptian civilisation were initially developed by the ruling élite of the Early Dynastic period. The mechanisms of rule which remained at the heart of Egyptian government for some three thousand years had their origin in the first three dynasties. They were formulated in response to the enormous challenge of ruling the world's first nation state. Their particular character suited not only the geography of Egypt but also the Egyptian psyche. Whether administrative structures, foreign relations, the ideology of divine kingship, royal mortuary architecture or the practice of religion, the solutions adopted by Egypt's early rulers to the problems of establishing authority moulded their country and profoundly influenced its subsequent development.
>
> (*Early Dynastic Egypt*)

As the country's outward appearance altered from the mighty archaic pyramidal structures to the monumental elegance of the later tombs and temples of the Middle Kingdom, the period was hailed as one of Egypt's three Golden Ages. The Middle Kingdom was also known as the 'Period of Reunification' as it was the time following a period of political division known as the First Intermediate Period, stretching from the reunification under the reign of Mentuhotep II in the 11th Dynasty to the end of the 12th Dynasty.

Pyramids were still the most important royal funerary buildings. At the beginning of the 12th Dynasty they were still built in stone, but under Senusret II the material for pyramid cores was mud-brick (with a limestone casing). A few temples of the period have been excavated. In the Middle Kingdom, limestone was the main building material for many temples, but mud was still an important material. Senusret I (of White Chapel fame) seems to have been the first king who rebuilt and enlarged the temples in a programme encompassing the whole country, although most of the buildings erected by him have been wrecked or disappeared.

Karnak, by contrast, is a Middle Kingdom temple complex located on the eastern bank of the Nile River, where the modern city of Luxor lies today. Karnak's grand temple construction began during the reign of Senusret I and took 1,500 years to complete, with as many as thirty successive pharaohs adding to it. This complex could reasonably be called a city of temples because its size covers an area of over 247 acres and it was bigger than some ancient cities. It is the largest temple construction in the world, with the largest room being the Great Hypostyle Hall with a surface area of 54,000 square feet and containing 134 gigantic columns.

During the Middle Kingdom Period, Osiris became the most important deity in popular religion. The modern reader must also constantly bear in mind that the Egyptian myths, unlike the Greek or the Roman, cannot be considered as fixed stories, explained Paul Hamlyn, since their function in the Egyptian religion was to provide a notation of symbols with which to express ideas; if the ideas changed, then the myths also had to change. And no myth is a better illustration of this principle than that of Osiris, which during the course of history underwent almost a complete reversal – of significance if not altogether of form ...

Chapter Six

The Second Golden Age

From its inception at the end of the fourth millennium BC, Egyptian civilisation had gone from strength to strength, according to Peter A. Clayton in *Chronicles of the Pharaohs*, in every sphere of the arts, sciences, and technology, reaching its zenith with Khufu's great monument at Giza.

> Small wonder then that the ancient Egyptians were complacent within sheltering and protective desert-backed cliffs of the Nile-Valley. The shock of the breakdown of that essential concept of stability. *Ma'at*, at the end of the Old Kingdom was therefore even greater because the unimaginable had happened. For 140 years chaos reigned only to be brought under control by a strong line of princes from Upper Egypt at Thebes. Just 250 years later central government and the concept of *Ma'at* broke down once again. The see-saw effect from one extreme to the other of the other was to become an unpleasant aspect of the structure of civilisation in the Nile Valley. Out of this period of disruption, now so dark and difficult to interpret, however, emerged the three luminous dynasties that were to comprise the New Kingdom.

The stage was now set for the Heliopolitan family to re-write history in favour of Osiris. The Great Ennead was only one of several such groupings of nine deities in ancient Egypt. Its claims to pre-eminence by its Heliopolitan priests, however, were not respected throughout Egypt. As close as Memphis was situated (also within modern Cairo), the priests of Ptah celebrated him as superior to the Nine... in addition to Memphis having its own creation myth, the Ogdoad/Hermopolitan grouping centred around physical creation and the eight primordial gods were another creation story that existed at the same time.

According to *Egyptian Mythology*, we suppose that Osiris was the first fetish of a conquering tribe which installed its god at Djedu, in the centre of the Delta region of Lower Egypt. This city was later named after him – Per-Usire, 'the House of Osiris' (Greek: Busiris). In Djedu, Osiris took the place of the former Lord of the City, Andjeti, a god associated with fertility cults, and represented him in human form as a king with the royal insignia of a long crooked sceptre, a whip in his hands and two feathers on his head. Identification of Osiris with Andjeti was strengthened by the fact that both were always represented as human; Osiris soon took the name Andjeti as an epithet and became known as 'Lord of Djedu'.

In the earliest times, the king was credited with the power to influence or control natural phenomena, simply because of his own great power. In later periods, the king was merely considered the intermediary between the gods, particularly the sun god, and human beings... and as such their only hope of securing the benevolence of the gods of nature and the benefits which they could confer. In either case, the benefits which the king brought to his land were benefits of nature. As recounted in the earlier discussions of the Osirian myth, he was originally supposed to have been an actual king of Egypt; in that case he would naturally transfer to his deified character attributes of a fertility god.

Whether it is because of this royal derivation or whether it is because of identification with Andjeti, who was always depicted as a living king and a god of fertility, Osiris was in fact associated with fertility cults from a very early stage. It seems, however, that as early as the period of the *Pyramid Texts*, Osiris was primarily a god of the dead. It was not until a much later stage, when he had usurped some of Re's functions, that he and his son Horus became the chief deities with which the pharaohs identified themselves, that the fertility associations were again to assume any great importance.

Heliopolitan Cosmogony

The Ennead or Great Ennead was a group of nine deities in Egyptian mythology worshipped at Heliopolis: the sun god Atum; his children Shu and Tefnut; his grandchildren Geb and Nut; and the great-grandchildren Osiris, Isis, Set, and Nephthys. An extension to this basic framework was the Osirian myth involving Osiris, his consort Isis, and their son Horus (the Younger); together with Anubis, whom Nephthys bore adulterously to Osiris. The murder of Osiris by Set, and the resulting struggle for power, won by Horus, provided a powerful narrative linking the ancient Egyptian ideology of kingship with the creation of the cosmos and the divinities of the 'First Time'.

According to the priests of Heliopolis, the sun god reposed, under the name of Atum-Re, in the bosom of Nun, the primordial ocean. He was originally a local god of Heliopolis, where his sacred animal was the bull Merwet (Greek, Mnevis). From very early times his priests taught that inside Nun, before the creation, there had lived a 'spirit, still formless, who bore within him the sum of all existence'. He was called Atum, and he manifested himself one day under the name of Re-Atum and drew from himself gods, men and all living things.

> Later Atum was personified as the setting sun and the sun before its rising. His cult spread widely through Egypt, co-jointly with that of Re, though the role of both was to change owing to the rival claims of other gods and other cults.
>
> (Egyptian Mythology)

His children were the first couple of the Ennead; Shu and his sister Tefnut being the first couple created by the creator god, through the practice of solitary procreation. The god of air, he represents more precisely the space that permits the sun's light to be diffused.

The god Shu is generally depicted anthropomorphically, wearing a single ostrich plume on his head, but is also frequently depicted as a lion. He is conventionally referred to as the god of the air, but Shu *is* air, not in an abstract elemental sense, but as life principle and as the void. Shu was the ancient Egyptian god of dry air, and so was considered a calming and cooling influence. In some Middle Kingdom texts, he was given the status of a primeval creator god; and later was frequently termed the 'Son of Re' (the sun god). He was also identified with Onuris, a warrior god, thus acquiring martial associations.

Shu belongs to the cosmic deities and as such no temples were dedicated to him since cosmic deities were never worshipped in a personified form. Many deities were represented only in human form: among these were such very ancient figures as the cosmic gods Shu of the air, Geb of the earth, the fertility god Min, and the craftsman Ptah. Although no temples have been traced dedicated to Shu, he was such an important god that small temples or chapels might well have built in his honour. Only the pharaoh and the priests of Shu were allowed inside the temple and the priests would undergo ritual purification in a deep stone pool before they entered the Inner Sanctum of the temple. This not only cleansed them but also gave them contact with the primeval moisture of life.

Ordinary Egyptians were only allowed to come to the gates, or forecourt of the temple of Shu to pay homage and offer gifts to the deities. The priests would collect the gifts and say prayers on behalf of the person in the confines of the temple. The priests would conduct ceremonies, make sacrifices, and chant magical incantations, sometimes referred to as spells. The temple of Shu would consist of heavy gates which accessed a massive hall with great stone columns, and then a series of many other rooms through which processions of priests would pass. These rooms, or chambers, were lit by lamps and incense would be burnt to purify the air of the temple. The chambers gradually decreased in size, the lighting in the temple was deliberately and significantly reduced to create an atmosphere of deepening mystery until the priests reached the chapel and the shrine which contained the *naos*. The *naos* was the stone tabernacle inside the shrine which housed the great statue of Shu, the god of wind and air.

This statue was situated in the inner sanctum of the temple. The statue of Shu would have been depicted with the body of a man and the head of a lion. This sacred statue, in the dwelling place of the god, was the embodiment of Shu. Food and drink would be offered to him. The high priest would conduct ceremonies and offer prayers and incantations but there was another important priest, called the *Medjty*, who was responsible for the toiletries. The statue of the god would have been washed and oiled; then dressed in fine linen and eye make-up, powder and rouge applied… with sacred oil rubbed on the forehead of the likeness. The statue of Shu, with its lion's head, was only seen by ordinary Egyptians at important festivals when the effigy was paraded in magnificent processions.

Shu was also the god of dry air, since his name meant 'dryness' or 'emptiness'. He was mentioned in both the *Coffin* and *Pyramid Texts*, but was not well known outside these religious areas until after the New Kingdom. As the air, Shu was considered to be a cooling, and thus calming, influence, and pacifier. Due to the association with dry air, calm, and thus *Ma'at* (truth, justice, order, and balance), Shu was depicted as the dry air/atmosphere between the earth and sky, separating the two realms after the event of the First Occasion. Shu was also portrayed in art as wearing between one and four feathers. The ostrich feather was symbolic of lightness and emptiness. Fog and clouds were also Shu's elements and they were often called his 'bones'. Because of his position between the sky and earth, he was also identified as the wind.

Generally, he was depicted as a well-built man holding the Egyptian symbol of life, the *ankh*, and was perceived as a very tranquil deity. He was the deity people prayed to whenever they needed calm and peace and for this role, he was revered as the 'Divine Pacifier'. In the underworld, Shu is one of the forty-two judges who judge the souls of the dead and, being the god of the wind, he was generally called upon by sailors for a safe and speedy voyage on the sea.

There are a number of variants to the myth of the creation of the twins Tefnut and Shu. In every version, Tefnut is the product of parthenogenesis, and all involve some variant of body fluid. In the Heliopolitan creation myth, Atum sneezed to produce Tefnut and Shu. *Pyramid Text* 527 says, 'Atum was creative in that he proceeded to sneeze while in Heliopolis. And brother and sister were born – that is Shu and Tefnut.' In some versions of this myth, Atum also spits out his saliva, which forms the act of procreation. This version contains a play on words, the *tef* sound which forms the first syllable of the name Tefnut also constitutes a word meaning 'to spit' or 'to expectorate'. The *Coffin Texts* contain references to Shu being sneezed out by Atum from his nose, and Tefnut being spat out like saliva. The *Bremner-Rind Papyrus* and the *Memphite Theology* describe Atum as sneezing out saliva to form the twins.

Tefnut was the goddess of moisture, moist air, dew, and rainfall. She was the twin sister-wife and female counterpart of the air god Shu. Tefnut was an early

Predynastic deity and worshipped as part of a system of gods in the ancient city of Heliopolis and the mother of Geb and Nut. She was also at times a lunar deity, associated with the cycles and power of the moon. As a water goddess in a desert civilisation, Tefnut was more directly responsible for maintaining life than nearly any other deity.

Tefnut is a leonine deity, and appears as human with a lion's head when depicted as part of the Great Ennead of Heliopolis. The other frequent depiction is as a lioness, but Tefnut can also be depicted as fully human. In her fully or semi-anthropomorphic form, she is depicted wearing a wig, topped either with a *uraeus* serpent, or a *uraeus* and solar disc, and she is sometimes depicted as a lion-headed serpent. Her face is sometimes used in a double-headed form with that of her brother Shu on collar counterpoises.

Heliopolis and Leontopolis (now Tell el-Muqdam) were her primary cult centres. At Heliopolis, Tefnut was one of the members of that city's great Ennead, and is referred to in relation to the purification of the *wabet* (priest) as part of the temple rite. Here she had a sanctuary called the Lower Menset.

> *I have ascended to you*
> *with the Great One behind me*
> *and [my] purity before me:*
> *I have passed by Tefnut,*
> *even while Tefnut was purifying me,*
> *and indeed I am a priest, the son of a priest in this temple.*
> (*Papyrus Berlin 3055*)

At Karnak, Tefnut formed part of the Ennead and was invoked in prayers for the health and well-being of the pharaoh. She was worshipped with Shu as a pair of lions in Leontopolis in the Nile Delta. Tefnut was also connected with other leonine goddesses as the Re. As a lioness she could display a wrathful aspect and is said to have escaped to Nubia in a rage, jealous of her grandchildren's higher worship. Only after receiving the title 'honourable' from Thoth did she return. In earlier *Pyramid Texts* she is said to produce pure waters from her vagina (sic). And, as Shu had forcibly separated his son Geb from his sister-wife Nut, Geb challenged his father Shu, causing the latter to withdraw from the world. Geb, who was in love with his mother Tefnut, took her as his chief queen-consort.

One of the most important deities in Old Egypt and one of the first goddesses to be created according to Egyptian religion, Tefnut was not only the goddess of water, but of rain and all moisture. She is an important figure within ancient belief because she is part of the original creation myth and is responsible for the birth of many gods and goddesses associated with Heliopolitan theology. Tefnut is commonly depicted in art alongside her twin brother and husband Shu and together they gave birth to Geb and Nut, the god of earth and goddess of the sky, respectively. These deities and the story of their creation are the roots of Egyptian religion and culture.

Water is an essential component of life, and as such Tefnut was a very important deity to the creation myth, as well as the sustainability of daily life in Egypt. She was worshipped as a goddess of creation, who shared the space between heaven and earth with her twin brother and sometimes associated with fertility and life-giving powers. In worship centres and sanctuaries such as Leontopolis in the Nile Delta, Tefnut is commonly portrayed as a lioness or a female with the head of a lion. Tefnut was typically worshipped through rituals or funerary rituals but there is also evidence of large feasts being held in her honour.

As Shu symbolises dry air and the force of preservation, Tefnut symbolises moist or corrosive air that brings about change, creating the concept of time. These two represent the Old Guard of the ancient Egyptian pantheon and of a stern or strict bearing or demeanour; forbidding in aspect. Their austere presence stresses an absence of warmth, colour, or feeling and may apply to rigorous restraint, simplicity, or self-denial.

As a lioness goddess she also incarnates, as does Sekhmet, the solar eye. More specifically, she represents the goddess who goes into self-exile in Nubia. It is Shu who is despatched to look for her, and Thoth is the one who, with his beautiful speeches, induces her to return to Egypt. The Wandering Goddess myth is also the source of a few fables and this is one of the stories Thoth and Shu told Tefnut to cheer her up. It is about a mouse and a lion with a thorn in its paw. Many people today know this story as the fable from a Greek writer named Aesop. Except in this case, Aesop was just repeating a story that was already popular in Egypt!

The fable is introduced as an illustration into a longer Egyptian myth in a papyrus of indeterminate date towards the start of the Common Era AD: a lion previously unacquainted with man comes across examples of his cruelty and exploitation of other animals and decides to hunt him down. On his way, the lion spares a mouse that comes beneath his paw and it promises to return the favour. This the mouse does by gnawing the lion free when he is netted in a trap set by man. In general, the evidence points to the tale being adapted from a Greek source. There was a long-established Greek trading colony in Egypt and the document appeared during the reign of the Ptolemaic dynasty, which was of Greek origin itself.

> Atum's grandson Geb is the god of the earth, the physical support of the world, and along with his sister, Nut formed the second generation in the Ennead of Heliopolis. In Egyptian art Geb, as a portrayal of the earth, was often depicted lying by the feet of Shu,

the air god, with Nut, the goddess of the sky, arched above them. Geb was usually portrayed as a man without any distinguishing characteristics, but at times he was represented with his head surmounted by a goose, the hieroglyph of his name. He was the third divine ruler among the gods; the human pharaohs claimed to be descended from him, and the royal throne was referred to as 'the throne of Geb'.

(Britannica)

Despite being an important figure in the Egyptian pantheon, portrayals of the earth god vary, sometimes even wildly. The most common depiction of Geb show him in a purely human form, often adorned with vegetation to symbolise his connection to fertility and farming, wearing the Red Crown of Lower Egypt and a goose sitting on top of his head. His is sometimes also depicted as having either pure green hair, another connection to his earth epithet, or even having completely green skin. The green skin could be another symbol for his earth connection, or it could also be in reference as the father of all snakes. He was also sometimes depicted in human form, shown with the head of either a snake or a goose.

Geb's depiction alongside his sister-wife remains more consistent. In these portrayals, Geb is depicted in his more human form, sometimes surrounded by vegetation or with his distinctive green hair. He is shown in a reclined position underneath his wife Nut, and with his phallus often pointing in her direction. This not only depicts the intimate relationship between the two gods which resulted in their five children, but also showcases Nut's role as a sky deity, being placed highly above Geb or the earth, and Geb's function as a fertility god with a large phallus. He was unusual because he was a male earth deity, while most ancient cultures regarded the earth as female.

Geb was associated with a wide range of powers in Egyptian mythology. These include powers over earthquakes, tides, fertility, and healing, as well as the power to pass judgement over the dead souls. He was also considered the father of snakes. One of the ancient Egyptian names for snakes stood for *son of the earth*. Because of this, people saw them as offspring of Geb. In some accounts, Geb was the spouse of Renenutet, the cobra goddess of the harvests. In these depictions, he was a deity associated with chaos.

Nut and her brother, Geb, may be considered enigmas in the world of mythology. In direct contrast to most other mythologies which usually develop a sky father associated with an earth mother (or Mother Nature), she personified the sky and he the earth.

Also known as 'Lady of the Starry Heavens', Nut secretly married her brother against Re's wishes, and as a result he had them brutally separated by Shu... and afterwards decreed that Nut could not bear a child in any given month of the year. Thoth, Plutarch tells us, happily had taken pity on the couple and, playing draughts with the Moon, he won in the course of several games a seventy-second part of the Moon's light, with which he created five new days. As these epagomenal days did not belong to the official Egyptian calendar of 360 days, Nut was thus able to give birth successively to five children: Osiris, Horus the Elder (Haroeris), Set, Isis, and Nephthys. These were also known as the 'Children of Disorder' because of the disruption their quarrels caused in the creation... a prophecy that Atum-Re had obviously foreseen!

She was usually depicted as an elegant woman bent over earth with her head in the west and feet in the east; represented as a woman with an elongated body, touching the earth with toes and fingertips, while her star-spangled body, held aloft by Shu, forms the arch of the heavens. When she is pictured as a woman, as opposed to the celestial cow – who carried Re to the sky after he turned his back on his rebellious subjects – she often wears a rounded vase on her head, this being the hieroglyph of her name. On the inner lid of a sarcophagus, her starry body stretches above the mummy, watching over him for eternity.

Also known by various other transcriptions, she is the goddess of the sky, stars, cosmos, astronomy, and the universe in the ancient Egyptian religion. She was seen as a slender star-covered nude woman arching over the earth. The pronunciation of ancient Egyptian is uncertain because vowels were long omitted from its writing, although her name often includes the unpronounced determinative hieroglyph for 'sky'. Her name *Nwt*, itself also meaning 'sky', forms *The Book of Nwt* – a modern title of what was known in ancient times as *The Fundamentals of the Course of the Stars*. This is an important collection of ancient Egyptian astronomical texts, perhaps the earliest of several other such texts, going back at least to 2000 BC. Nut, being the sky goddess, plays the big role in the *Book of Nut*. The text also tells about various other sky and earth deities, such as the star deities and the decans deities. The cycles of the stars and the planets, and the time keeping, are covered in the book.

These Heliopolitan quintuplets made up what is perhaps the most dysfunctional family in the history of divine kingship. According to *Egyptian Mythology*, hieroglyphic texts contain numerous allusions to the life and deeds of Osiris (Asir) during his sojourn on earth; but it is above all thanks to Plutarch that we know his legend so well. At his birth a loud, mysterious voice proclaimed the coming of the 'Universal Lord', which gave rise to shouts of gladness, soon followed by tears and lamentations when it was learned what misfortunes awaited him. Re rejoiced in the news of his birth in spite of the curse he had pronounced against Nut; and, having Osiris brought into his presence, he recognised his great-grandson as heir to his throne...

There were various versions of the Osirian legend and it underwent great changes through the course of history. In early times, certainly, he was a localised god before becoming one of the most important gods of ancient Egypt.

The origin of Osiris *is* obscure; he was a local god of Busiris, in Lower Egypt, and may have been a personification of chthonic (underworld) fertility and did not originally belong to any of the great cosmogonies, but being merged at a later stage to the family of gods venerated at Heliopolis, Hermopolis, Memphis, and Thebes, because the priests of those centres were anxious that the Osirian cult should not entirely engulf their own. As Paul Hamlyn points out: 'As Osiris in this powerful and universal form does not properly belong to the early Egyptian religious systems, we must leave full consideration of it to its rightful place.'

> As a vegetation spirit that dies and is ceaselessly regenerated, Osiris represented the corn, the vine, and the trees. He is also the Nile, which rises and falls every year; and the light of the sun, which vanishes in the shadows every evening to reappear more brilliantly at dawn. The struggle between the two brothers, Set and Osiris, is the war between the desert and the fertile earth, between the drying wind and the vegetation, between aridity and fecundity and between darkness and light.
>
> (*Egyptian Mythology*)

He was worshipped throughout Egypt in company with his sister-wife Isis and Horus, his posthumous son, who formed a Triad. He is represented tightly swathed in white mummy wrappings and his greenish face is surmounted by the high white mire flanked by two ostrich feathers of the *Atef* crown of Upper Egypt. In *Daily Life of the Egyptian Gods*, the authors observe:

> Osiris could seem colourless and excessively narcissistic, not to say egotistical. His precious self, power and privileges were his chief preoccupations. is wife was absent from his thoughts, while his son existed for him only insofar as he would ensure his [father's] triumph in the hereafter while seeing to it that he [Osiris] also maintained his power everlastingly in this world.

Isis (Asest) was originally a modest localised goddess of the Delta, the protective deity of Perehbet, north of Busiris, where she always retained a renowned temple. In later days her popularity became such that she finally absorbed the qualities of all the other goddesses and replaced them in the scale of importance. In the Nile Valley, Isis kept her worshippers until well into Christian times. It was not until the middle of the sixth century, in the reign of Justinian, that the temple of Philae – her chief sanctuary in the extreme south of the country – was closed to her cult and turned into a church. Great festivals were celebrated in spring and autumn in the honour of Isis. The splendours of the processions which then took place have been described to us by Apuleius, who was an initiate in the Mysteries. Thanks to him we can raise a corner of the veil which conceals the secret ceremonies of initiation.

> Isis, the mother and weeping widow, sometimes overplayed her role, profiting from her situation to monopolise the attention of her peers. In fact, she was rather cold and proud. She was not in the habit of letting her scruples get in the way of her objectives, but in this, she was quite like her fellow gods. It was universally acknowledged that she was perfectly faithful to her deceased husband and whole-heartedly loved his child, even if her love was not devoid of tactical considerations.
>
> <div align="right">(<i>Daily Life of the Egyptian Gods</i>)</div>

Isis is normally represented as a woman who bears on her head a throne, the hieroglyph of her name. Later, when Isis was identified with Hathor, she was represented with a headdress of a solar disc, set between cow's horns and sometimes flanked with two feathers. Despite the maternal imagery always associated with her, there is an instance of her interference over his dealing with Set that sent the Elder Horus into such a fit of rage that he cut off his mother's head – which Thoth had to put right by the use of powerful enchantments.

Isis also became known as a sly and a potent magician. It is recorded that when she was still only a simple woman in the service of Re, she persuaded the great god to confide to her his secret name in order to obtain immense magical power. In the Egyptian view, however, heka is the energy that underlies, interpenetrates, and empowers all things. Nevertheless, Thoth taught Isis all the Mysteries and magic she knows and she subsequently acted as Thoth's instrument to deliver the teachings in a form humanity could use.

The Heliopolitan priesthood carried out the ultimate 'hatchet-job' on Set's reputation when establishing the Ennead and in the Osirian myth he figures as the eternal adversary. All that is creation and blessing comes from Osiris; all that is destruction and perversity arises from Set. In primitive times, however, the evil character was not so accentuated. The old *Pyramid Texts* make him *not* the brother of Osiris, but the brother of Horus the Elder, and speak of terrible struggles between them which were terminated by the judgement of the archaic gods, who proclaimed Horus the victor and banished Set to the desert. It was only later, when the Osirian myth had become established, and when the two Horuses had become confused, that Set was made the uncle of Horus (the Child) and the eternal enemy of Osiris.

Originally Set seems to have been the Lord of Upper Egypt, who was overthrown by the worshippers of the falcon god and the legendary struggles between the brothers may reflect historical events. The bas-reliefs of the Old and Middle Kingdoms show the pair together at the base of the royal throne binding the plants of Upper and Lower Egypt around the emblem that expresses the idea of union of the two countries. A function which Set no doubt preserved from his earlier character in the tradition of the solar myths was that of one of the crew of the solar *barque*, who stood in the prow to defend Re against his enemies.

> One finds few character traits indicating distinctive, sharply etched personalities and Set stands out as the sole exception. It must be said that he was an 'excessive' god, and that this lent him a profile that his reputedly perfect fellows lacked. Violent, aggressive, given to drink, he was also brave, and a pitiful victim of his own passions.
>
> (*Daily Life of the Egyptian Gods*)

Along with the objective of discovering the original Set *before* he was drawn into the Osirian mythos – which can only be achieved by attempting to cut through the Osirian façade that obscures the real Set to allow us to see this primal *neter* in his own right. Yet Set was also possessed of another quality that the Egyptians could not, and would not, dismiss so easily. This was his tremendous strength and courage, and his ability to defend his fellow *neteru* against greater forces than themselves. Once he had been excluded from the Osirian family, Re adopted him as his son... and had a very good reason for doing so...

Apophis was said to wait for Re's boat at a place called Bakhu, the furthermost mountain in the west. As the boat sank into the western horizon at Bakhu, Apophis rose up and hypnotised all the occupants of the boat with his stare – with the single exception of Set. Set is usually depicted as standing in the prow of the boat with spear in hand ready to defend Re and repel the attacker. Set is said to either charm Apophis with a spell or else spears him and renders him incapable of harming or impeding Re. The boat then continues on its journey over the vanquished body of Apophis into the Twelve Hours of Night.

Horus the Elder (Haroeris) was the god the Egyptians referred to as the falcon they saw soaring above their heads, and many thought of as a divine bird whose two eyes were the sun and the moon. The hieroglyph which represents the idea of 'god' was a falcon on its perch. In the course of time and in different sanctuaries which were dedicated to him, his role and attributes varied. Thus we find in the Egyptian pantheon some twenty Horuses, among whom it is important to distinguish Horus the Elder and other falcons of a solar character from Horus, son of Isis of the Osirian legend and infant avenger of his father; Egyptians of the later periods were to confuse the solar Horus and the Osirian god of the same name.

In the *Pyramid Texts*, Haroeris is the son of Re and brother of Set. In the early texts, the Horus of this legend was Horus the Elder, but later sources make the epic battle take place between Set and Horus the Child. Behdety is another name of the great celestial Horus, who was worshipped at Behdet, a district of ancient Edfu. Behdety is usually represented in the form of a winged sun disc and often appears in battle scenes hovering above the pharaoh like a great falcon with outspread wings,

Nephthys had obviously inherited some of her sister's slyness, since it was her role in the Osirian myth to seduce her brother-in-law. The fruit of this union was Anubis. Nephthys helped Isis bring Osiris back to life after he was killed by Set, so she is often depicted in tombs and on coffins as a protector of the dead, specifically associated with the organs placed in canopic jars. Nephthys and Isis look very similar and can only be differentiated by their headdresses. Nephthys is shown with a basket on her head, however she is also sometimes depicted as a hawk or a mourning woman; Isis wears a throne. According to *Britannica* she plays practically no part outside the myth of Osiris, in which her only function is to bewail with Isis the death of Osiris and seduce him. The meaning of her name ('Mistress of the Castle') suggests that she is a mere personification of Osiris's residence, while Isis (meaning 'Seat') personifies his throne.

Like Isis, Nephthys was believed to have great power through her knowledge of sacred words and magical spells. She knew charms that could raise the dead and keep them from harm. Nephthys's healing skills and status as direct counterpart of Isis, steeped, as her sister in 'words of power', are evidenced by the abundance of faience amulets carved in her likeness and by her presence in a variety of magical papyri that sought to summon her famously altruistic qualities to the aid of mortals. She was appealed to as Mistress of the Gods, Lady of Life, Lady of Heaven, Mistress of the Two Lands, and Great Goddess.

There can be little doubt that a cult of Nephthys existed in the temple and great town of Herakleopolis, north of Sepermeru. A near life-sized statue of Nephthys (currently housed in the Louvre) boasts a curiously altered inscription. The basalt image originally was stationed at Medinet Habu as part of the cultic celebration of the pharaonic 'Sed Festival', but was transferred at some point to Herakleopolis and the temple of Herishef. The cult-image's inscription originally pertained to 'Nephthys, Foremost of the Sed [Festival] in the Booth of Annals' (at Medinet Habu), but was re-inscribed or re-dedicated to 'Nephthys, Foremost of the [Booths of] Herakleopolis'. A 'prophet of Nephthys' is indeed attested for the town of Herakleopolis in the 30th Dynasty.

Nephthys was considered the unique protectress of the Bennu bird. This role may have stemmed from an early association in her native Heliopolis which was renowned for its House of the Bennu temple. In this role, Nephthys was given the name 'Nephthys-Kheresket' and a wealth of temple texts from

Edfu, Dendera, Philae, Kom Ombo, El Qa'la, Esna, and others corroborate the late identification of Nephthys as the supreme goddess of Upper Egyptian seventh nome, where another shrine existed in honour of the Bennu. Nephthys also was the goddess of the Mansion of the Sistrum in Hwt-Sekhem (Gr. Diospolis Parva), the chief city of seventh nome. There, Nephthys was the primary protectress of the resident Osirian relic, of the Bennu Bird, and of the local Horus/Osiris manifestation, the god Neferhotep.

She was most widely and usually worshipped in ancient Egypt as part of a consortium of temple deities. Therefore, it should not be surprising that her cult images could likely be found as part of the divine entourage in temples at Kharga, Kellis, Deir el-Hagar, Koptos, Dendera, Philae, Sebennytos, Busiris, Shenhur, El Qa'la, Letopolis, Heliopolis, Abydos, Thebes, Dakleh Oasis, and indeed throughout Egypt. In most cases, Nephthys found her typical place as part of a triad alongside Osiris and Isis, Isis and Horus, Isis and Min, or as part of a quartet of deities.

An extension to this basic framework was the Osiris myth involving Osiris, his consort Isis, and their son Horus the Child (Harsiesis), who was conceived after her husband's death. The Osirian legend recounts the posthumous birth of the child which Isis had of Osiris by magical means, reanimating the corpse of the murdered god. Harsiesis was originally a minor falcon god from the neighbourhood of Buto, who was called Horus the Younger in order to distinguish him from the great sky god Horus the Elder.

Anubis, whom Nephthys bore adulterously to Osiris, is represented as a black jackal or as a black-skinned man with the head of a jackal. In the *Pyramid Texts*, he is the 'fourth son of Re' and his daughter Kebehut is the goddess of freshness. But later he was incorporated into the family of Osiris, having been abandoned by his mother at birth and found by Isis, who undertook to bring up the baby.

Chapter Seven

The Unconquerable Sun

A solar god or sun deity is a being who represents the sun, or an aspect of it. Such deities are usually associated with power and strength, and can be found throughout most of recorded history in various forms. Sun worship was, of course, prevalent in ancient Egyptian religion.

For example, Shu and Tefnut are sometimes called Ruti, or 'the two lions'. In their lion forms, with the sun (Re) between them, they form the horizon-god Aker or Akeru, who guarded the eastern and western borders of the netherworld. This leads to another nickname for them: Yesterday and Tomorrow, or the sides of the horizon. The Aker symbol was so popular that the Greeks and Romans took it from Egypt, and we can see houses and buildings with lions on either side of the doorway even today.

Khepri is a scarab-faced god who represents the rising or morning sun. By extension, he can also represent creation and the renewal of life. There was no cult devoted to Khepri, and he was largely subordinate to the greater sun god Re. The sun god was, however, included in the creationist theory of Heliopolis and later Thebes. Often, Khepri and another solar deity, Atum, were seen as aspects of Re: Khepri was the morning sun, Re was the midday sun, and Atum was the sun in the evening.

> As a deity, Khepri's four main functions were creator, protector, sun-god, and the god of resurrection. The central belief surrounding Khepri, however, was the god's ability to renew life, in the same way he restored the sun's existence every morning. Mummified scarab beetles and scarab amulets have been found in pre-Dynastic graves, indicating that Khepri was respected early on in Egypt's history.
>
> (*The Presence and Significance of Khepri in Egyptian Religion and Art*)

Re (also given as Ra) is the sun god of ancient Egypt. He is one of the oldest deities in the pantheon and was later merged with others such as Horus, becoming Re-Horakhty (the morning sun), Amun (as noonday sun), and Atum (the evening sun) associated with primal life-giving energy. According to scholar Richard H. Wilkinson, Re is 'arguably Egypt's most important deity', not only because of his association with the life-giving sun but also through his influence on the development of later gods. Amun, who would become so popular that his cult was almost monotheistic in devotion and the most powerful in ancient Egypt, developed from Re and shares much of his mythology. Horus, who was associated with the living king, followed this same paradigm as Re, being known as 'king and father of the king'. He was also associated with the creator god Atum and the two deities' names are used interchangeably in some versions of the creation myths.

There are some twenty Horus personages with a solar character and it is important to differentiate between those of the Early Dynastic Period and those of the later era. Horus is one of the earliest known Egyptian gods, because there are mentions of this god going back to the beginning of Egyptian history, and he is depicted in the oldest known cult statue in existence. The most common form in which Horus appears in iconography is the falcon. Sometimes, and especially from the Middle Kingdom onward, Horus is shown as a winged sun disc, representing the Horus of Behdet, a town in the Nile Delta and an important cult centre of the falcon god. This is one of the most widespread images in Egyptian religious architecture, and there are thousands of examples in museums and in monuments.

In *World History*, Professor Wilkinson suggests breaking any discussion of Re (for example) into five separate sections in order to address his various roles and functions:

- Re in the Heavens
- Re on the Earth
- Re in the Netherworld
- Re as Creator
- Re as King and Father of the King

This course of study is suggested for this deity more so than others because of the scope of his powers, the important part he played in Egyptian religion, and his long history. Worship of Re was already established by the time of the Old Kingdom and continued for almost 2,000 years until, like the other pagan gods, he was eclipsed by Christianity.

Re is first mentioned in the *Pyramid Texts*, the oldest religious works in the world, which were inscribed on the sarcophagi and walls of tombs at Saqqara. In these, Re gathers the soul of the king to himself and takes him to the paradise of the Field of Reeds in his golden barque. Worship of Re was already well established at the time these texts were inscribed – which are thought to derive from a much earlier oral tradition. His cult centre was at the city of Iunu (better known as Heliopolis, the Greek name, which means 'city of the sun god').

Understanding the Egyptian Gods and Goddesses

Re is depicted in the *Pyramid Texts* not only as the supreme ruler of the gods, nor simply a comforter of the newly arrived soul in the afterlife, but as the embodiment of divine order and balance.

Horus was also directly linked with Egyptian kingship since the earliest times when his image appeared in the rectangular devices known as *serekhs*. *Serekhs* were emblems of the earliest pharaohs and showed the falcon god perched on the façade of a palace enclosure. This implied a direct association between Horus and the kings, and indeed the 'Horus name' was one of the many titles of the king. As well as being characterised by a Horus name, the king was typically depicted with a form of the falcon hovering above his head.

Because of the life-giving qualities of the sun, the Egyptians worshipped it as a god; the creator of the universe and the giver of life. Re is therefore associated with this transformative power, which linked him with the sun that allowed for growth. Once associated with the sun, he was also linked with Horus the sky god and solar deity (as Re-Horakhty) while, as creator god, he was almost synonymous with Atum and, finally, as the champion of order and the seen and unseen world, with Amun, the ineffable representation of the nature of existence; in this capacity, he was known as Amun-Re. And it is not surprising that Horus was acknowledged as his son by the goddess Hathor.

Re is almost always depicted as the falcon-headed male Re-Horakhty with the solar disc above his head, although sometimes also shown as the scarab beetle below the solar disc (in this form he is known as Re-Khepri). His worship was already well established by the 2nd Dynasty and took the form of sacrifices made in temples dedicated to him. By the time of the 5th Dynasty, kings associated their reigns with Re, resulting in the construction of the Sun Temples of the period built to honour the god. From an early date, he was worshipped at Heliopolis in the form of the Mnevis bull, the living embodiment of Re, comparable to the better-known Apis bull.

Appearing in many manifestations over thousands of years, Horus is one of the only deities whose precise origin is known. He was born in the city of Nekhen (Hierakonpolis in Greek), where he was worshipped in the Old Kingdom as 'Horus of Nekhen'. His cult expanded rapidly throughout the country, and thus the falcon god appeared in many places as a local god, under different epithets and names. He was, for instance, Harakhtr (Horus of the Horizon), a second son of Re and his daughter Hathor.

There are many depictions of Horus as an old man in the Temple of Kom Ombo, near the First Cataract of the Nile. The name that accompanies the paintings and statues is Haroeris, 'Horus the Elder', a figure of wisdom and experience. Finally, the falcon god was worshipped in many towns and cities as Harakhte, and closely associated with Re, as the sun god. Later, both figures blended into one, Re-Horakhty, who was almost invariably depicted as a winged solar disc. Later still, a third deity was added to the composite god, making him the most powerful god of the Late Period, Re-Horakhty-Atum. When Horus merged with Re, he came to be known as Re-Horakhty, the Morning Sun. Most depictions of this composite god show him in anthropomorphic form, with the head of a falcon and a solar disc above his head. One rare ivory comb, dating to the 1st Dynasty, shows a boat with a falcon over a pair of outstretched wings, implying that this was the solar barque and that the falcon god traversed the sky as the sun god.

The conception that the reigning king was a manifestation of Horus arose sometime during the 1st Dynasty, at Nekhen. Afterward, when Upper and Lower Egypt became united by the Nekhen kings, this notion became an accepted dogma. Proof of this is the fact that Horus was equally worshipped in the Delta (for example, in Behdet) and in Upper Egypt. At Edfu, for example, there were many ceremonies to celebrate the falcon god. During the annual Coronation of the Sacred Falcon, held at the beginning of the fifth month of the Egyptian calendar, a real-life falcon was selected to represent Horus as king of all Egypt. The rituals held during this important festival symbolised the unification of the Two Lands by Horus.

Similarly, when the Ennead awarded Horus the Younger the kingship of Osiris, he became known as Harsomptus, 'Horus the Uniter', for he was supposed to keep together both parts of the country: Upper and Lower Egypt. The falcon god gladly fulfilled the role of ruling over the unified land, but in some texts found at Kom Ombo and Edfu, a different story is told. Here, Horus the Elder has a son with Hathor, called by the name Panebtawy, 'Lord of the Two Lands', and who is in charge of maintaining unity and peace in the whole country.

Re was associated with the sky in the *Pyramid Texts* and already linked with the sun and life-giving energy, but a later text, known as the *Book of the Heavenly Cow*, provided the details of how Re left the earth, which he once ruled directly, and ascended to heaven. The *Book of the Heavenly Cow* is thought to have existed in some form during the First Intermediate Period and written during the Middle Kingdom. All the extant texts, however, come from the period of the New Kingdom. The story relates how Re has grown old and his human subjects begin to plot his overthrow. Re is upset and calls a council of the other gods who encourage him to smite the humans for their ingratitude. Re summons The Eye of Re, usually personified as a goddess, which is a powerful force that alternately does Re's bidding or breaks free of his control to wreak havoc. Either way, The Eye of Re always brings about some form of transformation and this story aligns with all others concerning the Eye in this regard.

When Re became tired of ruling over humans, he asked the goddess Nut to carry him into the heavens. Nut turned herself into a celestial cow and took him skyward on her back. On his way, Re created the 'Field of Reeds' and organised the administration of the world, leaving it to the other gods. Human beings would henceforth be responsible for maintaining order in keeping with the will of these lesser gods and Re, having retired, will only concern himself with driving his great *barque* across the sky.

Prior to his departure, Re ruled over his creation directly from earth, creating the laws which were later bequeathed to humanity by Osiris. Re's presence on earth was recognised by sunlight and the growth of crops as well as the changing seasons, since a specific and important example of his influence on the earth was seen in that the god was said to direct the three seasons of the Egyptian year – thus influencing the annual inundation of the Nile and the subsequent growing and harvest seasons.

Re was honoured through Houses of Life, scriptoria attached to temples, where the works of scribes were kept under the protection of the god of writing Thoth and his consort (and sometimes daughter) Seshat. These written words, which recorded the past and so helped to maintain balance and order in the present, were given to humanity by Thoth but, as Creator of All, ultimately came from Re; the Houses of Life were considered emanations of Re himself who also inspired correct *interpretation* of the written works.

Following the abdication of the Creator, Re sailed across the sky in his *barque* throughout the day and then descended down into the underworld at night. The solar *barque* now transformed into the evening *barque* was known as the 'Ship of a Million Souls' – which picked up the newly arrived and justified dead to bring them to the paradise of the Field of Reeds. Re at this time became merged with Osiris, the judge of the dead; Osiris was seen as the 'corpse' and Re as the 'soul' of a single deity, Re-Osiris.

As the *barque* sailed on through the underworld, it was attacked by the serpent Apophis who tried to kill Re and prevent the sunrise. Led by a spear-wielding Set, the gods onboard fought the serpent off with the help of the justified dead – while on earth, the living encourage the defenders through ritual ceremonies, channelling positive energies to strengthen those on board. Every night Apophis attacks, and every night he is defeated by Set and his spear, Re and his crew sail on toward dawn, the justified dead are delivered to their destination, and the sunrise was then seen as the sign that Re was again victorious, and that Egypt would see another day.

This was only one version of the soul's journey toward paradise. In the New Kingdom work known as the *Book of the Dead*, the soul must stand in judgement before Osiris who weighs the soul's heart against the white feather of truth (the feather of *Ma'at*, goddess of harmony and balance) and, if the scales remained even, the soul was allowed to proceed (after Osiris confers with the Forty-Two Judges and other gods); if the heart was heavier than the feather, the soul would cease to exist. Re was considered present at the judgement in his form as Re-Osiris or invisibly as inspiration for Osiris's just decision. *Ma'at*, as one of Re's daughters, also embodied his presence at the judgement and was among his defenders on board the *barque* which, once dawn came, again transformed into the solar *barque*.

To add to the confusion, Egyptian mythology gives credit to a number of different gods for establishing order and making the world, but whichever gods are named, they always have the same characteristics and power as Re, and it is thought that Re was present – and alone – at the birth of creation no matter what name he was known by later. Although the priests of Ptah (for example) might claim it was their god who created all things, therefore, the Ptah they cite would actually be Ra. In the case of Atum, he was essentially Re only by another name, and the same could be said for Neith in her creative capacity.

Balance was the most important cultural value of ancient Egypt, and it was modelled and maintained by the king. The ruler was thought to have been sanctified by the gods for his ability to keep order which was understood as balance/harmony. The founder of the 5th Dynasty of the Old Kingdom, the king Userkaf, epitomised this ideal in elevating the Cult of Re to the position of almost a state religion and encouraging his subjects to maintain Re's values. Userkaf built the Nekhenre – the Sun Temple of Re – near Abusir and established a tradition venerating Re which continued throughout the dynasty.

Userkaf was the first king to erect a temple to Re but all of his successors would follow suit, creating a model for the tradition of erecting temples in Re's honour which continued throughout Egypt's history. The 5th Dynasty is best known for the sun temples as well as firmly establishing the link between a monarch and the gods. Userkaf and his successors referred to themselves as 'sons of Re' and were understood as literally being the children of the god. At this time, Re was already recognised as king of the gods but was now known as 'King and Father of the King' who maintained order through the just rule of his sons.

This policy established the king (known as 'pharaoh' only in the New Kingdom) as the god's own emissary on earth and demigod in his own right. By the time of the New Kingdom, Re had been replaced by Horus as the god of the king while he lived and reigned, and as Osiris after his death. In keeping with the belief that Re was the Self-Created from whom all else came, however, it would still have been the power of Re behind both Horus and Osiris, Professor Wilkinson tells us.

> Re as the unseen power behind all other powers extended to every god in the Egyptian pantheon. Famous goddesses such as Bastet (protector of hearth and home), Hathor (goddess of joy, dance, music, and love), and Isis (goddess of magic, the moon, and healing) were all aspects of the life force of Re as were their male consorts. Ra was the Giver of Life in the form of the sun who became associated with the Breath of Life in his form of Amun. He is sometimes depicted as Ra-Horakhty presenting the gift of life to a monarch by placing the symbol of the *ankh* to the king's lips.

It is a testament to Ra's enduring popularity that, during the reign of the so-called heretic king Akhenaten, who closed down and outlawed every other cult, he allowed the cult of Re to remain and worship to continue. This is no doubt because Akhenaten's personal god, Aten, was a solar deity patterned closely on Re and developed from both his and Amun's attributes.

Once Akhenaten's successor, Tutankhamun restored the old religion, Re's cult resumed its place among the many others and influenced their iconography. Even in depictions of other gods during the New Kingdom, images of Re such as solar discs and falcon heads and sun's rays make an appearance. The cult continued to exert this kind of influence, gradually waning during the Roman Period, until the old gods went into the Shadows...

(*Encyclopedia of World History*)

Eye of Re

The Eye of Re was an entity in Egyptian mythology that functioned as a feminine counterpart to the great sun god and a violent force that subdues his enemies. The eye was an extension of Re's power, equated with the disc of the sun, but often behaved as an independent – if virulent – goddess. This was the symbol of the omnipotence of the creator god Re and one of the most important emblems of ancient Egypt.

Hathor was a major goddess in the ancient religion who played a wide variety of roles. As a sky deity, she was the mother or consort of the sky god Horus and the sun-god Re, both of whom were connected with kingship, and thus she was the symbolic mother of their earthly representatives, the pharaohs. She was one of several goddesses who acted as the Eye, being his feminine counterpart, and in this form she had a vengeful aspect that protected him from his enemies.

Her beneficent side represented music, dance, joy, love, sexuality, and pleasure, and she acted as the consort of several male deities and the mother of their sons. These two aspects of the goddess exemplified the Egyptian conception of femininity. Her images were depicted as being slightly voluptuous and in mythology she was shown as being a bit of a 'flighty piece' – she crossed boundaries between worlds, helping the deceased in the transition to the afterlife – she was one of the forty-two state gods of Egypt, and one of the most popular and powerful. She was the protector of women, though men also worshipped her. She had priests as well as priestesses in her temples, one of the best-preserved complexes being at Dendura.

Hathor in the guise of the Eye of Ra here is released to destroy humanity. She kills thousands before Re realises what he has done and repents, begging her to stop. Hathor has lost all reason through the slaughter, however, and become the savage Sekhmet who, in her rage, cannot hear him. With the aid of Thoth, Re orders 7,000 jugs of beer to be dyed red with pomegranate juice to resemble blood and has them poured out on the plains of Dendera. Hathor-Sekhmet drinks the blood-beer, passes out, and wakes as Hathor, who pledges herself as a friend to humanity henceforth.

In Egyptian mythology, Sekhmet is a warrior goddess as well as goddess of healing, who is depicted as a lioness. She is a solar deity, sometimes called the daughter of Re and often associated with the goddesses Hathor and Bastet. As the vengeful manifestation of Re's power, in the Eye of Re, Sekhmet was said to breathe fire, and the hot winds of the desert were likened to her breath. She was also believed to cause plagues (which were called as her servants or messengers), although she was also called upon to ward off disease.

The myth surrounding the end of Re's rule on the earth, the same story was also described in the prognosis texts of the *Calendar of Lucky and Unlucky Days* of *Papyrus Cairo 86637*. In other versions of this story, Sekhmet grew angry over a deception and left Egypt, diminishing the power of the sun. This threatened the power and security of the world – thus, she was persuaded by the god Thoth to return and restore the sun to its full glory.

Tefnut was also connected with leonine goddesses and the Eye of Re. As a lioness, she could display a wrathful aspect and is said to have escaped to Nubia in a rage, jealous of her grandchildren's higher worship. Only after receiving the title 'honourable' from Thoth did she return. In the earlier *Pyramid Texts*, she is said to produce pure waters from her vagina (Geraldine Pinch, *Handbook of Egyptian Mythology*).

As an ancient goddess of moisture, she was strongly associated with both the moon and the sun. She was known as both the left (moon) and the right (sun) 'Eyes of Re' and represented moisture (as a lunar goddess) and dryness (or the absence of moisture, as a solar goddess). For Egyptians, the Eye of Re represented the sun, specifically its destructive power. Many also used it to protect themselves and their buildings, so it had different meanings for everyone involved. People also painted it on amulets, and some myths even suggest that it was an ancient weapon.

Eye of Horus

The 'Eye of Re' is often confused with the 'Eye of Horus'. However, the two are quite distinct. The Eye of Re represents the right eye, and the Eye of Horus the left eye. Re is the sun god, his power is quite close to the almighty gods of the monotheistic religions. According to later traditions, the right eye represented the sun and so is called the 'Eye of Re' while the left represented the moon and was known as the 'Eye of Horus' (although it was also associated with Thoth and Tefnut).

The *left eye* (which has the 'tail' trailing off to the right side) is the *Eye of Horus*, which represents the *moon*.

The *right eye* (which has the 'tail' trailing off to the left side) is the *Eye of Re*, which represents the *sun*.

In the Old Kingdom, originally the right eye and the left eye were both associated with Horus. However, over time, the right eye became solely associated with Re, but after Hathor restored Horus's eye, the classic 'Eye of Horus' symbol took on the meaning of an incredibly powerful force of protection. Early on in the history of Egypt, the Eye of Horus symbol was only permitted to be worn by pharaohs and because only pharaohs wore the symbol, it became associated with divine royalty. Like many ancient symbols, however, they commonly have multiple meanings, and the Eye of Horus was no exception.

Amulets shaped into the Eye of Horus first appeared in the late Old Kingdom but by the time of the New Kingdom, Eye of Horus amulets became more popular and were used as a symbol of protection on a wide range of mummified bodies. Today 'the Eye' has fallen quite a bit from its original status of 'pharaoh only', although the symbol is still widely recognised and seen as both ancient and mysterious.

The stylised symbol was used interchangeably to represent the Eye of Re but Egyptologists often simply refer to this symbol as the *wedjat* eye. Amulets in this shape first appeared in the late Old Kingdom and continued to be produced up to Roman times. Ancient Egyptians were usually buried with amulets, and the Eye of Horus was one of the most consistently popular forms. It is one of the few types commonly found on Old Kingdom mummies, and it remained in widespread use over the next 2,000 years, even as the number and variety of funerary amulets greatly increased. Up until the New Kingdom, funerary *wedjat* amulets tended to be placed on the chest, whereas during and after the New Kingdom they were commonly placed over the incision through which the body's internal organs had been removed during the mummification process.

Chapter Eight

Thrice Great Thoth

Thoth – the ancient Khemetic god of multiple names and titles – Thoth, Tahuti, *Djehuty*, Sheps, Lord of Khemennu, Asten, Khenti, Mehi, Hab, A'an... His roles in Egyptian mythology were many. He served as scribe of the gods, and is credited with the invention of writing and hieroglyphs. In the underworld, *Duat*, he appeared as an ape, Aani, the god of equilibrium, who reported when the scales weighing the deceased's heart against the feather, representing the principle of *Ma'at*, was exactly even.

The Egyptians regarded Thoth as One, self-begotten, and self-produced. He was the master of both physical and moral (i.e. divine) law, making proper use of *Ma'at* and credited with making the calculations for the establishment of the heavens, stars, earth, and everything in them. The Egyptians also credited him as the author of all works of science, religion, philosophy, and the arts of magic. The Greeks further declared him the inventor of astronomy, mathematics, geometry, surveying, medicine, botany, theology, civilised government, the alphabet, reading, writing, and (*phew!*) oratory. They further claimed he was the true author of every work of every branch of knowledge, human and divine!

In addition, Thoth was also known by specific aspects of himself, for instance the Moon god Iah-Djehuty (*j3ḥ-ḏḥw.ty*), representing the Moon for the entire month. The Greeks related him to their god Hermes due to his similar attributes and functions. One of Thoth's titles, 'Thrice Great', was translated to the Greek – making Hermes Trismegistus. He played many vital and prominent roles in Egyptian mythology, such as maintaining the Universe, and being one of the two deities (the other being *Ma'at*) who stood on either side of Re's solar *barque*. In later mythology, he became heavily associated with the arbitration of godly disputes.

Throughout his life, Thoth's name was linked with other goddesses other than *Ma'at*, who refers to the ancient Egyptian concepts of truth, balance, order, harmony, law, morality, and justice and was also the goddess who personified these concepts, and regulated the stars, seasons, and the actions of mortals and the deities who had brought order from chaos at the moment of creation. Another consort was Seshat, goddess of writing, the keeper of books, and patron goddess of libraries and librarians who was – alternately – his wife and/

or daughter. She was often depicted with the notched palm rib that represented the passing of time.

As a reward for his services, Thoth was also given the goddess Nehemtawy as a consort who, Geraldine Pinch claims, was 'a pacified version of the Distant Goddess'. Nehmetawy was a protector goddess whose name means: 'She Who Embraces Those in Need'. She was worshipped at Hermopolis where she was considered the wife of the snake deity, Nehebkau; in other regions, she was the consort of Thoth. In fact, Thoth's chief temple was located in the city of Hermopolis – 'Khemenu': Coptic: *Shmun*. Later known as *el-Ashmunein* in Arabic, it was partially destroyed in 1826. At Hermopolis, Thoth led 'the Ogdoad', a pantheon of eight principal deities. Needless to say, he also had numerous shrines in other cities.

With all these attributes, it's not surprising that Egypt's long-suffering 'Mr Fix-it' endured long past the collapse of his own ancient civilisation and into the twenty-first century, courtesy of the various esoteric Orders that continued to honour him down through the millennia. Being one of the oldest deities of the Egyptian pantheon, he is attested in many sources from the earliest periods of Egyptian history up to the Roman Period. The etymology of his name remains unexplained, possibly due to the name's antiquity. Perhaps it is his age as a divine figure that led to a rather confusing mythology with a series of contradicting traditions concerning his descent and his reputation as a benevolent versus atrocious or mistrusted deity (UCLA, *Encyclopaedia of Egyptology*).

Thoth is known from the earliest historical periods onwards: he already played a prominent role in the oldest religious texts of Egypt, the *Pyramid Texts*, and continued to appear almost everywhere in Egypt up to the end of Egyptian religion some 4,000 years later. Throughout this long period, the god is overwhelmingly present in a vast body of documentation that yields an extraordinarily colourful picture of his nature and functions within the Egyptian pantheon.

The more data and sources are collected, the more Thoth's picture becomes blurred and it seems that he embodies almost every possible aspect one could imagine a god to have within any mythology: in addition to the characterisations mentioned above, he is found acting as a cosmic deity, a primeval creator, and a warlike divinity.

The creation myth promulgated in the city of Hermopolis focused on the nature of the Universe *before* the creation of the world. This was a place of infinite watery waste, chaotic and dark, stagnant and immobile. This darkness was not that of night, for day and night had not yet been created and a concept of 'nothingness' did not exist in the ancient Egyptian psyche.

According to the theologians of Hermopolis, Thoth was the true universal Demiurge, the divine ibis who hatched the world-egg at Hermopolis Magna.

They taught that he had accomplished the work of creation by the sound of his voice alone.

> When he [Thoth] first awoke in the primordial waters of Nun, he opened his mouth and from the sound that issued forth, four gods materialized and then four goddesses. For this reason the future Hermopolis was called Khnum – 'City of the Eight'. Without any real personality these eight deities perpetuated the creation of the world by the word: Logos and the texts tell us that they sang hymns morning and evening to assure the continuity of the sun's course.
>
> (*Egyptian Mythology*)

The inherent qualities of the primeval waters were represented by those eight entities, called the Ogdoad. The goddess Naunet and her male counterpart Nu represented the inert primeval water itself; Huh and his counterpart Hauhet represented the water's infinite extent; Kek and Kauket personified the darkness present within it; and Amun and Amaunet represented its hidden and unknowable nature, in contrast to the tangible world of the living. The primeval waters were themselves part of the creation process; therefore, the deities representing them could be seen as creator gods.

According to the myth, these eight beings were originally divided into male and female groups. They were symbolically depicted as aquatic creatures because they dwelt within the water: the males were represented as frogs, and the females as snakes. These two groups eventually converged, resulting in a great upheaval, which produced the Sacred Mound, from which the sun rose into the sky to light the world.

As we have seen, even from primitive times, the Sacred Mound was an integral part of the evolution of Egyptian temple design. This mound is of particular significance as it may have been regarded as a symbol of the original mound of creation, from which the primordial falcon god was said to have surveyed the world. The location of the Osireion in the temple of Seti I at Abydos is due to the proximity of a natural spring. This seems to have been used to provide a pool of water around the subterranean 'grave' in order to make it a model of the mythical mound of creation, which the Egyptians believed rose from the primeval waters.

> In the world of giant metaphors which was the Egyptian temple, each element in the architectural programme played a role in symbolizing some aspect of the origins and function of the cosmos itself. There is no single model by which we may understand the symbolic complexities of the Egyptian temple,

> for the ancient structures often represented many concepts that had evolved over time and in different locations and settings. In the developed temple, individual features might be designed and decorated to appeal to or to strengthen any one or more of those ideas. This is because Egypt's mythology was complex, many-faceted and replete with different, and even contradictory, ways of viewing the same facts – a situation that was nevertheless acceptable within the overall system of Egyptian religion.
>
> *(The Complete Temples of Ancient Egypt)*

Little remains of the Temple of Thoth at Hermopolis Magna, the main cult centre and an important pilgrimage site; the main temple may have been quite ancient but over the passage of time it was constantly undergoing extensive changes and structural alterations. Hermopolis was the administrative centre of the nome of Hermapolites, which belonged to the larger administrative unit of the Upper Egyptian region of Thebais. It was also at times called Wenu, 'the City of Hares', probably derived from the name of the fifteenth Upper Egyptian nome, which had as its emblem the royal hare standard.

During its entire history, Hermopolis was always an important administrative city and also, because of its Thoth temple, a significant religious centre. The nomarch (governor), who was often also the high priest and thus controlled the temple, must certainly have played a decisive role in the unification of the kingdom of Thebes under Montuhotep I, and again later during the unrest that occurred when Amenemhet I was removed from the throne.

During the New Kingdom, the temple of Thoth was constantly rebuilt and expanded; an altar of Amenhotep II stood near the entrance at the Dromos. In the foundations of the temple of the 13th Dynasty were found pieces of the colossal baboons made of quartzite, dating from the time of Amenhotep III, which have since been erected in the northern sector. Horemheb erected a new southern entrance pylon for the temple and, nearby Tell el-Amarna, with the easily accessible blocks of the residence of Akhenaten, provided the material for the numerous new buildings erected under Ramesses II.

In the temple area, Ramesses II erected an entrance pylon, cobbled the court to the south of the Horemheb pylon and re-dedicated the cult to Amun. The temple took into consideration the cemetery of the First Intermediate Period, which had long existed, and possibly this slightly elevated spot was seen as the place of the primeval hill in the myth of creation. The location of the sacred lake is unknown, but it must have corresponded to the Lake of Fire, or the Island of the Hermopolitan Creation.

Another sacred complex, dating from the time of Ramesses III, possibly contained chapels of various gods, as texts refer to numerous buildings in honour of Osiris, Ptah, Horus, Hathor, Mut, and the southern version of Thoth.

There were also statues of the protector gods of the city in the shape of baboon and ibis which stood in the courts, although as yet it has been impossible to locate most of the chapels (*Tour Egypt*).

In year eight of Nectanebo I's reign, the New Kingdom temple of Thoth was demolished and work begun on a new temple measuring 55 by 110 metres with a huge *pronaos* – a vestibule before the sanctuary. It was at this time that the two colossal baboon statues from the reign of Amenhotep III were dismantled and buried in the foundations of the new *pronaos*. Today, the general outline of the original Thoth structure can be detected, but is apparently underwater.

> The Temple of Thoth must have been a building of great magnificence and the whole of the temple was roofed with stone since light had to be excluded as much as possible. Horizontal slit-windows were made at the top of the walls immediately below the ceiling for the purpose of ventilation and illumination. The only light which entered the building was the reflection from the white limestone walls of the shafts, cast down through the slits which was arranged to fall on the rows of statues against the walls.
>
> (*Egyptian Temples*)

In all Egyptian temples a 'dim religious light' was as essential to the cult of the god, as the offerings themselves. The brilliant glare of the sunshine and the glowing sand outside made the contrast with the darkness within still more marked. In the dim twilight of the halls, where the dark red walls and columns would absorb rather than reflect light, the statues of polished stone would be clearly seen against the dark background, every detail softened by the subdued light which fell upon them from above. Barefooted, white-robed priests and worshippers would be lost to sight in the gloom…

It is here, in the ambiance of an ancient temple that we will catch up with the god of magic and mystery, who will lead us to the hidden *Book of Thoth*, which contains all the magic in the world.

The Egyptians stored many texts, on a wide range of subjects, in 'Houses of Life', the libraries contained within temple complexes. As Thoth was the god of knowledge, many of these texts of knowledge were claimed to be his work and the Egyptian historian, Manetho credited him with writing 36,525 books. Christian theologian, Clement of Alexandria, in the sixth book of his work *Stromata* – intended for a limited, esoteric readership – mentions forty-two books used by Egyptian priests that he claimed contained 'the whole philosophy of the Egyptians'. All these books he attributed to Hermes – a pre-existing god that the Greeks likened to Thoth, claiming they were one and the same, having similar qualities. The translation from the Egyptian language and concepts into Greek were not entirely accurate, which meant that much of the Egyptian authenticity was lost. Among the subjects they covered were hymns, rituals, temple construction, astrology, geography, and medicine.

The Egyptologists Jasnow and Zauzich dubbed a long Demotic text from the Ptolemaic Period the *Book of Thoth* – known from more than forty fragmentary copies, it consists of a dialogue between a person called 'The-one-who-loves-knowledge' and a figure that the historians identify as Thoth. The topics of their conversation include the work of scribes, various aspects of the gods and their sacred animals, and the *Duat*, the realm of the afterlife.

The *Book of Thoth* appears in a short story from the Ptolemaic Period, known *as Setne Khamwas and Naneferkaptah* or *Setne I*. The book, written by Thoth himself, is said to contain two spells, one of which allows the reader to understand the speech of animals, and one of which allows the reader to perceive the gods themselves. According to the story, the book was originally hidden at the bottom of the Nile near Coptos, where it was locked inside a series of boxes guarded by serpents. The Egyptian prince Neferkaptah fought the serpents and retrieved the book, but in punishment for his theft from Thoth, the gods killed his wife Ahwere and son Merib. Neferkaptah committed suicide and was entombed along with the book.

Generations later, the story's protagonist, Setne Khamwas (a character based on the historical prince Khaemwaset), stole the book from Neferkaptah's tomb despite opposition from Neferkaptah's ghost. Setne then met a beautiful woman who seduced him into killing his children and humiliating himself in front of the Pharaoh. He discovered that this episode was an illusion created by Neferkaptah, and in fear of further retribution, Setne returned the book to Neferkaptah's tomb. At Neferkaptah's request, Setne also found the bodies of Neferkaptah's wife and son and buried them in Neferkaptah's tomb, which was then sealed. The story reflects the Egyptian belief that the gods' knowledge is not meant for humans to possess.

Worship of Thoth began in Lower Egypt most likely in the Predynastic Period and continued through the Ptolemaic Period, the last dynastic era of Egyptian history, marking Thoth's veneration as the longest of the Egyptian gods – or any deity from any civilisation. His name was often taken by the kings of Egypt (example, Tuthmoses – 'Born of Thoth'), scribes, and priests.

He is most commonly depicted as a man with the head of an ibis or a seated baboon, with or without a lunar disc above his head. He was the patron god of scribes and it was said that scribes would pour out one drop of their ink in Thoth's honour before they began their daily work.

According to one story, Thoth was born 'from the lips of Re' at the beginning of creation and was known as the 'god without a mother'. In another tale, Thoth is self-created at the beginning of time and, as an ibis, laid the cosmic egg which holds all of creation. He was always closely associated with Re and the concept of divine order and justice – although they didn't always see eye to eye! Re was not known for his sense of humour and it must have taken Thoth infinite patience to bear the provocation without loss of temper when it came to sorting out the problems caused by this dysfunctional pantheon. Re, himself, wasn't the most emotionally stable of the deities, who could swing from weak and indecisive to stubborn and unscrupulous.

He created Shu, god of air, and the goddess of moisture, Tefnut. The siblings symbolised two universal principles of humans: life and right (justice). Re was believed to have created all forms of life by calling them into existence by uttering their secret names. Additionally, he had three daughters, Bastet, Sekhmet, and Hathor, who were all considered the eyes of Re. Sekhmet was the Eye of Re and was created by the fire in her father's eye. She was violent and sent to slaughter those who betrayed Re, but when calm she became the more kind and forgiving goddess Hathor. Sekhmet was the powerful warrior and protector, while Bastet, who was depicted as a cat, was shown as gentle and nurturing.

By contrast, Thoth could be seen as wise but boring. Or even a wee bit pompous... but then he was also, by necessity, something of a con artist! These gods with virtually unlimited powers fought like adolescents still trying to find their direction in life. Nevertheless, it was Thoth who was sent to bring back Sekhmet after she'd gone on a rampage to kill those who had rebelled against Re. So enthusiastic was she that Re feared for the extinction of the human race. Knowing that she liked a tipple, Thoth flooded the land with beer coloured with pomegranate juice that Sekhmet mistook for blood and became roaring drunk! Thus incapacitated, Thoth was able to drag her back home... only to find that Re's saucy daughter Hathor had lifted her skirts in front of him, displaying her nether parts, which restored the old god to good humour, and all was well with the world once more.

We can perhaps visualise Thoth sitting in the sanctuary of his temple in the light of oil lamps with his head in his hands, wondering what in the *Duat* could next go wrong! Or with a cigarillo in one hand and a glass of Macallan twenty-one-year-old fine oak whisky in the other, contemplating how he's going to deal with the succession between Shu and Geb – Geb having sexually abused his mother, Tefnut, and been badly burned in the process! Not to mention the curse Re laid upon Nut – that she should not be able to bear any child upon any day in the year.

Re had overheard a prophecy that the goddess of the sky would one day have a son who would replace him on the throne. Outraged, he cast a spell that forbade Nut to ever give birth to any child on any day of the year. Nut was naturally upset by this so she turned to Thoth – because if anyone could outsmart the spell, it would be him!

Thoth hatched a plan and challenged Khonsu, the moon god, to a game of *senet*, and Khonsu couldn't resist – after all, he was confident that he was the best *senet* player of all, and would enjoy boasting about his victory over the god of wisdom. So when Thoth said that he wanted to play for some of Khonsu's moonlight, Khonsu was not at all worried.

Thoth easily won the first game and got an hour of moonlight as a reward. Anxious to win back his light, Khonsu agreed to another game… and another… and another… but he kept losing. When Thoth finally had won enough hours of light to equal five days, he called it quits. Khonsu was left so exhausted that from that moment on, he could no longer shine a full moon every night. Thoth returned to Nut with five extra days' worth of light, which he inserted between the last day of one year and the first day of the next.

Since these days were not part of any year, Nut was able to use them to have her children despite Re's curse! Osiris – who would indeed go on to replace Re as the ruler on earth – was born on the first day. On the second day, she had Set, followed by Isis on the third day, Nephthys on the fourth, and Horus (the Elder) on the fifth.

By pretending that he knew less about something than he really did, Thoth was being somewhat disingenuous as well as cynical. His duplicity showed over and over again that he was almost like two people, saying one thing but then doing something very different, even contradictory; able to cloak his intentions under the guise of wisdom. Even though Re had been angry with his granddaughter, he relented and honoured Thoth for his part in getting around the decree. Thoth was given a seat of honour in the solar barque, which crossed the heavens by day and, by night, Thoth joined with Set in helping to drive away the serpent of chaos, Apophis, who sought to destroy the sun god. This participation in the overthrowing of Apophis linked Thoth to the cycle of day and night and so intimately to the lives of human beings.

Thoth also played an active role in the eternal squabbling between Horus and Set, using all his magical arts to restore eyes, testicles, and other body parts; and to act as mediator over the Osiris and Set disputes. Osiris could seem excessively narcissistic, not to say egotistical; his precious self, power, and privileges were his chief preoccupations. Set, by contrast, was violent, aggressive, given to drink, he was also brave and often a victim of his own passions. The Elder Horus was also a fearless warrior, who had earned his stripes as a god 'greater than the others'. Isis, the weeping mother and widow, sometimes overplayed her role, profiting from her situation to monopolise the attention of her peers. In fact, she was rather cold and proud. She was not in the habit of letting her scruples get in the way of her objectives, but, in this, she was quite like her divine siblings. In *Daily Life of the Egyptian Gods*, Nephthys is dismissed as greedy and perhaps a bit of a simpleton!

Thoth played a prominent role in many of the Egyptian myths. In the Osiris myth, he is seen as being of great aid to Isis. After she gathered together the pieces of Osiris's dismembered body, he gave her the words to resurrect him so she could be impregnated and bring forth Horus. After a battle between Horus and Set in which the latter plucked out Horus's eye, Thoth's counsel provided him the wisdom he needed to recover it.

Thoth taught Isis all the mysteries and magic she knew and we see here an echo of the later Merlin-Vivienne mythology, mirroring Isis tricking Re into revealing his 'Secret Name' because 'she longed in her heart for that power, that she should be greater than the gods and have dominion over men' (*Sacred Texts*). Her appeal to the general populace was based in her protective character, as exemplified by the magical healing spells. In the Late Period, she was credited with ever greater magical power, Thoth appeared regularly at the side of Osiris and Anubis in the Hall of Truth as the scribe who had kept accounts of the life of the soul of the deceased and who recorded the outcome of the weighing of the heart against the feather of truth. Scholar Richard H. Wilkinson writes:

> In vignettes of the *Book of the Dead* [Thoth] stands before the scales which weigh the heart of the deceased and records the verdict. This role gave Thoth a reputation for truth and integrity and is seen in the common assertion that a person had conducted his life in a manner straight and true like Thoth. His home in the afterlife, known as the Mansion of Thoth, provided a safe place for souls to rest and receive magic spells to help them against the demons that would prevent them from reaching paradise. His magic was also instrumental in the revitalization of the soul which brought the dead back to life in the underworld.

The association of writing with magic gave rise to the belief that Thoth had written magical treatises based on all he knew of the heavens, the earth, and the afterlife, and that these books were hidden away to be found by the initiates of later generations. Geraldine Pinch writes:

> All funerary spells could be regarded as works of Thoth. A tradition grew up that Thoth had written forty-two books containing all the knowledge needed by humanity. Some of this was occult knowledge to be revealed only to initiates who would not misuse the power it gave them. The Greeks identified Thoth with their messenger god, Hermes. The body of literature known as the *Hermetica* claimed to preserve the teachings of Hermes Trismegistus (Thoth the Thrice Great), who was eventually reinterpreted as a great thinker who had lived thousands of years in the past.

Nevertheless, there was a darker side. One source implies that, according to a Letopolitan tradition, Thoth was not exactly free of blame in the murder of Osiris, whom he, together with Horus, killed accidently during the primordial battle against the cosmic enemies, Thoth actually completing the murder. Such a violent action is not alien to Thoth, surprising though it may seem for the 'god of wisdom'. He predominantly appears as a slaughterer of inimical beings in the older sources (particularly those of the Old Kingdom) and this feature was retained throughout Egyptian history.

In Spell 175a of the *Book of the Dead*, a dialogue between the solar creator (here named Atum) and Thoth is preserved and best understood in the context of the *Myth of the Celestial Cow*. Atum complains about the rebels and asks the advice of Thoth, who promises to solve the problem and introduces mortality to mankind. Thus, Thoth is not an unequivocally beneficent god, but also an entity who was distrusted at times (UCLA, *Encyclopaedia of Egyptology*).

Like many Egyptian gods, Thoth had multiple roles. One of the most important was maintaining the Universe, which focused on mediation. He served as a mediator between the forces of good and evil; it was his job to ensure that neither side gained the upper hand, which would disrupt the balance.

He was known as the scribe of the gods, as he created the writing system and, having created the hieroglyphs, it is said he created the act of writing itself. It was believed that without his creation of words, the gods would not exist. Plato mentions Thoth in his dialogue, *Phaedrus*. He uses the myth of Thoth to demonstrate that writing leads to laziness and forgetfulness. In the story, Thoth remarks to King Thamus of Egypt that writing is a wonderful substitute for memory; Thamus remarks that it is a remedy for reminding, not remembering, with the appearance but not the reality of wisdom. Future generations will hear much without being properly taught and will appear wise but not be so.

The priests of Thoth were highly educated scribes and his cult was closely associated with the ruling class. It was not only the monarchy or the educated elite who admired him, however, as Richard H. Wilkinson points out: Thoth's appearance in the names of several New Kingdom monarchs shows important royal acceptance and patronage of the god's cult, but earlier references to offerings made in private tombs on the festival of Thoth also show the importance of this god to non-royal individuals and his worship appears to have always had a wide base among ancient Egyptians. Amulets of the god as an ibis or an ibis-headed man – sometimes holding the divine *wedjat* eye occur, though those depicting him as a baboon were more common. These amulets were worn in life, many presumably by scribes. The wisdom and magical powers ascribed to Thoth meant that he was naturally invoked in many spells utilised in popular magic and religion.

The continued fascination with Thoth and his far-ranging knowledge is a testament to his enduring popularity. Even today, Thoth is recognised as an important spiritual entity. Aside from those in the New Age, Wiccan, or neo-pagan communities who revere the god, he is one of the better-known Egyptian deities in popular culture. The University of Cairo features Thoth on his throne as their logo and statuary of the god remains one of the most popular and recognisable, after images of Tutankhamun, Nefertiti, and the goddess Bastet, in the modern world.

Nevertheless, we should not forget that the archaic Thoth-cult of the Predynastic era was a long way removed from the sophisticated theology of Ptolemaic times. Neither is my shadowy concept of Thoth enjoying a fine single malt and a cigar any more incongruous than the anthropomorphic images carved in the stone of the ancient temples. In historical terms, the death of Cleopatra was nearer to man's landing on the moon than it was to the magnificence of the pyramid-building era of ancient Egypt – but through all these times of change, Thoth's popularity endured. Still holding the brush and palette of a scribe, the wisdom of which he is the Master is contained in all sacred texts.

All religions without exception, however, appear to go through periods of evolution and devolution; they also go through times of amalgamation with other beliefs. Some enlightened and often great personality formulates and teaches a theory of the meaning of life and a code of ethics to go with this theory; the persons taught seldom, if ever, grasp the whole of its meaning, and never remember *all* of it. The next stage follows when the cult gathers impetus and former members of other cults join it – some of these invariably bringing parts of their earlier beliefs and adding them to the Master's teaching.

This chapter was previously published in Mélusine Draco, *Thrice Great Thoth* (Ignotus, 2021).

Chapter Nine

Heka – Magic By Any Other Name

Heka, among the oldest of the gods, is said to have been present at the act of Creation. Each of the gods was given their own sphere of influence so that order would be strictly maintained, and, in today's parlance, there would be no duplication of services. The gods would ultimately care for the people and, in gratitude, the people would worship and obey the will of the gods. This relationship produced balance and harmony between the people, their gods, the earth, and the afterlife – all of which emanated from Re.

> He was known as the Self-Created-One who appears in creation myths as the deity (interchangeably known as Atum) who stands on the primordial mound amidst the swirlings of chaos and establishes order, gives birth to the other gods, and creates the world. Re is enabled in this through the power of Heka who was both the god of magic and magic itself. Magic, to the ancient Egyptians, was a divine force which allowed for all that exists to be and also enables transformation. Re, as the first god, created heka and harnessed it, resulting in the birth of Heka who then maintained and controlled the divine magic afterwards.
>
> (*Encyclopedia of World History*)

Heka (ancient Egyptian: ḥk³(w) also transliterated Hekau) was the deification of magic and medicine: the name being the Egyptian word for 'magic'. According to literature (*Coffin Text*, Spell 261), Heka existed 'before duality had yet come into being' – the term *ḥk3* was also used to refer to the practice of magical rituals. This hieroglyphic spelling includes the symbol for the word ka – the ancient Egyptian concept of the vital force. Heka, holding two serpents crossing each other with the hindquarters of a lion on the nome-standard, represents his name on his head in the magical form.

Old Kingdom *Pyramid Texts* depict Heka as a supernatural *energy* that the gods possess. The 'cannibal pharaoh' must devour other gods to gain this magical power. Eventually, Heka was elevated to a deity in his own right, and a cult devoted to him developed. By the time of the *Coffin Texts*, Heka is said to have been created at the beginning of time by the creator Atum. Later, he is depicted as part of the tableau of the divine solar *barque* as a protector of Osiris capable of blinding crocodiles. Then, during the Ptolemaic dynasty, Heka's role was to proclaim the pharaoh's enthronement as a son of Isis, holding him in his arms.

Heka also appears as part of a divine triad in Esna, capital of the Third Nome, where he is the son of ram-headed Khnum and a succession of goddesses. His mother was alternately said to be Nebetu'u (a form of Hathor), lion-headed Menhit, and the cow goddess Mehetweret, before settling on Neith, a war and mother goddess. Other deities connected with the force of Heka include Hu, Sia, and Weret Hekau, whose name means 'she who has great magic' – the latter appearing in cobra-form in the snake-shaped wands carried by certain priests to distinguish those who were skilled in this type of sorcery.

Weret Hekau also served as the personification of supernatural powers, her power being one of the inherent qualities of the Crowns of Egypt. As goddess of the crowns, she was a snake or a lion-headed woman and dwelt in the state sanctuary. As the wife of Re-Horakhty, she is depicted with his solar disc on her head and 'Weret Hekau' was an epithet frequently conferred on Isis, Sekhmet, Mut, and others. Hu and Sia were partners. Sia was the personification of Divine Knowledge/Omniscience, the mind of the gods; Hu was the personification of Divine Utterance, the voice of authority. During ancient times, Weret Hekau accompanied these two gods and together, they were very important to the rulers of Egypt.

Hu was one of the minor gods in some respects, but he was one of the most important gods for those serious about Egyptian deities. Hu is the power of the spoken word. He personifies the authority of utterance. He was particularly important because he was the epitome of the power and command of the ruler. Even after death, Hu was of the utmost importance to the kings of ancient Egypt, acting as the king's companion as the king entered the Afterlife. Through Hu, the king maintained his royal authority as Hu allowed the king to cross the waters of his canal and acknowledged the king's authority and supremacy.

As the personification of Divine Utterance, however, some legends maintain that Hu was not just a part of creation, but that he was the Creator. It is said that as Hu drew his first breath, there was in that sound the essence of his name, hence, we have the name Hu, which sounds remarkably like the sound of an expelling breath. With each breath Hu expelled, creation took place. The first breath created the Divine Being and his last creation was the sun. So it is said that Hu is the Word of God, the first and the last breaths, *Hu Hu*.

The Egyptians recognised the Sphinx at the Giza Plateau as an image of Hu. The lion was a symbol of power and strength; used as the body of the Sphinx, this was perfectly acceptable to them. The face of the Sphinx wore the distinctive Red Crown of the Creator and the Beard of Kingship: these were hallmarks of the time. Sia represents 'personification of mind' and 'deification of wisdom' and she is born from one drop of blood from Re – as was Hu in the 'deification of the word of creation'. Both Sia and Hu represents insight and wisdom of Re.

As Egyptologist Ogden Goelet explains, magic in *The Egyptian Book of the Dead* is problematic: the text uses various words corresponding to 'magic', for the Egyptians thought magic was a legitimate belief. '*Heka* magic is many things, but, above all, it has a close association with speech and the power of the word. In the realm of Egyptian magic, actions did not necessarily speak louder than words – they were often one and the same thing. Thought, deed, image, and power are theoretically united in the concept of *heka*.'

In modern times, a clear distinction is usually made between the use of prayers, medicine, or magic, but in ancient Egypt (and many other cultures) these three categories were regarded as overlapping and complementary. Thus, a single problem, whether a disease or a hated rival, might be solved by a combination of magical rituals or treatments (*seshaw*), medicinal prescriptions (*pekhret*), and religious texts (*rw*). There was also another type of magic called *akhu* for enchantments, sorcery, and spells which were associated with the dead.

According to *Henadology*, Heka or sometimes *Hike*, possibly in closer accord with the actual pronunciation in Egyptian, is generally translated as 'magic', and the god Heka is the anthropomorphic divine personification of this power. Occasionally Heka may be depicted holding a snake in each hand. Being a personification does not mean that Heka was without his own cult in diverse places (e.g. at Esna as the child of Khnum and Menhyt), but his relationships to other deities are conceptual rather than mythical.

> Heka is one of the key concepts of Egyptian religious thought. Gods and humans alike draw upon the power of heka, and it is a constitutive force in the cosmos. The word heka contains as its principal component the word ka, which is frequently translated either as 'spirit' or as 'double', the latter because the ka of an individual is sometimes depicted as their twin. Ka is the force of vitality or of will in the individual, comparable to the Roman concept of the personal genius, of varying strength depending upon the individual's degree of accomplishment or self-realization, while heka is the instrumentalization of that force.
>
> Although 'to go to one's ka' means to die, one's ka is what supports one all through life as well as beyond. Food-offerings for the dead were directed to their kas, just as offerings to the Gods were directed to their kas. Since the ka is the source of sustenance and vitality, heka is in some sense the primary activity, the mobilization of vital energy as a movement of will

prior to all other modes of activity. One's ka is both one's innate nature, and also the best that one can be, and heka manifests the striving to actualize the potential of one's ka. The ka can also be understood as one's luck or fortune, and heka as the effort to affect this element of 'destiny' or to deploy it as an effective force in the moment, in the now.

(Henadology)

In *Pyramid Texts* Utterance 539, the king, asserting his right to ascend to the sky, makes a series of what appear to be threats directed to the gods if they do not assist him, the threats concerning for the most part the withholding of offerings. He states, however, that 'It is not I who says this to you, you Gods, it is Heka who says this to you, you Gods.' This is not in the nature of a refusal of responsibility any more than the threats are an attempt at coercion. Rather, the invocation of Heka identifies the lack of offerings which the Gods will experience if the king is not helped to ascend as a function of the very structure of the cosmos. If the king is not able to ascend to the sky, then the cosmic project resulting in the cult of the gods has in essence come to naught and all that has been invested in the constitution of the human spirit shall be lost rather than being recovered and returned to the gods who are its origin. Heka is in this sense synonymous with the cosmic order and the will of the gods themselves. The king threatens the gods, therefore, with nothing more than their own failure to carry out their own will, which is meant to be manifestly impossible.

Spell 261 of the *Coffin Texts* is for becoming Heka, and reveals much about how the Egyptians conceived this magical exercise. Here, Heka is identified with the primordial speech of Atum when he was yet alone, at the very moment in which the differentiated cosmos begins to emerge, and as the ongoing protection of that which Atum has commanded. Heka is thus at once the means by which the cosmos comes forth as well as the means of its maintenance and preservation. Heka says, 'I am "If-he-wishes-he-does", the father of the Gods', the effective will being essential to the nature of a god.

Indeed, Heka here identifies himself as 'the son of Her who bore Atum', thereby placing himself prior even to the eldest among the gods, 'who was born without a mother'. This paradox, typical of Egyptian religious thought, expresses that Heka is essential to the nature of the gods and is therefore in a sense prior to them, albeit not in a generative sense, but simultaneous to their own timeless existence. The relationship between Heka and ka is underscored in Heka's styling himself 'Greatest of the owners of kas, the heir of Atum', and in the reference to the two functions of the mouth of Atum, 'the august God who speaks and eats with his mouth'.

In Spell 945 of the *Coffin Texts*, a spell for the divinisation of the members of the body, the eyes are identified with Heka, and correlatively, a spell against crocodiles affirms that their eyes are blinded by Heka. Heka can symbolise the powers of perception and cognition combined, as can be seen from the tendency for Heka to appear sometimes in place of Hu and Sia, the gods representing the faculties of thought and perception respectively, in the boat of Re as it travels through the night in the Amduat books. In the *Teaching for Merikare*, it is said that Heka was made by the divine for humans 'as a weapon to oppose the blow of events'.

As in many other cultures, the techniques employed by Egyptian magicians were based largely on the concept of imitation – the belief that the replication of a name or image of a mythical event could produce an effect in the real world. The imitation meant that verbal trickery, such as puns, metaphors, and acrostics, were regarded as powerful forms of magic rather than simply literary devices. In the case of 'execration texts', the act of smashing *ostraca* or figures bearing the names of enemies was considered to be an effective way of thwarting them.

These textual spells occur from the late Old Kingdom onwards and were inscribed on statuettes of prisoners or pottery jars, which were often broken and buried as part of a magical process of triumphing over the persons or places listed. Most of the surviving examples were found in the vicinity of tombs at Thebes and Saqqara; the execration texts having helped Egyptologists identify those who were considered to be enemies of Egypt at different periods in their history. An execration figure consisting of a schematic statuette of a bound captive inscribed with a hieratic cursing ritual was one of five similar figures thought to have been found at Helwan. The text lists various Nubians and Libyans as well as two Egyptian rebels from the 12th Dynasty.

Similarly, the creation of statuettes or figurines of gods or enemies, which could then be either propitiated or mutilated, was regarded as an effective way of gaining control over evil forces. In a sophisticated combination of verbal, visual, and physical imitation, it was believed that water poured over *cippi* of Horus the Child (a stelae depicting the god defeating snakes, scorpions and other dangers) would confer healing on those who drank it.

Imitative magic, also known as sympathetic magic, is a type of magic based on imitation or correspondence. Both homoeopathic and contagious magic can be conveniently placed under the heading of sympathetic magic. Both work on the principle of events being controlled from a distance by utilising an item to represent the recipient, or by arranging to place an item in close proximity to the target. Both types of sympathetic magic can be used to cure or curse. Unfortunately, much of Sir James Frazer's writing is concerned with folklore from around the globe, but he does manage to categorise magical application in a way that would probably never occur to a native practitioner of the time. Purely for teaching purposes, we will utilise Frazer's magical division as follows:

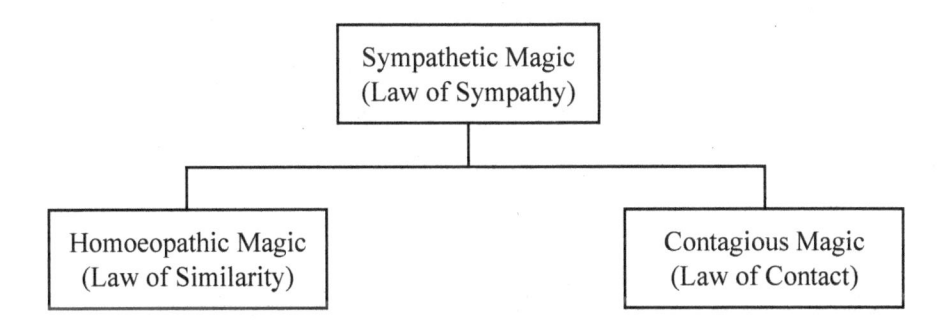

```
                    ┌─────────────────────┐
                    │  Sympathetic Magic  │
                    │  (Law of Sympathy)  │
                    └──────────┬──────────┘
                ┌──────────────┴──────────────┐
    ┌───────────────────────┐      ┌───────────────────────┐
    │  Homoeopathic Magic   │      │   Contagious Magic    │
    │  (Law of Similarity)  │      │   (Law of Contact)    │
    └───────────────────────┘      └───────────────────────┘
```

Positive magic says: 'Do this in order that so and so may happen', while negative magic says: 'Do not do this, lest so and so may happen.' The aim of positive magic is to produce a desired event; the aim of negative magic is to avoid an undesirable one. Both consequences, however, the desirable and the undesirable, are brought about in accordance with Frazer's laws of similarity and contact. A simple explanation... but an effective one.

As with the later Western Tradition of magic, a great number of the spells were for protective measures and/or amuletic, similar to the curved 'magic' wands incised with figures of deities and mythical beasts. Probably intended to protect the owner from harm like the hippopotamus ivory example dating from the Middle Kingdom in the British Museum. These objects are often called magic knives but they are nothing like the knives held by protective deities. The shape may be derived from a type of throw-stick used against birds, since flocks of wild birds were a symbol of the forces of chaos in Egyptian art, so the throw-sticks could symbolise the victory of order over chaos.

In private magic they were emblems of the control of a magician hoped to have over demons, according to *Magic in Ancient Egypt*. Another term that has been used to describe these objects is 'apotropaic wand', which refers to something that turns away evil, particularly evil spirits. The ivory from which most wands are made placed the formidable power of the hippopotamus in the hand of the magician. The earliest known wands go back to around 2800 BC – but around 2100 BC a new type came into use, with elaborate incised or carved decoration on one or both sides.

> The wands even pre-date the appearance of many of the same gods and demons in the royal Underworld Books. It appears that at this period, ordinary people enjoyed closer contact with their gods during magical rites than they could through the official cults of the state-run temples. It is perhaps significant that the wands disappear at around the time the great state temples became more accessible to ordinary people.
>
> (*Magic in Ancient Egypt*)

Similarly, sets of four magic bricks were often placed on the four sides of the tomb during the New Kingdom in order to protect the deceased from evil. Surviving examples date from at least as early as the reign of Thutmose III until the time of Ramesses II. A socket in each brick supported an amulet, the form of which depended on the cardinal point where the brick was placed: the brick beside the western wall included a faience *djed* pillar, that beside the eastern wall incorporated an unfired clay Anubis, and those beside the southern and northern walls contained a reed with a wick resembling a torch and a mummi-form *shabti*-like figure respectively. The amulets themselves usually faced towards the opposite wall; the bricks were inscribed with sections of the hieratic text of the *Book of the Dead*, describing the role they played in protecting the deceased from the enemies of Osiris (*British Museum Dictionary of Ancient Egypt*).

Most common, however, were the small prophlactic charms which the Egyptians called *meket*, *nehet*, or *sa* (all words deriving from verbs meaning 'to protect'), although the term *wedja* ('well-being') was also used. As well as offering protection, they may have been intended to imbue the wearer with particular qualities: the bull and the lion, for instance, may have been intended to provide strength and ferocity respectively. During the First Intermediate Period, parts of the human body were used as amulet shapes, perhaps serving as replacements for actual lost or damaged anatomical elements.

Amulets frequently depicted sacred objects and animals, and, from the New Kingdom onwards, they portrayed gods and goddesses, not just state and powerful local deities but also 'household' deities such as Bes and Tauret. The range of funerary amulets increased greatly from the Saite Period onwards. Amulets could be made from stone, metal, glass, or, more commonly, faience, and the materials were selected for their supposed magical properties. Specific combinations, or correspondences, shapes, and colour were prescribed for particular amulets in funerary texts from as early as the 5th Dynasty, although recognisable types of amulets were being made from Predynastic times onwards.

A broad distinction can be made between those amulets that were worn in daily life, in order to protect the bearer magically from the dangers and crises that might threaten him or her, and those made expressly to adorn the mummified body of the deceased. The second category can include funerary deities such as Anubis, Serket, and the Sons of Horus, but rarely (surprisingly enough) figures of Osiris. The *Book of the Dead* includes several formulae with illustrative vignettes that endow prescribed amulets with magical powers; particularly those placed at specific points within the wrapping of a mummy. Late Period funerary papyri sometimes end with representations of the appropriate position of each amulet on the body.

Many amulets represented abstract concepts in the form of hieroglyphs, as in the case of the *ankh* ('life') and the *djet* pillar ('stability'); other forms included the *tyet* ('buckle of Isis'), the *was* sceptre, the *akhet* ('horizon'), the *wedjet*-eye, and the scarab. Similarly the *shen*, a circle or ring of rope folded and knotted at the bottom, came to denote 'infinity'; when the *shen* sign was depicted encircling the sun, it appears to have symbolised the eternity of the universe.

In ancient Egypt, magic permeated all corners of the civilisation and evidence for its practice can be found in the medical, magical, and religious texts, funerary artefacts, and sacred jewellery. All elements of life – whether human, flora, or fauna, even the gods – were considered to be animated by a spiritual force that could be manipulated; and all objects both animate and inanimate were also imbued with magical power. This pantheonic assemblage was of epic proportions but it boiled down to an almost simple animistic belief that all objects, places, and creatures possess a distinct spiritual essence. Potentially, animism perceives all things – animals, plants, rocks, rivers, weather systems, human handiwork, and perhaps even words – as animated and alive.

The spiritual and material were believed to be woven from the same substance, and it was considered possible, by using magic, to control the order of the cosmos and to modify individual destiny by combating negative trends. Amongst the priesthood, however, magic was regarded as an exact science in its highest form; its secrets were revealed only to the highest orders within the temple who had the ability to control and regulate these events and actions. Nevertheless, it has long been the practice of professional Egyptologists to reject the magical elements of ancient Egyptian discoveries, despite the fact that evidence for the importance of indigenous magic spans almost 4,500 years. Written spells are the main source material, but objects sometimes provide evidence for types of magic scarcely recorded in the text, explains Geraldine Pinch:

> These objects would have been even more useful if all early archaeologists had appreciated the need to record the exact context of their finds. The large number of well preserved tombs and the sheer quantity of tombs objects on view in museums have ensured that funerary magic has been the subject of much research. Ritual magic performed in temples and everyday magic – the spells and rites enacted for individuals in life – have been studied far less. These three types of magic were closely related and influences passed back and forth between them. The insights that everyday magic can give into the personal lives of the ancient Egyptians makes it of far more than marginal interest.
>
> (*Magic in Ancient Egypt*)

Some past studies of Egyptian magic have been contemptuous in the extreme, with one scholar punnishly claiming that 'magic, after all, is only the disreputable basement in the house of religion' – while another liberally sprinkled a text supposedly about the Egyptian religion by using references to magic as examples of a form of senile dementia! As a result, most descriptions of magic attempt to separate it from religion, while in reality, in ancient Egypt, magic and religion enjoyed a symbiotic relationship.

According to Christian Jacq,

> dessicated theory is the only result of hostility to Egyptian religion and inevitable if an Egyptologist lacks sympathy with its civilization. Even in the sciences, intellectual brilliance alone can achieve nothing without sudden leaps of awareness. The greatest scientists are those who have some insight into the mysteries of the universe and attempt to express this knowledge or understanding which matures over the years ... It is even more vital in Egyptology if the student is to avoid the trap of examining his subject with icy reason and historical 'detachment' alone.
>
> In Egypt, as we have seen, magic was considered to be an exact science. Although some amateurs, such as the village 'wise' men and women used some simple spells and charms, the great magic of Egypt was only revealed to the elite of scribes who we can compare to today's atomic scientists. This magic, in fact, is intended to preserve the order of the world. Such an act is not the fruit of improvisation or some piece of conjuring. It depends upon a precise sequence of actions which are controlled by the magician.
>
> <div align="right">(<i>Egyptian Magic</i>)</div>

First Steps on the Path

Since many of the Egyptian deities were merely personifications of abstract concepts or natural phenomena, they were never generally the focus of cult worship or private devotion. Nevertheless, all deities, great and smaller, had their own Heka, which was considered as much part of them as their forms or their names. When we begin our quest into understanding the gods of ancient Egypt, we tend to get bogged down worrying about choosing an appropriate Path or patron deity, when in fact it is the Path or deity that selects us, not the other way around.

It really doesn't matter when or where our choice settles, because it is essential to feel comfortable and at ease when a particular image of a deity appears to be pushing itself into our subconscious. Like kittens or puppies vying for the attention of a prospective owner, involuntary mental images will keep popping up in the most unexpected places – this may (or may not) be the deity we come to refer to as our 'patron'. The gods choose us for *their own* designs and purposes – in reality we *do not* choose them. And, once we begin to delve into the world of the old gods and magic, we re-activate these ancient energies...

Once we begin to explore *magic* in any context, we start to transmit esoteric pheromones onto the astral that act as a beacon for all manner of magical entities to home in on. We all develop different personalities when we expand our magical persona but unless our magical abilities are capable of dealing with the more volatile and unpredictable members of the pantheon, such as Sekhmet, Wadjet, or Set, it would be unwise to view any of these as our patron until we fully understand the 'nature of the beast'. Call upon them in times of trouble, by all means, but to work with them on a permanent basis can be extremely exhausting, due to the vampiric nature of the Old World gods.

Having said that, it would also be unwise to look upon the Hermopolitan Path under the influence of white light and holiness, since the whole Mystery of the devotional Path requires us to also work with the darker aspects of a deity. Similarly, the early or localised *nome* gods would not be recognisable to Egyptians of the New Kingdom, who would not have been familiar with their primitive energies. All the Egyptian deities were creatures according to the light of their own times and it would be unwise to attempt to bend them to our own world-view of the history of this remarkable nation.

A number of the deities involved in the central myths were specifically linked to magic but the god who possessed the power of Heka more than any other deity was Thoth. His temple at Hermopolis had a library which was famous for its ancient records and books on magic. Thoth was said to be the inventor of both magic and writing and he was the patron deity of scribes. He was particularly associated with the hieroglyphic script, for which the Egyptian name was 'the divine words'.

In the regional myths collected in *Jumilhac Papyrus*, the incantations of Thoth feature as a powerful weapon on the side of order. This is a religious monograph devoted to the myths and rites of the 17th and 18th nomes of Upper Egypt and dated to the late Ptolemaic or early Roman Period. The text in hieroglyphic script is accompanied by numerous illustrations and is written on a papyrus which was 9 metres long before being cut into twenty-three sheets for the purposes of better preservation. This compilation was written during the Ptolemaic Period, at a time when the priests, in a search of the past, decided to preserve its traditions. To this end, they copied documents dating from the Old Kingdom which had been partly eaten by worms or mice, which is revealed by the texts themselves.

This papyrus, despite some gaps, is well preserved as a whole and was purchased in 1870 by consul Raymond Sabatier, then stationed in Egypt. In 1945, it was sold by his grandson, Odet de Jumilhac, to the Louvre Museum (ref. E. 17110) which has since kept it away from light and mould; in 1961, the text was translated into French by Jacques Vandier .This document explains at length the various legends current in the 18th *nome* (*nome* of the falcon with outstretched wings) of Upper Egypt and to a lesser extent those of the 19th *nome* (*nome* of the jackal) located opposite, on the other side of the Nile.

Be assured that it really doesn't matter if we find we cannot immediately identify with a particular deity at this stage. Few who come to Temple of Khem wishing to dedicate themselves to a particular god or goddess, for example, find that they stick with that choice. This is because the popular concepts of deities have probably been influenced by Greek, Roman, and modern pagan views, which bear little or no resemblance to the way the original Egyptian people actually viewed their gods.

Nevertheless, to work with the magic of Old Egypt, we need to fully understand these ageless deities and disregard the views of those of a more scholarly nature who would reject the importance of the Old One's importance in the scheme of things. Preconceived ideas about magical/mystical matters can be counterproductive in terms of esoteric study, as we only waste time in trying to merge our own ideas, without having the full understanding of true Egyptian belief. For the time being, perhaps we can suggest that you work with the 'magician's magician' (Thoth) and the big black dog (Anubis), as your best guides in these preliminary stages of discovery. The rest will come…

Chapter Ten

State Religion and Popular Magic

The ancient Egyptian religion was a complex system of polytheistic beliefs and rituals that formed an integral part of the culture that centred on the Egyptians' interactions with many deities believed to be present in and in control of the world, with rituals such as prayer and offerings being provided to the gods to gain their favour. Formal religious practice centred on the rulers of Egypt, believed to possess divine powers by virtue of their position and who acted as intermediaries between their people and the gods. These lofty individuals were obligated to sustain the gods through rituals and offerings so that they could maintain *Ma'at*, the order of the cosmos, and repel *isfet*, which was chaos. The state, therefore, dedicated enormous resources to these religious rituals and to the construction of magnificent temples.

The state religion had its roots in Egypt's prehistory and lasted for 3,500 years. The details of this religious belief changed over time as the importance of particular gods rose and declined, and their intricate relationships shifted. At various times, certain gods became pre-eminent over the others, including the sun god Re, the creator god Amun, and the mother goddess Isis. For a brief period, the theology promulgated by the pharaoh Akhenaten, of a single god, the Aten, replaced the traditional pantheon but his successor was not interested in disrupting the status quo.

A state or official religion is that endorsed by a sovereign state. *Official* religions have been known throughout human history in almost all types of cultures, reaching into the ancient Near East and pre-history. The religion of ancient Egypt was a polytheistic (many faceted) belief – with one short period of monotheism (one god) – and hosted about 700 different deities, although it was not uncommon for deities to be combined to form a new individual. Government and religion were inseparable in Egypt, bringing order to society through the construction of temples; the introduction of laws and taxation; the organisation of labour and trade with neighbours... not to mention the defence of the country's military interests.

As Margaret Murray observed, it must be borne in mind that the Egyptian religion was never static.

> Social conditions affect religion as much as, perhaps more than, religion affects social change; and as those conditions change, the

spirit and therefore the outward form of religion changes also. During those many centuries through which the history of Egypt can be traced, religious changes occurred as they occurred in any other country, and these must be taken into account.

Ancient Egypt grew, as other countries have grown, from an aggregation of little states, each little state being entirely independent and having its own chief and its own deity. The early deities of Egypt – often in animal form – numbered more goddesses than gods; but whether male or female the local deity was supreme in his or her own district. This was, of course, the form of monotheism common to all primitive societies. The deity had, however, no jurisdiction outside his own principality, and in war it was the god and not the tribe that was defeated or victorious. In the course of time one district tended to merge into another; the result to the deities of the districts concerned depended upon whether the union was due to peace or war. If the union had come about by peaceful means the deities, became either husband and wife, or parent and child.

(*The Splendour That Was Egypt*)

Thirty years earlier, Dr Murray had written:

All Egyptian temples are remarkable as being entirely rectangular, both in plan and elevation; at no period was a curved structure used. This is perhaps due to the fact that the landscape of Egypt is a landscape of lines, vertical, horizontal or diagonal; and, as the artist knew nothing else, his buildings conformed to their surroundings. This was the reason of the vertical columns, horizontal roofs and sloping pylons of Egyptian architecture.

The rainless skies and continuous sunshine of Egypt are points to be considered in the architecture. It is a country of violent contrasts; the flat plain and vertical cliffs, the fertile fields and the dreary waste of desert, the brilliant sunshine and the dark shadows, the river which harboured edible fish and murderous crocodile; all these naturally had their effect on the mind of the Egyptian architect and showed themselves in the architecture.

(*Egyptian Temple*)

While the state cults were meant to preserve the stability of the ancient world, lay individuals had their own religious practices that related more directly to daily life. This popular aspect of religion left less evidence than the official cults, and because this evidence was mostly produced by the wealthiest portion of the Egyptian population, it is uncertain to what degree it reflects the practices of the populace as a whole.

Individuals could interact with the gods for their own purposes, appealing for help through prayer or compelling the gods to act through magic. These practices were distinct from, but closely linked with, the formal rituals and institutions. The popular religious tradition grew more prominent over the course of history as the status of the pharaoh declined. Egyptian belief in the afterlife and the importance of funerary practices is evident in the great efforts made to ensure the survival of their souls after death – via the provision of tombs and funerary temples, grave goods and offerings to preserve the bodies and spirits of the deceased.

Popular religious practice included ceremonies marking important transitions in life. These included birth, because of the danger involved in the process, and naming, because the name was held to be a crucial part of a person's identity. The most important of these ceremonies were those surrounding death, because they ensured the soul's survival beyond it. Other religious practices sought to discern the gods' will or seek their knowledge. These included the interpretation of dreams, which could be seen as messages from the divine realm, and the consultation of oracles. People also sought to affect the gods' behaviour to their own benefit through magical rituals.

Individuals also prayed to gods and gave them private offerings. Evidence of this type of personal piety, however, is sparse before the New Kingdom, probably due to cultural restrictions on depiction of non-royal religious activity, which relaxed during the Middle and New Kingdoms. Personal piety became still more prominent in the late New Kingdom, when it was believed that the gods intervened directly in individual lives, punishing wrongdoers and saving the pious from disaster. Official temples were important venues for private prayer and offering, even though their central activities were closed to laypeople. Egyptians frequently donated goods to be offered to the temple deity and objects inscribed with prayers to be placed in temple courts. Often they prayed in person before temple statues or in shrines set aside for their use.

Yet in addition to temples, the populace also used separate local chapels, smaller but more accessible than the formal temples. These chapels were very numerous and probably staffed by members of the community. Households, too, often had their own small shrines for offering to gods or deceased relatives. The deities invoked in these situations differed somewhat from those at the centre of state cults. Many of the important popular deities, such as the fertility goddess Tauret and the household protector Bes, had no temples of their own, while Bastet protected the home from evil spirits and disease, especially diseases associated with women and children.

- Bastet first appears in the third millennium BC, where she is depicted as either a fierce lioness or a woman with the head of a lioness; two thousand years later, during the First Intermediate Period, she began to be depicted in a more domestic role. Cats were very important to the ancient people and were even considered to be demi-deities and those who killed them, even by accident, could be sentenced to death. Not only did they protect the crops and slow the spread of disease by killing rodents, they were also thought to be the physical form of the goddess Bastet, who was the daughter of Re, sister of Sekhmet, the wife of Ptah, and the mother of Mihos. Since the 2nd Dynasty, she was worshipped as a deity, most commonly in Lower Egypt, although her form and powers changed over the years. Bastet was the goddess of protection, pleasure, and the bringer of good health. She had the head of a cat and a slender female body. Bastet was one of the most popular deities of ancient Egypt as she was the protector of everyone's home and family.
- Tauret was the protective goddess of childbirth and fertility. Her name (*T3-wrt*) means 'she who is great' or simply 'great one', a common pacificatory address to dangerous deities. She is typically depicted as a bipedal female hippopotamus with feline attributes, pendulous female human breasts, the limbs and paws of a lion, and the back and tail of a Nile crocodile. Protective amulets bearing the likenesses of female hippopotamuses have been found dating as far back as the Predynastic Period and the tradition of making and wearing these amulets continued throughout the history of Egypt into the Ptolemaic Kingdom and the Roman Period. It was not until the Middle Kingdom of Egypt that Tauret became featured more prominently as a figure of religious devotion. Her image adorns magical objects, the most notable of which being a common type of 'magic wand' or 'knife' carved from hippopotamus ivory that was likely used in rituals associated with birth and the protection of infants. Similar images appear also on children's feeding cups, once again demonstrating Tauret's integral role as the patron goddess of child rearing.
- Bes was a minor god of ancient Egypt, represented as a dwarf with large head, goggle eyes, protruding tongue, bowlegs, bushy tail, and usually a crown of feathers. The god's figure was that of a grotesque mountebank and was intended to inspire joy or drive away pain and sorrow, his hideousness being perhaps supposed to scare away evil spirits. He was portrayed on mirrors, ointment vases, and other personal articles. He was associated with music and with childbirth and was represented in the 'birth houses' devoted to the cult of the child god. Contrary to the usual rule of representation, Bes was commonly shown full-faced rather than in profile, since full-faced figures were marginal to the normal, ordered world.

Predynastic and Early Dynastic Periods

The beginnings of Egyptian religion extend into pre-history, though evidence for them comes only from the sparse and ambiguous archaeological record. Careful burials during the Predynastic imply that the people of this time believed in some form of Afterlife. At the same time, animals were ritually buried, a practice which may reflect the development of zoomorphic deities like those found in the later religion. The evidence is less clear for gods in human form, and this type of deity may have emerged more slowly than those in animal shape.

Each region of Egypt originally had its own patron deity, but it is likely that as these small communities conquered or absorbed each other, the god of the defeated area was either incorporated into the other god's mythology or entirely consumed by it. This resulted in a complex pantheon in which some deities remained of only locally importance – while others developed more universal significance. Archaeological data has suggested that the Egyptian religious system had close cultural affinities with Eastern African populations and arose from an African substratum rather than deriving from the Mesopotamian or Mediterranean regions.

The Early Dynastic Period began with the Unification around 3000 BC. This event transformed Egyptian religion, as some deities rose to national importance and the cult of the divine pharaoh became the central focus of religious activity. Horus was identified with the king, and his cult centre in the Upper Egyptian city of Nekhen was among the most important religious sites of the period. Another important centre was Abydos, where the early rulers built large funerary complexes.

Old and Middle Kingdoms

During the Old Kingdom, the priesthoods of the major deities attempted to organise the complicated national pantheon into groups linked by their mythology and worshipped in a single cult centre, such as the Ennead of Heliopolis, which linked important deities such as Atum, Re, Osiris, and Set in a single later creation myth. Meanwhile, pyramids, accompanied by large mortuary temple complexes, replaced mastabas as the tombs of pharaohs. In contrast with the great size of the pyramid complexes, temples to gods remained comparatively small, suggesting that official religion in this period emphasised the cult of the divine king more than the direct worship of deities. The funerary rituals and architecture of this time greatly influenced the more elaborate temples and rituals used in worshipping the gods in later periods.

The Egyptians continued to regard the sun as a powerful life force. The sun god Re had been worshipped from the Early Dynastic Period, but it was not until the Old Kingdom that he became the dominant figure in the pantheon, growing in influence, and his cult centre at Heliopolis became the nation's most important religious site. By the 5th Dynasty, Re was the most prominent god in Egypt and had developed the close links with kingship and the Afterlife that he retained for the rest of the country's history.

Around the same time, Osiris became an important Afterlife deity. The *Pyramid Texts*, first written at this time, reflect the prominence of the solar and Osirian concepts of the Afterlife, although they also contain remnants of much older traditions. The texts are an extremely important source for understanding early Egyptian theology. Symbols such as the 'winged disc' took on new features. Originally, the solar disc with the wings of a hawk was originally the symbol of Horus and associated with his cult in the Delta town of Behdet. The sacred cobras were added on either side of the disc during the Old Kingdom. The winged disc had protective significance and was found on temple ceilings and ceremonial entrances.

The Old Kingdom collapsed into the disorder of the First Intermediate Period, until rulers from Thebes reunified the Egyptian nation in the Middle Kingdom. These Theban pharaohs initially promoted their patron god Montu to national importance, but during the Middle Kingdom, he was eclipsed by the rising popularity of Amun. In this reunified Egyptian state, personal piety grew more important and was expressed more freely in writing, a trend that continued in the New Kingdom.

New Kingdom

The country was reunited by the Theban rulers, who became the first pharaohs of the New Kingdom. Under this new regime, Amun became the supreme state god. He was syncretised with Re, the long-established patron of kingship, and his temple at Karnak in Thebes became Egypt's most important religious centre. Amun's elevation was partly due to the great importance of Thebes, but it was also due to the increasingly professional priesthood. Their sophisticated theological discussion produced detailed descriptions of Amun's universal power. Increased contact with outside peoples in this period led to the adoption of many Near Eastern deities into the pantheon. At the same time, the subjugated Nubians absorbed Egyptian religious beliefs, and, in particular, adopted Amun as their own.

This New Kingdom religious order was disrupted when Akhenaten acceded, and replaced Amun with the Aten as the state god. Eventually, he eliminated the official worship of most other gods and moved Egypt's capital to a new city at Amarna. In doing so, Akhenaten claimed unprecedented status: only he could worship the Aten, and the populace directed their worship toward him. The Atenist system lacked well-developed mythology and afterlife beliefs, and the Aten seemed distant and impersonal, so the new order did not appeal to ordinary Egyptians. Thus, many probably continued to worship the traditional

Above and overleaf: Two views of the Great Sphinx of Giza, Egypt.

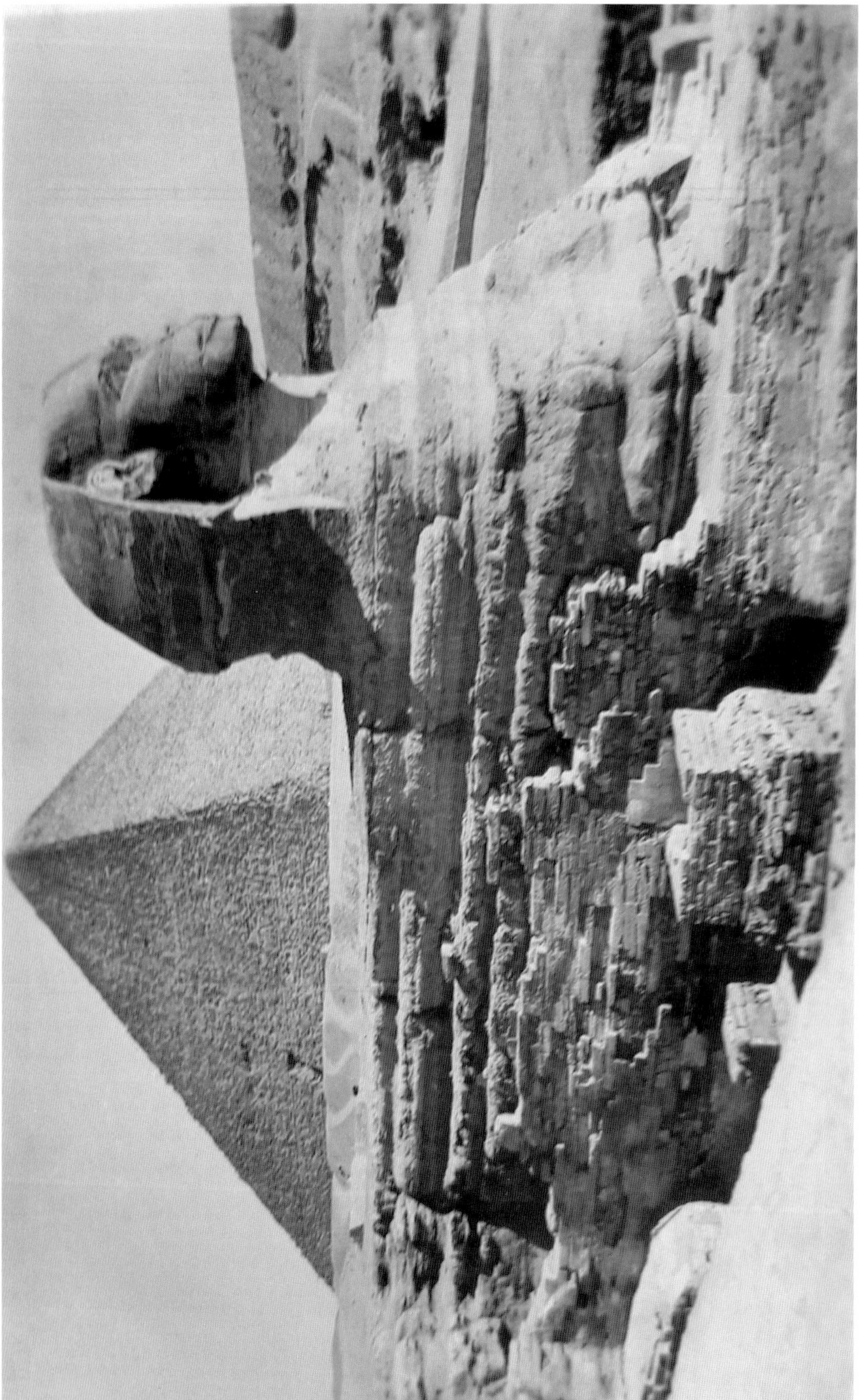

A reflected image of the Pyramid at Giza.

An Egyptian snake charmer.

Above: A crocodile of the Nile.

Below: Statue of the falcon-headed deity Horus, located at the Temple of Edfu on the west bank of the Nile.

A depiction of the crocodile god Sobek at the Temple of Kom Ombo, Upper Egypt.

A statue of Khonsu, the Ancient Egyptian god of the moon.

Relief carving of the goddess Isis, located at the Philae temple complex.

Above: A depiction of Hathor, the bovine goddess of the sky.

Below: Representations of Thoth and Hathor at Kom Ombo, Upper Egypt.

Above: A statue of the solar deity Sekhmet, the Egyptian warrior goddess of conflict and medicine.

Below: Carving of a scarab beetle at the Temple of Hatshepsut, West Bank, Luxor, Egypt.

Above and below: Examples of statues at Karnak Temple, Luxor.

The Great Temple of Ramesses II at Abu Simbel, Upper Egypt.

The small Temple of Hathor and Nefertari at Abu Simbel.

Pylon at the Philae temple complex depicting King Ptolemy XII before Isis, Osiris, Horus and Hathor (upper section) and Horus between Hathor and Isis (lower section).

The Temple of Kom Ombo, in Aswan Governorate, Upper Egypt.

The Temple at Edfu, located on the west bank of the Nile in Upper Egypt.

gods in private. Nevertheless, the withdrawal of state support for the other deities severely disrupted Egyptian society.

Akhenaten's successors restored the traditional religious system, and eventually, they dismantled all Atenist monuments.

Before the Amarna Period, popular religion had trended toward more personal relationships between worshippers and their gods. Akhenaten's changes had reversed this trend, but once the traditional religion was restored, there was a backlash. The populace began to believe that the gods were much more directly involved in daily life. Amun, the supreme god, was increasingly seen as the final arbiter of human destiny, the true ruler of Egypt. The pharaoh was correspondingly more human and less divine. The importance of oracles as a means of decision-making grew, as did the wealth and influence of the oracles' interpreters, the priesthood. These trends undermined the traditional structure of society and contributed to the breakdown of the New Kingdom.

Later Periods

In the first millennium BC, Egypt was significantly weaker than in earlier times, and in several periods foreigners seized the country and assumed the position of pharaoh. The importance of the pharaoh continued to decline, and the emphasis on popular piety continued to increase. Animal cults, that characteristically Egyptian form of worship, became increasingly popular in this period, possibly as a response to the uncertainty and foreign influence of the time. Isis grew more popular as a goddess of protection, magic, and personal salvation, and became the most important goddess in Egypt.

Hence the emergence of a syncretistic combination of many of the other original gods and, as ancient Egyptians could easily merge two gods into one, Isis gradually took on other goddesses' attributes, particularly those of Hathor. Originally, Isis only was associated to others in the temples but, a sign that her importance was on the up, temples specifically dedicated to her were built in the country's later stages. Isis was initially an obscure goddess who lacked her own dedicated following, but she grew in importance as the dynastic age progressed, until she became one of the most important deities of ancient Egypt.

During the fourth century, Egypt became a Hellenistic kingdom under the Ptolemaic dynasty, which assumed the pharaonic role, maintaining the traditional religion and building or rebuilding many temples. The kingdom's Greek ruling class identified the Egyptian deities with their own. From this cross-cultural syncretism emerged Serapis, a god who combined Osiris and Apis with characteristics of Greek deities, and who became very popular among the Greek population. Nevertheless, for the most part the two belief systems remained separate, and the Egyptian deities remained singularly Egyptian.

Ptolemaic-era beliefs changed little after Egypt became a province of the Roman Empire with the Ptolemaic kings replaced by distant emperors. The cult of Isis appealed even to Greeks and Romans outside Egypt, and in Hellenised form it spread across the empire. In Egypt itself, as the empire weakened, official temples fell into decay, and without their centralising influence religious practice became fragmented and localised. Meanwhile, Christianity spread across Egypt, and in the third and fourth centuries AD, edicts by Christian emperors and the missionary activity of Christians eroded traditional beliefs.

Nevertheless, the traditional Egyptian religion persisted for a long time. The traditional worship in the temples of the city of Philae apparently survived at least until the fifth century, despite the active Christianisation of Egypt. In fact, the fifth-century historian Priscus mentions a treaty between the Roman commander Maximinus and the Blemmyes and Nobades in AD 452, which among other things ensured access to the cult image of Isis.

In Rome, her cult was a 'mystery cult' and after episodes of repression and destruction, Isis and Serapis (Osiris-Apis) cults came under the protection of the emperors. By the third century, there were several temples and sanctuaries to Isis and Serapis in Rome and a Roman didn't need to travel to Egypt to see obelisks, pyramids, and original statuary; towering above the city, the Serapeum was the most important Roman temple to Egyptian deities and Rome was the largest centre for Egyptian gods outside Egypt.

The temple of Isis at Philae, built during the era of Greek pharaohs, is still one of the best-preserved temples of Egypt, and at the southern reaches of the Roman Empire, it saw the end of the old 'pagan' religion. After 3,500 years of use, the last hieroglyphic inscription was etched on its walls in AD 394. Three years earlier, it was made illegal to 'go around the temples; [to] *revere the shrines*'. The very last words carved in hieroglyphs were that of the 'Second Priest of Isis, for all time and eternity'. The final record of the cult of Isis in Philae is a Greek inscription dated AD 456: the temple was closed in AD 535.

According to the sixth-century historian Procopius, the temples in Philae were closed down officially in AD 537 by the local commander Narses the Persarmenian, in accordance with an order of Byzantine emperor Justinian I. This event is conventionally considered to mark the end of ancient Egyptian religion and while it persisted among the populace for some time, the Egyptian religion slowly faded away until it was revived in the twentieth century.

In ancient Egypt, every day in every temple, specially designated persons performed a ritual focused on making offerings of food, drink, clothing, and ointment, to a divine being (deity, king, or blessed dead), made accessible in the form of images. Through this ritual, the Egyptians sought to maintain the fabric and process of the universe. According to their own writings, the Egyptians did *not* worship idols – they did not consider the images themselves to be divine forces; rather, the image provided a visible and tangible form in

State Religion and Popular Magic

which the offerings and service of human beings could be channelled into the divine forces. In order to make an inanimate item into a possible channel for offerings, it had to be consecrated by the ritual of Opening the Mouth.

The two principal surviving sources for the words and actions of the daily offering ritual were:

- Depictions with accompanying hieroglyphic inscriptions, in the temple for the cult of King Sety I at Abydos.
- Full record of the words in the hieratic script, without illustrations, on papyrus manuscripts referring to the cult of the god Amun and the goddess Mut at Karnak, East Thebes – these manuscripts date to the first part of the 22nd Dynasty, and are preserved in the Egyptian Museum and Papyrus Collection, Berlin (nos. 3014 and 3053 for the cult of Mut, and the better-preserved no. 3055 for the cult of Amun).

From these and other sources, Alexandre Moret compiled an outline of the course of the daily offering ritual (1902). In the Amun ritual recorded on *Papyrus Berlin 3055*, the daily offering ritual comprises the following sections:

- It begins with the burning of incense before going to the shrine;
- The sealed shrine is then opened, by breaking the seal and untying the cord around the door-knobs;
- The person conducting the ritual bows in front of the image of the deity with two main gestures: (1) kissing the ground and (2) raising his arms while singing hymns;
- Offerings of incense and scented oil are made;
- Stages 2–4 are repeated, for an inner shrine or perhaps for a second time on the same day;
- Central offering of the goddess personifying What Is Right (expressed in the Egyptian language by the single word *Ma'at*);
- The image is robed, with offerings of four lengths of cloth, each with a different name;
- The image is offered scented oil and green (copper) and black (lead) eye-paint;
- The person conducting the ritual withdraws from the shrine, sweeping away his footprints, and offering natron, incense, and water.

Although there are some sixty-six episodes recorded in the Amun ritual manuscript detailed below, this would not have been enough to provide all the necessary information for every step and gesture. Additional details, such as the preparation of material for the ritual, appear in a later version known from two fragmentary copies preserved at the temple of Sobek at Tebtunis (Gloria Rosati, 1998).

In every shrine, the offering of food and drink must have played a large part in daily activity, but this is marginal to the surviving manuscript versions. More in-depth information about the quantity of offerings made at individual shrines is covered by *Temple Festival Calendars of Ancient Egypt* by Sherif El-Sabban at El-Minia University. The temple was the god's home on earth and the daily offerings made to the deity were equivalent to the meals of his worshippers. For special festivals, depending on the particular deity and the wealth of a particular temple, special additional supplies were brought in and the custom became established of making calendars, which have been compiled here from a group of specialised documents.

The daily offering ritual for the cult of Amun at Karnak, as recorded in manuscript *Papyrus Berlin 3055*:

> Beginning of the formulae of offerings to the god made at the temple of Amun-Re king of the gods in the course of every day by the principal pure-priest who is in his day of service.

Preparations
1. Formula for lighting the fire
2. Formula for taking the censer
3. Formula for placing the offering-cup on the censer
4. Formula for placing the incense on the flame
5. Formula for proceeding to the sacred place
6. Another formula

Formula for opening the shrine
7. Formula for breaking the seal-tie
8. Formula for breaking the clay seal
9. Formula for untying the seal-cord

Facing the image – hymns to the deity
10. Formula for opening the face (= introducing light to the face of the image)
11. Formula for seeing the deity
12. Formula for kissing the earth
13. Formula for placing oneself on one's stomach
14. Formula for placing oneself on one's stomach and stretching out
15. Formula for kissing the earth, face down
16. Another formula
17. Another formula
18. Formula for adoring Amun
19. Another adoration of Amun

Ointment and incense
20. Formula for the oil-festival-perfume with honey
21. Formula for incense

Entry
22. Formula for entering the temple
23. Formula for entering the sanctuary of the deity
24. Another formula
25. Formula for going to the stairway

Facing the image
26. Formula for opening the face in festivity (= introducing light to the face of the image)
27. Formula for opening the face (= introducing light to the face of the image) (= no. 10)
28. Formula for seeing the deity (= no. 11)
29. Formula for kissing the earth (= no. 12)
30. Formula for placing oneself on one's stomach (= no. 13)
31. Formula for placing oneself on one's stomach and stretching out (= no. 14)
32. Formula for kissing the earth, face down (= no. 15)
33. Another formula (= no. 16)
34. Another formula (= no. 17)

Incense
35. Formula for incense
36. Another formula

Hymns to the deity
37. Adoration of Amun
38. Another
39. Another
40. Another adoration of Amun
41. Another adoration of Amun at dawn

The offering of the goddess personifying What is Right (*Ma'at*)
42. Formula for the offering of Ma'at

Incense
43. Formula for incense for the Nine Gods (= the other deities in the same temple)

Robing the deity
44. Formula for placing one's hands on the deity
45. Formula for placing one's hands on the box for performing the purification

46. Formula for the four purifications of the four nemset-vessels of water
47. Formula for the four purifications of the four red vessels of water
48. Performing the purification with incense
49. Formula for the white cloth
50. Formula for donning the cloth
51. Formula for donning the plant-fresh cloth
52. Formula for donning the cloth of red-soaked linen
53. Formula for donning the idemi-cloth

Adorning the deity with scented oil and eye-paint
54. Formula for the offering of oil
55. Formula for the offering of oil for the daily offerings
56. Formula for offering the copper eye-paint
57. Formula for offering the lead eye-paint

Closing the ritual
58. Formula for spreading the sand
59. Formula for smin-natron at circuiting four times
60. Formula for the cup of natron
61. Formula for the cup of incense
62. Performing the purifications
63. Formula for smin-natron (= abbreviated version of no. 59)
64. Formula for the cup of water
65. Formula for incense (= version of no. 21/48)
66. Formula for censing with antyu (= myrrh?)

Additional formulae in other sources for the daily offering ritual
Among the formulae omitted in the ritual for Amun on *Berlin 3055* (Moret, 1902, 229–246), the versions in the temple of Sety I at Abydos include the following at the robing and anointing of the image:

Formula for tying the nemes-headcloth on the body
Formula for the was-sceptre, crook, flail, armlets, and anklets
Fastening the Double Plume crown on the head
Formula for placing the necklace (?) and counterpoise
Formula for tying the broad collar and rectangular pectoral
    (UCL, Digital Egypt: www.ucl.ac.uk/museums-static/
        digitalegypt/religion/dailycult.html)

Chapter Eleven

Anthropomorphism and Zoomorphism

Anthropomorphism is the methodology of attributing human-like mental states to animals. Zoomorphism is the converse of this: it is the attribution of animal-like mental states to humans. 'Though it is difficult to say the Egyptians thought one thing or another, since so much change happened across their 3000+ years of history, the ancient Egyptians, in general, did *not* worship animals,' says Julia Troche, an assistant professor of history at Missouri State University and author of *Death, Power, and Apotheosis in Ancient Egypt: The Old and Middle Kingdoms*. 'Rather, [they] saw animals as representations of divine aspects of their gods.'

Anthropomorphism is derived from the Greek anthropos ('human') and morphe ('form'). The term was first used to refer to the attribution of human physical or mental features to deities. By the mid-nineteenth century, however, it had acquired the second, broader meaning of a phenomenon occurring not only in religion but in all areas of human thought and action, including daily life, the arts, and even sciences. Anthropomorphism may occur consciously or unconsciously. Most scholars since the time of the English philosopher Francis Bacon have agreed that the tendency to anthropomorphise hinders the understanding of the world, but it is deep-seated and persistent.

> People in all cultures have attributed human characteristics to deities, often including jealousy, pride, and love. Even deities with an animal form, or with no physical form at all, are thought to understand prayer and other symbolic communication. The earliest known commentator on anthropomorphism, the Greek poet and religious thinker Xenophanes criticized the tendency to conceive of the gods in human terms, and later theologians have sought to reduce anthropomorphism in religion. Most contemporary theologians, however, concede that anthropomorphism cannot be eliminated without eliminating religion itself, because objects of religious devotion must have features to which humans can relate. For example, language,

widely considered a human characteristic, must also be present in deities if humans are to pray to them.

(Britannica)

In the context of art, it could be said to describe art that imagines 'humans as non-human animals'. In the ancient Egyptian religion, deities were depicted in animal form, which is an example of zoomorphism in not only art but in a religious context, too. That approach actually continued also in other cultures, and we need to understand why it is so common in ancient art and in populations with traditions completely different from each other.

> The best known are probably the deities of the Egyptians – Anubis and Horus. Anubis, with his jackal head and human body, was the god of death. Jackals had been strongly associated with cemeteries because they were scavengers which uncovered human bodies and ate their flesh. Death was really important in the Egyptian culture, so the creation of the god in charge of it was fundamental. In fact, one of the main reasons why gods were created was to justify some natural events that nowadays are explained by science, but back then were still a mystery. Horus for example, often depicted as a man with a falcon head, served many functions: most notably god of kingship and the sky. Being the sky, he was considered to also contain the sun and moon. Egyptians believed that the sun was his right eye and the moon his left, based on which side he was flying. So even here the zoomorphism was used to explain a natural event.
>
> *(Exploring Art)*

Sobek, the crocodile god, for example, must have been the scariest of all their deities. The Nile crocodile is a massive reptile and probably the most feared predator in Africa. And with good reason: it is one of the very few animals for which human beings regularly feature on the menu. One of ancient Egypt's many significant and symbolic animals, it was among the most dangerous and enduring species that still exists today. It is also the largest species of crocodile found in Africa, maintaining a reputation for aggression that is on par with a hippopotamus.

In ancient Egypt, the crocodile was revered for its might and agility; it was also closely associated with the Nile, where it often dwelled. One of Egypt's many deities was a river god depicted as a man with the head of a crocodile, whose cult centre was in Fayoum. The crocodile was thus perceived as a symbol of Sobek, with thousands of mummified crocodiles found in Greco-Roman dated excavations of Tebtunis, even though crocodiles were deemed a great threat to everyday Egyptians. Indeed, Nile crocodiles were far more populous in ancient times. Their semi-aquatic nature gave them easy mobility across Egypt's marshy lands and swamps, not just the river. Observant Egyptians memorialised their existence in art and on funerary structures, etching figures of the elongated creatures, particularly in scenes in the tombs of Mereruka and princess Idut in Saqqara.

The discovery of these crocodile mummies also contributed to learning more about life in ancient Egypt, since the papyrus found with the mummies detailed how Egyptians dealt with these creatures as mentioned. Many of these mummies today are on display in museums in different countries worldwide, namely the Cairo Museum in Tahrir. In Aswan, an entire museum is consecrated entirely to them, containing twenty-two mummified crocodiles. The British Museum in London houses one crocodile but the Phoebe A. Hearst Museum of Anthropology in California is more well known for displaying nineteen mummies that were among the thousands discovered in Tebtunis.

It is difficult to definitively tell which crocodile species inspired Sobek. The god's fearsome reptuation is more like a Nile crocodile, but Crocodylus suchus was easier to catch, keep, and mummify. Perhaps both contributed to the imagery. Either way, these grinning reptiles were important symbols to the people of ancient Egypt, and they knew more about them than biologists did for centuries. Modern science stumbled upon what the Egyptians already knew, and there is still much left to learn about these reptiles that so inspired generations of people.

Since the crocodile was one of Egypt's most dangerous and feared animals, it comes as no surprise that it came to hold an impressive degree of religious and mythological status to the ancient Egyptians, who sought to find ways to protect themselves from the wrath of such deadly creatures through their deification. This deity had a most impressive pedigree with Set, the god of thunder, storms, war, and chaos being his father; Neith, the goddess of war, hunting, and wisdom was his mother; and his wife Renenutet was goddess of plenty, who brought good fortune to the native people.

The cult of Sobek was probably one of the earliest in ancient Egypt. He first appeared on a seal from the reign of King Narmer, the first king of the 1st Dynasty. The seal shows crocodiles facing a distinctively shaped shrine that later became the symbol for the city of Shedet (modern-day Fayum). In the Old Kingdom, Sobek was established as one of the significant gods and was frequently mentioned in the funerary *Pyramid Texts*. Despite the occasional literary references to Sobek, his prominence at that time was focused on his cult centre at Shedet.

During the Middle Kingdom, when Sobek was merged with the sun god, Re, such mergers of local and broader deities were not uncommon during this period. Sobek-Re's name first appeared at the entrance to the Theban tomb of Daga, an official during Montuhotep II's reign. Even the *Coffin Texts*, the funerary texts used primarily during the Middle Kingdom, address Sobek as 'he who rises in the east and sets in the west'. By this merger, Sobek was no longer just a local god of inundation and fertility but *the* creator god through his association with Re; in his crocodile form crowned with the solar disc and uraeus (the symbolic cobra), he became the creator who rose from the primeval waters, *Nun*, and formed the rest of the gods and the world. This role was frequently evoked in the cycle of hymns for Sobek, which were recorded during the late Middle Kingdom. Whether Sobek's popularity led to his merger with Re or whether the merger was a political move by the priests of Sobek to gain power remains a mystery.

At Shedet, however, the new administrative capital of the 12th Dynasty, the cult of Sobek saw yet another plot twist. Amenemhat II began to evoke an early dynasty, merging the form of Sobek and Horus. Horus of Shedet was shown as a crocodile on a seal from the reign of Khasekhmwy of the 2nd Dynasty. Amenmhat II was the first to see this merging of Sobek and Horus of Shedet as the perfect syncretism to affirm the king's divinity. But it was Amenemhat III who brought the role of 'Sobek of Shedet-Horus residing in Shedet' to the highest significance.

The crocodile god Sobek, whose name means simply 'crocodile', was a powerful deity worshipped from the Old Kingdom through to the Roman Period. His sanctuaries were vast and widespread, but the two main cult centres were located in the ancient town of Shedet (Greek Crocodileopolis), in the Faiyum region, and at the temple of Kom Ombo, in Upper Egypt (home to various 12th Dynasty rulers). Within the temples dedicated to Sobek it was usual to have pools full of sacred crocodiles, which were mummified after their death and placed in temples, tombs, and burials.

> He was a crocodile-headed god with several important connotations, including his association with the colour green. The worship of Sobek peaked in the Middle Kingdom, and his name is lent to several 12th and 13th Dynasty pharaohs such as Sobeknefru and Sobekhotep I–IV. In mythology, as written in the *Pyramid Texts*, he is referred to as the 'raging one' who 'takes women from their husbands whenever he wishes according to his desires', but was also responsible for making green the grass in the fields and river banks, tying him to both procreativity and vegetative fertility. Most notably Sobek was the god of water and other areas where crocodiles were frequently found such as river banks and marshland, and it was believed that the Nile arose from his sweat. He was linked to cults of other gods such as Osiris and Amun and in particular the sun god when in the form of Sobek-

Re, which later lead to him being identified with Greek god of the sun Helios. Sobek was also closely associated with the king and could act as a symbol of pharaonic power and might.

(Wikipedia)

Sobek was represented as either the reptile itself, often seated upon a shrine or altar, or as a crocodile-headed man. In either form he usually wears a sun disc headdress with horns and tall plumes, and he may also wear a wig when in human form. Confusingly, another crocodile-headed deity was Ammit, known as 'devourer of the dead'. She was a crocodile-headed demoness and goddess with a body that was part hippopotamus and part lion, which were the three largest and most dangerous animals feared by ancient Egyptians. She can be most commonly seen in the 'Weighing of the Heart' ceremony, waiting to devour impure hearts of the deceased, in doing so dooming their safe passage into the afterlife.

Similarly, the hippopotamus was the largest animal indigenous to Egypt, but sadly, it has been completely extinct there since the early nineteenth century. From prehistoric times, the hippo inhabited the Nile; however, their relationship with the ancient Egyptians was somewhat hesitant – they were both admired and heavily feared. Being highly unpredictable, they were a danger to boats travelling along the river, as well as the people working along the riverbanks. Their sheer size (weighing up to 4 tonnes), sharp teeth, large jaw and speed made them an extremely powerful mammal, and when feeling threatened they can become aggressive, particularly when protecting their young.

This sense of protectiveness over offspring is the main quality displayed by the most well-known and benevolent of the hippopotamus goddesses, Taueret (meaning 'the great one'). Taueret was identified as the 'protector of mothers and children', in particular pregnant women and newborn babies, being strongly associated with childbirth and fertility. She is most often shown standing upright on her hind legs, with the head and body of a hippo, the tail of a crocodile and the paws of a lioness, with a rounded pregnant belly and heavy breasts. Usually, she carries the symbol of protection. Her image (or more generally that of a hippo) often appears on household objects, magical 'wands', amulets, and figurines. 'Wands' were usually carved from hippopotamus ivory, maintaining a curved shape. Taweret is often depicted on them, brandishing a knife, imbuing them with the power to ward off evil forces and provide a source of protection for the intended mother and child.

Hippopotamus also appear in tomb scenes, where they are often being hunted in the marshes by the pharaoh with a harpoon. This displayed the strength, power, and bravery of the king, symbolising his ability to overcome chaotic forces and maintain *Ma'at* (world order). Hippos were hunted not only for food and their ivory, but also because of their destructive nature. They have the ability to decimate fields of crops with their huge appetites, often grazing overnight – perhaps this explains the meaning of 'hungry hippos'!

The hippo is also often found within grave goods, in the form of a blue faience model decorated with examples of river plants such as the lotus flower. This promotes a connection with growth, new life, and cosmogony, rather than an image of chaos and ferocity. Hippos have the ability to continuously submerge themselves underwater for several minutes before resurfacing – a wonderful metaphor for rebirth and regeneration. When underwater, sometimes only their back is visible. This is reminiscent of the Egyptian creation myth where the first primeval mound rises up from the chaotic waters of Nun. The Egyptians believed that placing hippopotamus models in their tombs would provide them with this renewing power and would guarantee their rebirth, by magically passing over these qualities. Interestingly, many hippo statues have been discovered with broken legs – it is possible that this was a deliberate attempt by the ancient people to avoid any unfortunate incidents with the animal after death, as it was believed that depictions in the tomb could magically come to life. For them, it was certainly better to be safe than sorry (Wikipedia).

Ipet or Ipy was a benign aspect of the hippopotamus goddess known as a protective and nourishing deity. Her name seems to mean 'harem' or 'favoured place'. Our first reference to her comes from the *Pyramid Texts*, where the king asks that he may nurse at her breast so that he would 'neither thirst nor hunger ... forever'. Afterwards, she is called 'mistress of magical protection' in funerary papyri. Under the epithet 'the great Opet', she is fused to some extent with Taweret, 'the great one', but she never completely loses all of her independent characteristics, regardless of the fact that many modern texts completely assimilate her with Taweret.

Today, hippos are still regarded as the most deadly land animal in the world – it is easy to see why the ancient Egyptians felt so threatened by them, and why they felt the need to placate them in any way that they could!

At the other end of the scale, the sacred scarab beetle was modelled on the indigenous dung beetle and is probably one of the most recognisable images from ancient Egypt. The insect spends its days rolling and crafting balls of dung, inside which the female beetle lays its eggs. The dung provides the larvae with not only a safe nest, but also a place for them to feed as they develop. The female beetle tends to the ball, eradicating mould and fungi, until the offspring surface as adults. A second ball is used for nourishment, sustaining the life of the beetle. This is rolled along the ground by the beetle's hind legs and then deposited in an underground chamber.

It is from this visual image that the idea was formed of the scarab beetle rolling the newly born morning sun disc across the sky, until it disappeared (or died) in the evening, only to be reborn again the next morning. Additionally,

Anthropomorphism and Zoomorphism

witnessing the emergence of new beetles from balls of dung would only further strengthen the connotations of scarab beetles with rebirth and regeneration. The ancient people seemed to believe that the dung beetle was spontaneously created in this way.

The artistic depiction of the scarab was also used as a hieroglyphic symbol in its own right. The verb 'to come into being' was written with the sign of a scarab beetle. The noun 'scarab' literally translates as 'that which comes into being' or 'manifestation'. It was these metaphors that caused the scarab beetle to assume the embodiment of the god Khepri – the 'god of the morning sun' who could bring about his own birth. Khepri was often depicted as a male figure with a whole beetle set onto his shoulders. This took on a different form to other hybrid deities, who would only utilise the head of the animal on top of a human body. Khepri was associated with creation and new life, as a subsidiary of the principal creator and sun god, Re.

Scarab beetles had several functions for the ancient Egyptians and came in various forms. Scarab amulets were probably the most common type, and replicas make rather popular souvenirs in Egypt and international museums today. They are mostly small and are usually pierced on either end, indicating that they were to be used in rings, necklaces, and bracelets by the owner. They could be made from a variety of stones, the most recognisable probably being the blue faience scarabs which were popular in the New Kingdom. The underside could be inscribed with personal names, titles, kings' names, protective sayings, or drawings. This compact size meant large-scale distribution was much easier.

A larger type of scarab amulet came in the form of the heart scarab. These were inscribed with a chapter from the *Book of the Dead* and were placed on top of the mummy or close to it. The function of the heart scarab was to prevent the heart of the deceased individual from speaking out against the owner during judgement in the underworld – this was crucial if the individual was to pass safely into the Kingdom of Osiris. It was thought that the heart scarab could control the memory and responsiveness of the dead. Large scarabs were also utilised by the royal family to make announcements – these were known as commemorative scarabs. Scarab beetles were clearly an important part of life and death, as a symbol of protection, creation, and regeneration for the ancient Egyptians – certainly not the flesh-eating villains portrayed in popular culture!

An animal that has an impressive image within contemporary esoterica is the hare. Originally, she had the form of a snake and was called 'the swift one'. She came from the 15th Upper Egyptian province, the Hare nome (called *Wenet* in Egyptian), and was worshipped with Thoth at its capital Hermopolis (in Egyptian: *Wenu*). Later she was depicted with a woman's body and a hare's head; firstly taken into the cult of Horus and later of Re, her name can be represented with five different hieroglyphs, but she rarely appears in literature and inscriptions. Her name was taken into the highest royal position just once in the long Egyptian history: the only king bearing her name was Unas. Her male companion is Wenenu, who was sometimes regarded as a form of Osiris or Re.

In Egypt, the hare was the goddess Wenet, whom the Egyptians venerated because of its swiftness and keen senses. The hare's form was also taken by other deities who had associations with the Otherworld. In one scene from the Egyptian *Book of the Dead*, a hare-headed god, a snake-headed god, and a bull-headed god sit side by side; a hare-headed deity also guards one of the Seven Halls in the Underworld.

Wenet is further described in a portion of Spell 17 of the *Book of the Dead*, which reads: 'Who is he? "Swallower of Myriads" is his name, and he dwells in the Lake of Wenet…' To interpret the meaning of this passage, one remembers that hares can swim, and the Egyptian creation first came about in the watery abyss of Nun, out of which rose the primordial mound where newly born gods manifested. To 'dwell in the Lake of Wenet' means to live renewed, revitalised, to be reborn, to live, forever and ever, renewed after death, as the god Atum-Re. Spell 17 goes on to identify the dweller in the Lake of Wenet as Atum-Re, the creator of all, whose father is said to be Nun, because he rose out of the 'watery abyss'.

Other passages in the *Book of the Dead* mention Wenet. Spell 149 describes the 'Mound of Wenet' through which the spirit travels to be reborn, rejuvenated while in the Otherworld or Duat:

> As for that Mound of Wenet which is in front of Rosetjau, its breath is fire, and the gods cannot get near it, the spirits cannot associate with it; there are four cobras on it whose names are 'Destruction.' O Mound of Wenet, I am the greatest of the spirits who are in you, I am among the Imperishable Stars who are in you, and I will not perish, nor will my name perish. 'O savour of a god!' say the gods who are in the Mound of Wenet. If you love me more than your gods, I will be with you for ever…

Not only is the Mound of Wenet a site of sacred creative energy, the ability of the hare to elude destruction shows the Goddess Wenet as associated with the hare, to provide a haven for the spirit, where it is rejuvenated on its journey through the Otherworld, a place where it cannot perish.

In Egyptian history, her name ('Unut') was used by only one king, the Pharaoh Unas, who was the first pharaoh to have the *Pyramid Texts* carved and painted on the walls of the chambers of his pyramid. The *Pyramid Texts* are possibly the oldest known religious texts in the world.

The antiquity of Wenet's worship is suggested by the *Book of the Dead* in Spell 137a (Heku Stories 3) as well as in the *Coffin Text* Spell 495, where the deceased states, 'I extend my arm in company with Shu, I am released in company with Wenet.' In Spell 720, 'To become a dawn-God and to live by means of magicians', the deceased affirms: 'I will act as one who is sent to the Gods, and my voice is that of Wenet.' In a fragmentary *Coffin Text* Spell 942, an unknown deity is identified with Wenet by the phrase: 'she has nothing which has been done against her, in this her name of Wenet' (*Henadology*).

An ancient text describes how Horus was injured after fighting with Set, and he asks his mother (Isis) to speak words of *heku* on his behalf, 'the name of Wenet was made, since words existed'. Elsewhere the same text refers to Wenet as 'the lady of fighting of the chamber of Nunet in the high hill of Khemenu which is on the island of fire', which means the point from which the sun rises. Carved mythological texts found in shrines and temples to Bastet describe Bastet projecting her magical fury to destroy evil-doers in the form of the 'Seven Arrows'. Each Arrow was attributed to a deity who controlled a group of supernatural beings (or demons). The full list of deities has been lost to history; however, Wenet is identified as the sixth of the 'Seven Arrows of Bastet'.

The hare's form was also taken by other deities who had associations with the Otherworld. In one scene from the *Book of the Dead*, a hare-headed god, a snake-headed god, and a bull-headed god sit side by side; a hare-headed deity also guards one of the Seven Halls in the Underworld. Like owls, the hare is a nocturnal animal that lives by night and sleeps by day. Which is a main reason why the hare has almost always been regarded as an agent of the supernatural: it is a creature of the night, the time of mystery and magic. Egyptians venerated the hare not just for its strength and swiftness, but because they believed it to be immortal: It 'died' every dawn but was 'resurrected' every evening. For a rather unknown deity of great antiquity, there remains a great deal of evidence as to the hare's god powers.

The owl also has a unique position because of all the birds used in the hieroglyphic system, the owl is the only one shown full face. More precisely, the hieroglyph shows the head full face, leaving the body in profile. According to *Hieroglyphics: The Writings of Ancient Egypt*, the reason for this uniqueness is probably to be found in the intense individuality of the owl's gaze, which the Egyptians undoubtedly perceived as a distinctive personality trait of the bird, such as that it unequivocally distinguished it from other species. However, it must also be noted that the owl, like all nocturnal birds of prey, has limited peripheral vision and compensates for this by the ability to rotate its head a full ninety degrees. A quality, according to Professor Betro, that perhaps did not escape the perceptive Egyptians!

Whether the owl was considered bad luck in ancient Egypt we do not know, although some evidence leads us to suppose that it might have been. Owls were associated with mourning and death. The ancient name for owl was *jmw*, 'one who laments'. 'To cut a bird's neck' was written by a composed hieroglyph of the owl with its body crossed by the alphabetic mark *k* (perhaps originally from the sign for knife, which is very similar), though more compelling is the curious fact that all the mummies of owls that have been examined have had their heads cut off. Even the Egyptians were not immune to the effect of the disquieting gaze of this bird of prey!

Nevertheless, inscriptions on the walls of Pharaonic temples show how it had become of greater significance under Ramesses II, who considered it his favourite bird. In addition, ancient Egyptians believed that the spirit of the deceased wanders at night in the air as a bird with a human head, much like an owl. The much interest and respect for the owl had been clear via women's jewellery, which had been in the shape of that bird. Egyptians also decorated their houses and temples with owl statues made of stone or copper. Some historians confirm that Egyptians had respected it until one slapped Ramesses II in the face with its wingtips, and for this *lese-majesty* he took revenge of it. Hence, it was called *umm queiq*, as a symbol of bad omen among Egyptians (*Egyptian Geographic*).

On the back of the Protodynastic 'Libyan palette' from the beginning of the 1st Dynasty found at Abydos, an owl within a fortified wall is depicted, representing a city and recording the victories of a ruler over seven fortified settlements. While in Predynastic times, a city named 'Eagle-Owl City' was mentioned on a schist palette in the Egyptian Museum (no. 1423869) and was discovered in Abydos. A fortress called 'Eagle-Owl City' was recorded among seven Predynastic fortresses that had been destroyed by the governors of Upper and Middle Egypt; four of these cities were located in the western region of the Delta and the so-called 'owl city' is the largest depicted that was attacked by the Falcon governor.

During the fifth century AD, the Egyptian philosopher Horapollo made the link between this bird and the concept of death. According to Horapollo, the night owl 'signifies death, for it suddenly pounces upon the young of the crows by night, as death suddenly overtakes men'. Furthermore, owl-shaped amulets were discovered in pharaonic tombs confirming its protective function. Being connected to the death, these amulets were apparently used to protect its wearer from the dangers that he might face after death. Examples of these talismans were excavated in the tomb of Amenhotep II in the Valley of the Kings (KV22) in 1915. One of these amulets is made of faience and is now preserved in the Metropolitan Museum of Art.

Since owls could not be sorted under the categories of pets or sacred animals, mummified owls were rather sacred birds of certain deities or votive species for these gods. However, the lack of any archaeological evidence hinders identifying which deity the mummified owl was dedicated to. Like other mummified animals, owls were ritually devoted as offerings to certain deities. After being relentlessly killed, throttled, beheaded, or even burnt, the bird was mummified and deified. Thus, its sacred body was preserved in its elaborate container. By the Ptolemaic Period, thousands of birds from different breeding sites were yearly mummified and presented in Hermopolis as votive offerings.

Animals of Mystery and Wonder

The Egyptians worshipped a multitude of gods and goddesses, and an understanding of this is crucial to unlocking the secrets of Egyptian religion and mythology. Worship of the gods often involved people making regular offerings, accompanied by invocation, in order to ensure a continued and benign presence in their lives. Animals were mummified in the thousands in order to appease the gods and seek their favour. The object of worship was not the animals themselves, but the gods that took on their forms – animals acted as a kind of messenger between the people and the gods.

In this book we have provided merely a taste of the many sacred animals that Egyptians chose due to their specific qualities and behaviours, and reflected in the deity that they epitomised. Utilising an animal's head on top of a human body ensured that the gods could still interact with the world, at the same time as providing a visual metaphor through the animal's characteristics. Hieroglyphs portray easily identified species and the accurate observation of the animals is always present, especially in the hieroglyphs of the Old Kingdom, which are the most detailed; scholars have been able to identify the exact species represented.

Almost no animal was considered too insignificant or unworthy of appearing in their graphic code. Religion and mythology were central to the lives of the ancient Egyptians, and central to their religion were the deities they worshipped. The physical form of the deities allowed cultic or personal interaction with their gods, and whether it be in full animal form or a mix of animal and human, those ancient sacred animals still to this day infuse a sense of mystery and wonder.

Chapter Twelve

Hieroglyphics – Language of the Gods

The hieroglyph is a character used in a system of pictorial writing, particularly that form used on ancient Egyptian monuments. Hieroglyphic symbols may represent the objects that they depict but usually stand for particular sounds or groups of sounds. Hieroglyph, meaning 'sacred carving', is a Greek translation of the Egyptian phrase 'the god's words,' which was used at the time of the early Greek contacts with Egypt to distinguish the older hieroglyphs from the handwriting of the day (demotic).

When Jean-François Champollion finally managed to decipher these ancient texts, he opened up the flood-gates on the world of ancient culture, mystery, and magic. The article entitled 'How Champollion Deciphered the Rosetta Stone' by Muriel Mirak Weissbach appeared in the autumn 1999 issue of *Fidelio* magazine, revealing that this was not merely a question of breaking a code, as a cryptographer might imagine. It was a matter of demonstrating that what had been considered a mysterious, pictographic cult object, manipulated by a sinister, elite priesthood to exert social control over the masses, was, in reality, a highly sophisticated, rational form of writing, which communicated the spoken language of Egypt.

> In addition, this also meant that the ancient Egyptian society which British scholarship had depicted as backward, slave-based, and devoted to a death cult, was instead a civilization with an advanced language-culture and science. By deciphering the hieroglyphic texts reaching back to the earliest dynasties, Champollion was able to prove the antiquity of this language-culture, and its extraordinary, unbroken continuity over twenty-two centuries. This established the fact that the Egyptians, far older than the Greeks, had invented writing, in the form of a beautiful alphabetical system, and given this great gift to mankind.
>
> (*Fidelito*, Vol. VIII, no. 3)

Historically, it was in summer 1799 that a Frenchman, working on fortifications in a town 30 miles from Alexandria, struck upon a stone in the ground with his pick. When the object he had hit was dusted off, it became clear that it was something of enormous value: although broken off in the upper portion, the basalt slab was inscribed with texts in three scripts: hieroglyphics at the top, demotic (popular Egyptian script) in the middle, and Greek at the bottom. After the capitulation in 1801, the British confiscated all the artefacts the French had collected – in particular, the Rosetta Stone, which they sent to the British Museum in London.

Not only did the British grab the Rosetta Stone through war, but they also controlled access to it. Through the offices of the Royal Society, the institution through which the British sought to control science, they initiated a project to decipher hieroglyphics. The ancient stone bears inscriptions in several languages and scripts; their decipherment led to the understanding of hieroglyphic writing. An irregularly shaped stone of black granite 3 feet 9 inches long and 2 feet 4.5 inches wide, being broken in antiquity, the Stone is a fragment of a larger stele and no additional fragments were found in later searches of the Rosetta site (*Britannica*).

The stele is composed of granodiorite inscribed with three versions of a decree issued in Memphis, Egypt, during the Ptolemaic dynasty on behalf of King Ptolemy V Epiphanes. It says that the priests at the temple in Memphis supported the pharaoh and translates as a summary of all of the good things he did for the priests and the people of Egypt. But how much of the Rosetta Stone is missing? Only the last fourteen lines of the hieroglyphic text can be seen; all of them are broken on the right side, and twelve of them on the left. 'The first people to look at the Rosetta Stone thought it would take two weeks to decipher,' says Edward Dolnick, author of *The Writing of the Gods: The Race to Decode the Rosetta Stone*. 'It ended up taking 20 years.'

By Ptolemy's time, some 3,000 years after the hieroglyphs' creation, the elaborate script was mainly used by priests (hence the Rosetta Stone's reference to 'the words of the gods'), with the general public more often using the simpler Demotic. (For a sense of just how long ancient Egypt thrived, writes Dolnick, consider this: 'Cleopatra came at the very end of Egypt's imperial run, 13 centuries after King Tut, 20 centuries after the golden age of Egyptian literature, 26 centuries after the Great Pyramid. To put it in another context, the reign of Cleopatra is closer to the year 2022 than it is to when the pyramids were built.')

The decipherment was largely the work of Thomas Young of England and Jean-François Champollion of France. The hieroglyphic text on the Stone contains six identical cartouches (oval figures enclosing hieroglyphs) and Young deciphered the cartouche as the name of Ptolemy and proved a long-held assumption that the cartouches found in other inscriptions were the names of royalty. By examining the direction in which the bird and animal characters faced, Young also discovered the way in which hieroglyphic signs were to be read.

In 1821–22 Champollion, starting where Young left off, began to publish papers on the decipherment of hieratic and hieroglyphic writing based on study of the Rosetta Stone and eventually established an entire list of signs with their Greek equivalents. He was the first Egyptologist to realize that some of the signs were alphabetic, some syllabic, and some determinative, standing for the whole idea or object previously expressed. He also established that the hieroglyphic text was a translation from the Greek, not, as had been thought, the reverse. The work of these two men established the basis for the translation of all future Egyptian hieroglyphic texts.

(*Britannica*)

The Rosetta Stone was found broken and incomplete, and with other sculptures was placed in temporary structures in the Museum grounds because the floors were not strong enough to bear their weight. After a plea to Parliament for funds, the trustees began building a new gallery to house these acquisitions. The Rosetta Stone has been on display in the British Museum since 1802, with only one break: towards the end of the First World War, in 1917, when the museum was concerned about heavy bombing in London, they moved it to safety along with other, portable, 'important' objects, which spent the next two years in a station on the Postal Tube Railway 50 feet below the ground at Holborn!

Jean-François Champollion, also known as 'Champollion le jeune', was a French philologist and orientalist, known primarily as the decipherer of Egyptian hieroglyphs and a founding figure in the field of Egyptology. He was able to decipher the ancient hieroglyphs through the oval shapes found in the text, which are known as *kharratis* and include the names of kings and queens. He was also able to compare these names with the Greek text to distinguish the name of Ptolemy and Cleopatra, which led to the decipherment of the hieroglyphic language.

Emblems of the Gods

In hieroglyphic writing, not many of the god names were written in a single symbolic sign, an ideogram that would synthetically render the essence of the deity. The gods were strongly associated from the ealiest times and the ancient deities tended to each have a distinctive headdress, which could be used to tell the gods and goddesses apart. These headdresses often seem to have been strongly linked to the attributes of the particular deity, giving the Egyptians a visual clue as to the powers of the individual god. This, then, led to the mix-up of emblems when different deities took over the attributes and powers of another. To the Egyptians it made sense – they could easily tell what the god was worshipped for – but it makes things difficult to identify deities today.

> **Aker** is the ancient Egyptian god of Earth and the horizon; he guarded the eastern and western borders of the netherworld. He protected Re, the sun god, when he entered the netherworld at sunset and when he returned to the world of the living at sunrise and bore the sun on his back through the underworld. Aker was thus often titled 'He who is looking forward and behind'. When depicted as a lion pair, a hieroglyphic sign for 'horizon' (two merged mountains) and a sun disc was put between the lions sitting back-on-back.
>
> (Ancient Egypt Online)

The name **Amun** means 'the hidden' or the 'hiddenness of divinity', whereas Re means 'the sun' or the 'divinity in the power of the sun'. The god Amun-Re is, therefore, a representation of these two ideas: the ever-present invisible power and radiant light of the divine force that sustains life. Amun's cult was the most powerful and popular in Egypt for centuries. He is usually depicted as a bearded man wearing a large headdress with a double plume or, after the New Kingdom, as a ram-headed man or simply a ram. Many deities in the official Egyptian pantheon can be recognised by their headdresses. When he appears with a solar disc at the base of the crown, he is known as Amun-Re, who possesses both hidden and solar creative powers.

> **Anqet** was generally depicted as a woman wearing a tall headdress made either of reeds or of ostrich feathers. It spreads out slightly at the top, where the ends of the feathers or reeds tip outwards. This headdress is thought to be of Nubian origin, linking her to the lands south of Egypt ... a foreign-looking crown of feathers standing upright in a close ring ... That such is the signification of Anqet is indicated by the crown of feathers, by the meaning of her name 'to surround', and by the determinative hieroglyphic of her name, a serpent, signifying 'knowledge'.
>
> (*The Correspondences of Egypt*, C. Th. Odhner, 1914)

> **Atem** is usually depicted as a man wearing the Double Crown (both of the crowns of Upper and Lower Egypt). The crowns signify that he is related to rulership over the Two Lands, giving him a close connection with the pharaoh. Horus is also depicted

as wearing this crown. The Double Crown – Pschent. With the unification of Upper and Lower Egypt, the red crown and the white crown were combined to become the double crown, known as the 'Two Mighty Ones'.

Royal Crowns and Headdresses (Egyptology Online)

Geb is often depicted wearing the headdress of a goose. Most often he is shown wearing no headdress at all. The goose was Geb's sacred animal, and it was also the hieroglyph used in his name. He was also sometimes shown wearing the red crown of Lower Egypt combined with the Atef crown and long, spiral horns. The Egyptians believed that Geb was one of the first pharaohs of Egypt, and so he was sometimes shown wearing the crown of Lower Egypt, combined with Osiris's Atef crown.

Hapi was also both god of Upper and Lower Egypt – this duality was shown by having twin Hapi deities, one wearing the papyrus of the north (Lower Egypt) as a headdress, the other wearing the south's (Upper Egypt) blue water lily as a headdress. When the two gods are shown together, they are usually using their respective plants to tie together a set of lungs and windpipe, symbolising the Two Lands together as one.

Heh was shown as a man wearing a notched palm frond on his head. The palm frond was an ancient Egyptian symbol for long life. Heh was the god of infinity, and so the palm could also stand for an infinite amount of time.

Many of the gods with the name of **Horus** were shown as hawk-headed men, each Horus having a different headdress. These headdresses did get confused, along with the gods, over time. Horus – son of Isis and Osiris – and Horus the Elder – brother of Isis and Osiris – both wore the Double Crown of Upper and Lower Egypt. Horakhty, Horus of the Horizon, wore the sun disc on his head with the uraeus. These gods could also be shown wearing the headdress of Amen or no headdress at all.

Isis was shown as a beautiful woman, wearing the hieroglyph of the throne of Egypt on her head. Later, when she took on the aspects of Hathor, she started to be shown wearing her headdress – the cow's horns with the sun disc between them – often combined with the vulture headdress of Mut. She took over many of the positions of the other goddesses, and so ended up taking on their headdresses as well, though the hieroglyph and the cow horns, solar disc, and vulture headdress combination were the most common.

Khonsu was generally depicted as a youth or a hawk headed man wearing a lunar disk and crescent on his head. Thoth and Yah, both moon-related deities, also wore this lunar headdress. Like the two most important other lunar gods, Yah, whose name simply means 'moon', and Khonsu, whose name 'the wanderer' refers to the cycles of the moon, Thoth is very closely associated with the calculation of time in specific and arithmetic in general ... As a lunar god, he was responsible for completing the moon during its cycle, that is to say, to make sure that time passes as it is supposed to.

(*Thoth*, Jacques Kinnaer)

Ma'at was shown as a woman with an ostrich feather – the Feather of Ma'at and the symbol of truth – on her head. The tall feather, attached by a headband, is the hieroglyph for truth, order, balance, justice and freedom. The reason for the association of the ostrich feather with Ma'at, the goddess of truth, is unknown, as it is also the primitive concept which underlies the name, but it is certainly very ancient, and probably dates from pre-Dynastic times.

(*The Gods of the Egyptians*, E. A. Wallis Budge)

Min was shown as a man wearing a crown with twin plumes, similar to that of Amen, occasionally with a long ribbon trailing down to his feet. When he took the form of Min-Amen, he wore the solar disc between the two tall feathers on his headdress. Min was one of the most ancient of Egyptian deities. He is always depicted with an erect phallus, sometimes ejaculating, and wearing a crown topped by two straight plumes: in his right hand he holds a raised flail used to thresh husks from the ears of corn to make it edible – hence the flail, or whip, is a symbol of power and fertility. Min was later joined with the great solar deity Amen to become the sun god's fertility aspect (*An Account of Phallic Survivals within the Christian Church and some of their Pagan Origins* by Ian McNeil Cooke). Min's other main distinguishing feature, though not part of a headdress, is his symbol, the flail. The way he holds his flail might be symbolic of sexual intercourse – the flail forms the V while his upraised forearm seems to thrust inside the V.

Mut was often shown wearing the double crown of Egypt or the vulture headdress of the New Kingdom queens. She wore the vulture crown because of the link between her name and the name for 'mother' in Egyptian – they were both mwt, and the vulture was the hieroglyph for mw. In Southern Africa, the name for an Egyptian vulture is synonymous with the term applied to lovers, for vultures like pigeons are always seen in pairs. Thus mother and child remain closely bonded together ... the wide wingspan of a vulture may be seen as all encompassing and providing a protective cover to its infants. The vulture when carrying out its role as a mother and giving protection to its infants may exhibit a forceful nature whilst defending her young. All these qualities inspired the imagination of the ancient Egyptians.

(*Ma-Wetu*, The Kiswahili-Bantu Research Unit for the Advancement of the Ancient Egyptian Language)

Nefertem was depicted as a beautiful young man with a water lily (lotus) flower on his head. The flower was the floral symbol of Upper Egypt – the Nymphaea caerulea – which the Egyptians related to the sun, healing, perfume, and sexuality. The Egyptian idea of sexuality was identified with creation.

Nekhbet was depicted as a woman wearing the crown of Upper Egypt or the vulture headdress, or a woman with the head of a vulture. She was shown to wear the vulture crown because she was believed to be the mother – the Egyptian word used the hieroglyph of the vulture – of the pharaoh. Her claim to the crown of Upper Egypt came from the fact that she was one of the pharaoh's 'Two Ladies' – nebty – who was the goddess of all of Upper Egypt. In later times, these two crowns were combined.

Nephthys was depicted as a woman with the hieroglyph of her name (a basket and a house on top of each other) on her head. Her name meant 'Mistress of the House' in ancient Egyptian ... but by the word 'house' we must understand that portion of the sky which was supposed to form the abode of the Sun-god Horus.

(Tour Egypt)

Neith was shown either wearing her emblem – either a shield crossed with two arrows, or a weaving shuttle – or the Red Crown of Lower Egypt. Linked to royalty since the 1st Dynasty, Neith was a guardian of the Red Crown of Lower Egypt itself. As for the shuttle, her name – nt – was linked to the root of the Egyptian word for 'weave' – ntt. The emblem also could be depicted as that of warfare – the shield and arrows that she was believed to have used to put evil spirits to sleep.

Nut was sometimes portrayed as a woman wearing her sign – the particular design of an earthenware pot on her head, though most often she was not shown wearing a headdress at all.

Osiris is generally shown as a green man wearing the Atef crown on his head. It seems that this was originally the crown of Re when the Egyptians believed that he ruled the earth. For Osiris to be pharaoh of Egypt, he had to wear this crown, though it produced much heat, as expected from an object belonging to the sun god. On the very first day that he wore it, Osiris had much suffering in his head from the heat of the Atef crown which [he wore] that men and gods should respect him ... and when Re returned in the evening ... he found Osiris sitting in his house with his head angry and swollen from the heat of the atef crown.

(R. T. Rundle Clark, *Myth and Symbol in Ancient Egypt*)

Ptah was shown as a mummiform man with a false beard, wearing a close-fitting skull cap that exposed only his face and ears. A golden statue of Ptah from the tomb of Tutankhamen has a blue faience cap on his head.

Satet was often shown wearing the crown of the south – Upper Egypt – and a pair of long antelope horns. This crown has a vulture's head and tail peeking out from within it, linking her to the mother goddesses of Egypt. The vulture beneath the crown is the symbol of maternal love and protection, and the horns signify the power of celestial love.

(C. Th. Odhner, *The Correspondences of Egypt*, 1914)

Serqet was often shown as a woman with a scorpion on her head. During later periods, she was sometimes shown wearing the headdress of Hathor – a solar disk with cow horns. Contrary, however, to popular beliefs, she was originally associated with the so-called water-scorpion, an aquatic animal that physically resembles but bears no relation to the real scorpion. Only through a (graphical) assimilation between the water-scorpion and the real scorpion in the 19th Dynasty, she would become associated with the real scorpion.

(*Serqet*, Jacques Kinnaer)

Seshat was depicted as a woman with a headdress that was also her hieroglyph, which may represent either a stylized flower or seven (or nine) pointed star on a standard that is beneath a set of down-turned horns or a down turned crescent of the moon. Much argument is made over whether the symbol over her head is a star or a rosette. An article recently has shed an interesting light on this issue. In 'Seshat and the Pharaoh' by G. A. Wainwright, in

> which he shows the development of Seshat's symbol over time. It first appeared ... on Seshat's palette, perhaps as part of a title, where it is clearly a flower-shape, and not a star.
>
> (D. A. Schaefer, Seshat: *A Goddess of Ancient Egypt*)

Shu was generally depicted as a man wearing an ostrich feather headdress, though sometimes he was shown wearing the sun disc on his head. The feather was the same ostrich feather of Ma'at, but his name might be derived from the word for dryness – shu, the root of words such as 'dry', 'parched', 'withered', 'sunlight' and 'empty'. His name could also mean 'He Who Rises Up'.

> **Thoth** was usually depicted as an ibis-headed man or as a full ibis, or with the face of a dog-headed baboon and the body of a man or, again, as a full dog-headed baboon. Each form could have the lunar disk and crescent on his head. Khonsu and Aah, both moon-related deities, also wore this lunar headdress.
>
> (*Mélusine Draco*, Thrice Great Thoth)

Wadjet was depicted as a woman wearing the crown of Lower Egypt or with a cobra on her head. Her claim to the crown of Lower Egypt came from the fact that she was one of the pharaoh's 'Two Ladies' – nebty – who was the goddess of all of Lower Egypt. In later times the crown of Lower Egypt was combined with the vulture headdress. The goddess Wadjet comes to us in the form of the living uraeus to anoint our head with her flames.

> The Egyptian State was much more than a bureaucratic organ occupied only with administration. Even at the beginning, the institution was thought by its very nature to be divine. As the State's means of communication, hieroglyphic immediately became a 'sacred' script, initially used only by a small elect class who also possessed magical powers. The evocative power of these signs was such that they were considered to possess the property of life; the scribes took care, in the wall inscriptions of the Old Kingdom burial chambers or on sarcophagi, to render the signs harmless. To do this, they represent in a mutilated form those animals or men which might be inimical to the dead, or eliminated them. Even in later epochs, dangerous animals such as crocodiles or serpents were shown with a lance piercing the spine. On the other hand, the hieroglyphs represented desirable qualities, such as longevity, prosperity, or divine protection, were made into valuable and commonly used amulets.
>
> (*Hieroglyphs*)

The total number of distinct Egyptian hieroglyphs increased over time from several hundred in the Middle Kingdom to several thousand during the Ptolemaic Period. Hieroglyphs were not just beautiful symbols, they represented a living, spoken language. From romantic poetry and international treaties, to shopping lists and tax returns, the hieroglyphic inscriptions and ancient handwriting revealed stories that were fantastically varied. As well as an unshakeable belief in the power of the pharaohs and the promise of the afterlife, it was obvious that ancient Egyptians enjoyed good food, writing letters, and making jokes.

The *Pyramid Texts*, for example, were carved on the walls of the pyramids of King Wenis of the end of the 5th Dynasty and the rulers of the 6th Dynasty, and constitute the oldest corpus of Egyptian religious and funerary literature now extant. Furthermore, according to R. O. Faulkner, they are the least corrupt of all such collections of funerary texts, and are of fundamental importance to the student of Egyptian religion. Despite the comparative rarity of corruptions, however, the *Pyramid Texts* provide problems and difficulties of their own. They include very ancient texts among those which were nearly contemporary with the pyramids in which they were inscribed, imposing on the modern reader problems of grammar and vocabulary; the orthography is apt to be unusual; and there are many mythological and other allusions of which the purport is obscure to the translator of today.

Their purpose was to ensure the welfare of the dead king in the hereafter, and they shed much light on contemporary religious beliefs, while embedded in them are fragments of temple ritual, traces of stellar cult, and glimpses of daily life. Nevertheless, according to Sir Alan Gardiner (*Egyptian Grammar*), the earliest inscriptions go back as far as the 1st Dynasty, which can in no case be placed later than 3000 BC, while some authorities favour a date many hundreds of years earlier. The same script lived on far into the Christian era; the latest hieroglyphs known are at Philae and dated to AD 394; the next latest show the names of the Roman emperors Diocletian and Traianus Decius. Thus the use of the earliest form of Egyptian writing, though confined to a narrow circle of learned priests, covers a period of 3,000 or even 4.000 years.

In the course of so many centuries, grammar and vocabulary were bound to change very considerably, and in point of fact the Egyptian spoken under the Roman occupation bore but little resemblance to that which was current under the oldest pharaohs. It is true that new modes of parlance which came into existence from time to time were by no means adequately reflected in the contemporary hieroglyphic inscriptions; for in Egypt the art of writing was always reserved to a conservative and tradition-loving caste of scribes, upon whose interests and caprice it depended how far the common speech of the people should be allowed to contaminate the 'gods' words'.

Chapter Thirteen

An Egyptian Bestiary

The significance drawn between animals and religion started long before bestiaries came into play. In many ancient civilisations there are references to animals and their meaning within that specific religion or mythology that we are familiar with today. These civilisations, of course, included Egypt and their animal-faced gods or Greece which had symbolic animals for their godly beings – an example being Zeus as both the bull and the eagle. With animals being an important a part of religion imagery before bestiaries and their lessons came out, they were influenced by past observations of meaning as well as older myths and their interpretations.

A mythological creature is a type of fictional entity, typically a hybrid, that has not been proven and that is described in folklore (including myths and legends), but may be featured in historical accounts before modernity. This imaginary creature, usually having various human and animal parts, plays no important role in ancient Egyptian history – because the Egyptians were notoriously accurate when it came to illustrating the different species of animals that were familiar to the people living in the Nile Valley, which were easily identifiable – with notable exceptions…

Unlike other totemic animals, the Set-animal is *not* easily identifiable in the modern animal world. Today, there is a general agreement among Egyptologists that it was *never* a real creature and existed only in ancient Egyptian imagination. In recent years, there have been many attempts by zoologists to find the Set-animal in nature and whether or not the animal ever existed is currently unknown, yet it had much significance for the Egyptians. The Set-animal is one of the most frequently demonstrated animal determinatives. According to Egyptologist Richard H. Wilkinson, the first known use of the Set-animal was upon the Scorpion Macehead of king Scorpion II of Naqada III; and thereafter portrayed mounted upon the *serekhs* of kings Seth-Peribsen and Khasekhemwy.

According to some scientists, the Set-animal hieroglyph does not actually represent a living animal, and it is currently not possible to determine from what living creature the hieroglyph derived. In art, Set is usually depicted as an enigmatic creature referred to in Egyptological circles as the 'Set-animal', a beast not identified with any known creature, although it could be seen as a resembling an aardvark, an African wild dog, a donkey, a hyena, a jackal, a pig, an antelope, a giraffe, an okapi, a saluki, or a fennec fox. The animal has a downward curving snout, slanting eyes, long ears with squared-off ends; a thin, forked tail with sprouted fur tufts in an inverted arrow shape; and a slender canine body. Mostly, Set is depicted as a well-proportioned human with the distinctive head.

According to *Britannica*, Set was the patron of the 11th nome, or province, of Upper Egypt and his worship originally centred at Nubt (Greek Ombos), near present-day Ṭūkh, on the western bank of the Nile River. Nubt, with its vast cemetery at nearby Naqādah, was the principal Predynastic centre in Upper Egypt. The town lost its pre-eminent position with the Unification of Egypt, which was carried out under kings whose capital was Abydos and whose royal god was Horus. Set was represented as the composite figure detailed above and because even the ancient Egyptians rendered his figure inconsistently, it is probably a mythical assortment. Originally he was a sky god, lord of the desert, master of storms, disorder, and warfare – in general, a trickster. Set embodied the necessary and creative elements of violence and disorder within the ordered world. The vicissitudes of his cult reflect the ambivalent attitude of the indigenous Egyptians toward him, as well as the shifting political fortunes of Egypt.

During the 2nd Dynasty, King Peribsen identified himself with Set for the first time, giving himself a Set title instead of the traditional Horus name. His successor, Khasekhemwy, gave both Horus and Set equal prominence in his titulary, reflecting the mythical resolution of the two gods. During the rule of the Hyksos invaders, Set was worshipped at their capital, Avaris, in the north-eastern Nile Delta, and was identified with the Canaanite storm god Baal. During the New Kingdom, he was esteemed as a martial god who could sow discord among Egypt's enemies. The Ramesside pharaohs, originating in the north-eastern delta, ranked him among the great gods of Egypt, used his name in their personal names (Seti I and Seti II, Setnakht), and promoted the image of Set as the protector of Re in the prow of his *barque*, slaying Re's enemy, Apophis. Set also joined Amon, Re, and Ptah as the fourth of the principal gods of the cosmos.

In later myth, Set was the brother of Osiris. There, too, his character was troublesome, for he was depicted as bursting out of the womb of his mother, Nut, being an unfaithful husband to his consort and sister, Nephthys, and murdering Osiris, whom he tricked into entering a chest, which he then closed and hurled into the river to be carried out to sea. After Osiris's murder, Horu the Child was conceived miraculously by Isis, the wife and sister of Osiris. Horus struggled with Set, who sought to dispossess him from his father's throne and this struggle forms the theme of the Ramesside text *The Contending of Horus and Set*, which borders on satire, and the later, much more sombre version recorded by Plutarch, in which Set is the embodiment of the Greek demon, Typhon.

> After the close of the New Kingdom, as Egypt lost its empire and later its independence, and as the cult of Osiris grew in prominence, Set was gradually ousted from the pantheon. In the 1st millennium BC his name and image were effaced from many monuments – and he was now identified as a god of the eastern invaders of Egypt, including the Persians. No longer able to reconcile Set with Horus, the Egyptians equated the former with evil. Elaborate rituals of the repeated defeat of Set as an enemy largely replaced the earlier ritual destructions of Apophis.
>
> *(Britannica)*

In the Early Dynastic Period, however, Set was a critical and benevolent god of Upper Egypt. People invoked his name for love spells and inscribed them on amulets that served as love charms. Moreover, Set also saved the sun god Re from the serpent Apophis. The snake was an evil creature who tried to stop Re's journey through the night sky towards morning. Set was the one who resisted the serpent's deadly stare and repulsed the evil creature with the thrust of a great spear. Hence, Set ensured that Re would rise the following day through this act. Set was also the benefactor who helped the people in life and provided for them after death.

Set can, therefore, be best described as 'magnificent' among the Egyptian gods, and someone we'd like to have at our backs in case of trouble. He might not be the most refined member of the pantheon, but he is certainly the most enduring... no matter what the later priesthoods may say!

Although hippopotami were greatly feared, Tauret appears to have developed a rather Walt Disneyish kind of character as a domestic goddess and protector of the home. She is also often seen with features from other predatory creatures, most notably being the tail of a Nile crocodile and the paws of a lioness. With the rise of popular piety during the New Kingdom, household deities like her gained even more importance, with her image being found on an array of household objects, demonstrating her central role in the home.

> In fact, such objects were even found at Amarna from the reign of Akhenaten, a pharaoh of the 18th Dynasty who re-organized the Egyptian religion into a monotheistic religion focused on the worship of the sun-disc, called the Aten. The worship of many traditional gods was proscribed during this period, so Tauret's survival in the artistic corpus found at the Aten's capital demonstrates her overwhelming significance in daily life.
>
> (Wikipedia)

Tauret's image served a functional purpose on a variety of objects. The most notable of these objects are amulets, which protected mothers and children from harm. Such amulets, appearing before 3000 BC, were popular for most of Egyptian history. She also consistently appeared on household furniture throughout history, including chairs, stools, and headrests. Apotropaic objects became popular in the Middle Kingdom and are thought to have been used in rituals related to pregnancy and birth. As is aforementioned, ivory wands and knives showing long processions of deities became widely used in this period. These objects have been shown on tomb paintings in the hands of nurses and wear patterns on the tips indicate that these nurses likely used them to draw protective patterns in the sand. Tauret is featured on almost all known wands, as her powers were invoked particularly to protect children and their mothers.

In the secret crypts of the Temple of Ipet at Karnak, the hippopotamus goddess was said to give birth to the solar form of Osiris who rose again as Amun-Re. In the *Pyramid Texts*, the reborn king is nourished by the sweet milk. This creation story consolidated by Geraldine Pinch is a probably why Tauret, also known as Ipet, is seen as a mother figure rather than a domestic goddess. If Tauret was one of the goddesses from the primeval marshes then her importance with the fertility of Egypt would be paramount. She would be an obvious protector of pregnant women and children because she is the mother goddess and in a sense the mother of ancient Egypt.

> To suggest that Tauret (Ipet) is a typical goddess would be an understatement that unravels the essence of the Egyptian artistic canon. She is not slender nor fits the traditional beautiful standard as the other goddesses. She is the Ammut parallel who is a savior to women and children. Her swollen belly is not meant to be realistic as to suggest that she is pregnant but to relate her to Hapi and the fecundity figures as to show the viewers that she is more than a mere domestic deity.
>
> (*A Guide to the Gods, Goddesses, and Traditions of Ancient Egypt*)

In Egyptian astronomy, Tauret was linked to the northern sky. In this role she was known as Nebetakhet, the Mistress of the Horizon – the ceiling painting of the constellations in the tomb of Seti I showed her in this capacity. She was thought to keep the northern sky – a place of darkness, cold, mist, and rain to the Egyptians – free of evil. She was shown to represent the never-setting circumpolar stars of Ursa Minor and Draco. The seven stars lined down her back are the stars of the Little Bear. She was believed to be a guardian of the north, stopping all who were unworthy before they could pass her by.

> In all of the ancient Egyptian astronomical diagrams there is one figure which is always larger than all the rest, and most frequently found at the center of what appears to be a horizontal parade of figures. This figure is Tauret 'The Great One', a goddess depicted as a pregnant hippopotamus standing upright. It is no mystery that this figure represents a northern constellation associated, at least in part, with our modern constellation of Draco the dragon.
>
> (Jim Fournier, *Precession and the Pyramid Astronomical Knowledge in Ancient Egypt*)

A fearsome goddess that is a composite of three of the most dangerous creatures in Egypt was rendered by adults as the loveable roly-poly protector of children!

By contras, Tauret and her fellow hippopotamus goddesses of fertility should not be confused with Ammit, another composite hippopotamus deity who gained prominence in the New Kingdom. Ammit was the Otherworld entity, responsible for devouring the unworthy before passing into the afterlife. Unlike Ammit, the other hippopotamus goddesses were responsible for nourishment and aid, not destruction. Ammit *'m-mwt* was the 'Devourer of the Dead', with the forequarters of a lion, the hindquarters of a hippopotamus, and the head of a crocodile – the three largest 'man-killing' animals known to ancient Egyptians.

Ammit literally means 'Swallower of the Dead', where *'m* is the verb 'to swallow' and *mwt* signifies 'the dead', or more specifically the dead who had been judged not to belong to the *akhu* or 'blessed dead' who had abided by the code of truth (*Ma'at*). 'Judgement of the Soul' from the *Papyrus of Hunefer* (*c.* 1375 BC) shows Hunefer's heart being weighed on the scale of *Ma'at* against the feather of truth, by the jackal-headed Anubis, and Ammit lying in wait to eat the heart if it fails the test. The ibis-headed Thoth, scribe of the gods, records the result.

She is usually depicted as attending the Judgement of the Dead before Osiris, in Chapter 125 of the *Book of the Dead*. Osiris presided over the judgement as the ruler of Duat, the Egyptian Underworld, in the depictions during the New Kingdom and judgement took place in the Hall of the Two Truths (or Two *Ma'ats*). The Forty-Two Judges were the divine beings of the Egyptian afterlife who presided over the Hall of Truth where the great god Osiris judged the dead. The Negative Confessions (also known as The Declaration of Innocence) is a list of forty-two 'sins' which the soul of the deceased can honestly say it has never committed when it stands in judgement in the afterlife. The soul would recite these in the presence of the gods who weighed their truth in deciding the deceased's fate.

Anubis, the Guardian of the Scales, conducted the dead towards the weighing instrument, so that the heart of the dead could be weighed against the feather of *Ma'at*. If the heart was judged to be impure, Ammit would devour it, and the person undergoing judgement was not allowed to continue their voyage towards Osiris and immortality. Once Ammit swallowed the heart, the soul was believed to become restless forever; this was called 'to die a second time'. Thus Ammit was often depicted sitting in a crouched posture near the scale, ready to eat the heart. However, the *Book of the Dead* served as both guide and guarantee, so that the dead buried with it always succeeded in the trial, leaving Ammit ever-hungry, and the consecrated dead were then able to bypass the 'Lake of Fire' of Chapter 126.

This ancient goddess Ammit (also known as Ammut and Ahemait) was, therefore, personification of divine retribution. She sat beside the scales, ready to devour the souls of those deemed unworthy. Those unfortunate enough to fail the judgement of the dead would suffer the feared second death, and have no chance of the blissful life of the field of reeds, instead roaming restlessly for eternity. In fact, this fearsome creature was never worshipped, and was not strictly a goddess, but her image was thought to ward off evil. She was the personification of all that the ancient Egyptians feared and a reminder to live by the principles of *Ma'at*. Although she was referred to as a demon, she was in reality a force for order. Moreover, each person was at least given the chance to defend their actions before being consigned to eternal damnation. The heart scarab was used to encourage the person's heart not to speak out against them and the negative confessions allowed a person to defend themselves by pointing out all of the evil actions they had *not* taken.

Apophis, also called Apep, Apepi, or Rerek was an archaic demon of chaos, who had the form of a serpent and, as the foe of the sun-god, Re, represented all that was outside the ordered cosmos. Although many serpents symbolised divinity and royalty, Apophis threatened the underworld and symbolised evil. Each night Apophis encountered Re at a particular hour in the sun god's ritual journey through the underworld in his divine barque. Set, who rode as guardian in the front of Re's barque, fought him off with a spear and slew him; but the next night Apophis, who could not be permanently subdued, was there again to attack Re. The Egyptians believed that the king could help maintain the order of the world and assist Re by performing such rituals against Apopis.

Egyptian serpents and/or dragons are highly complex and integral to Egyptian mythology. The dates of Egyptian myths vary, but they tend to be within 3000 BC and 2000 BC; the foremost dragon/sea serpent is Apep (also known as Apophis in Greece) was the living embodiment of chaos and was the greatest nemesis of the Egyptian gods and the concept of *Ma'at* (order). The few descriptions of Apep's origin in myth usually demonstrate that it was born after Re, usually from his umbilical cord – but generally Apep was commonly believed to have existed from the beginning of time in the waters of Nu of primeval chaos.

Apep was first mentioned in the 8th Dynasty, and honoured in the names of the 14th Dynasty king Apepi and of the Greater Hyksos king, Apophis. Apep was seen as a giant snake or serpent leading to such titles as *Serpent from the Nile* and *Evil Dragon*. Some elaborations said that he stretched 16 yards in length and had a head made of flint. Already on a Naqada I (*c*.4000 BC) bowl (now in Cairo museum) a snake was painted on the inside rim combined with other desert and aquatic animals as a possible enemy of a deity, possibly a solar deity, who is invisibly hunting in a big rowing vessel. In an annual rite called the *Banishing of Chaos*, priests would build an effigy of Apep that was thought to contain all of the evil and darkness in Egypt, and burn it to protect everyone from Apep's evil for another year.

In present times, 99942 Apophis is a near-earth asteroid and potential astral hazard with a diameter of 370 metres that caused a brief period of concern in December 2004 when initial observations indicated a probability up to 2.7 per cent that it would hit earth on 13 April 2029.

> Named after Apophis, the Greek name of Apep, the enemy of the ancient Egyptian sun-god, he is the Uncreator, an evil serpent that dwells in the eternal darkness of the Duat and tries to swallow Re during his nightly passage. Apep is held at bay by Set, the ancient Egyptian god of storms and the desert. The new radar-derived orbit shows that 99942 Apophis will pass 288 m (945 feet) farther from Earth in 2029 than had been expected, enough to assure that it will miss the 600-m-wide 'keyhole' in near-Earth space that would have deflected it onto a collision course in 2068.
>
> (*Sky & Telescope*)

Possibly one of the most curious animals from Egypt's ancient world, *Ovis longipes palaeo-aegyptiacus* is a type of the extinct wild barbary sheep found in southern Egypt and Nubia. The *ovacaprines* were domesticated and often depicted on the stone tomb murals of the pharaohs for religious or aesthetic purposes. *Ovis longipes palaeo-aegyptiacus* was one of the two most commonly domesticated sheep utilised on the reliefs of early pharaonic tombs mostly because of its unique loosely spiralling horns which came out of the sides of the skull. A similar form of the sheep called *Ovis platyura aegyptiaca* had horns that developed downward and curled forward.

> Later on, these two variants of sheep came to assume important religious significance as well as domestic use. Herodotus recounts that early Egyptians did not wear wool, but some scholars argue that it was meant only for the priests and that there is archaeological evidence, including the body of a man wrapped in wool dating to

the 1st Dynasty in a burial at al-Helwan, that argues this point. The use of this sheep is also unique in Egyptian depiction of their early deities. In fact, 'the standard representation of Egyptian gods, were first developed, and naturally the ram-headed deities wore the horns of the then prevailing *Ovis longipes palaeo-aegyptiacus* and retained them even long after the sheep itself had become extinct.'

(Wikipedia)

For example: Khnum was worshipped from the 1st Dynasty into the early centuries AD. He was represented as a ram with horizontal twisting horns or as a man with a ram's head, and was believed to have created humankind from clay like a potter – a scene, with him using a potter's wheel, was depicted in later times. The god's first main cult centre was Herwer, near Al-Ashmūnayn in Middle Egypt. From the New Kingdom onwards, however, he was the god of the island of Elephantine, near present-day Aswān, and was known as the lord of the surrounding First Cataract of the Nile River. At Elephantine he formed a triad of deities with the goddesses Satis and Anukis. Khnum also had an important cult at Esna, south of Thebes.

Banebdjedet (Banebdjed) was an ancient Egyptian ram god with a cult centre at Mendes: Khnum was the equivalent god in Upper Egypt. The Goat of Mendes introduced by Eliphas Lévi, possibly following Herodotus's account that the god of Mendes – the Greek name for Djedet, Egypt – was depicted with a goat's face and legs. The earliest rams to depict gods were heavily built and had long, wavy horns. Two gods thus represented were Khnum, who created both man and gods on his potter's wheel, and Banebdjedet.

The latter was the manifestation of the Lord of Djedet and of the 'ba', or soul, of Osiris, one of the most renowned of the ancient Egyptian deities. The second, later species of ram, which was the earthly incarnation of Amun, had curved horns and didn't appear until the 12th Dynasty of Egypt's Middle Kingdom. The processional avenue leading to the Temple of Amun at Luxor (ancient Thebes) was flanked by ram-headed lion sphinxes, each guarding a statue of the pharaoh between its front legs.

The Oracle of the Lamb

This text describes how a lamb, representing the god Khnum, speaks to a man called Pasaenhor; after the lamb dies, Pasaenhor recites his prophecies to the pharaoh Bakenranef (Bocchoris), who orders that the lamb should be buried in a shrine, 'in the manner of a god'. Various historical interpretations of the prophecies have been offered by modern writers – but none of them can be regarded as certain. The prophecies of the lamb were already well known in the third century BC, when the historian Manetho referred to them (as quoted by Eusebius, *Chronicle*, p. 147). This version was probably composed during the Ptolemaic Period, and the surviving copy was written in the reign of the emperor Augustus. (The translation is taken from R. K. Ritner, in *The Literature of Ancient Egypt: An Anthology*, pp. 445–449.)

A kind of encyclopaedia of animals, the bestiary was among the most popular illuminated texts in northern Europe during the Middle Ages. Because medieval Christians understood every element of the world as a manifestation of God, the book largely focused on each animal's religious meaning. The bestiary brought creatures both real and fantastic to life before the reader's eyes, offering devotional inspiration as well as entertainment. The beasts and their tales became so familiar that they often escaped from the pages to inhabit an array of works of art, ranging from ivories and metalwork to stained glass and tapestries. The bestiary also provided the basis for the emerging field of natural history in the late Middle Ages and established a far-reaching legacy that still impacts the visual arts today.

For all its mighty animal-based pantheon, however, Egypt had no great monsters compared with the rest of its neighbours. Of all the world's early civilisations, it was Egypt that fostered the closest relationship with the animal world. Here, all aspects of life, both secular and sacred, gave prominent place to man's vital involvement with living creatures of every kind. Nevertheless, *An Egyptian Bestiary: Animals in Life and Religion in the Land of the Pharaohs* by Jacques Livet and Philippe Germond – a large-format publication from the Metropolitan Museum of Art – portrays the pantheon of animal-headed gods and the sacred and fabulous creatures that inhabited their devotional, funerary, and magic world... but no real monsters.

Chapter Fourteen

Power of the Bull and the Celestial Cow

The bull of the ancient world is best summarised by Michael Rice in his *Power of the Bull* as the divine bull in the characteristic of the huge and ferocious wild bovine, which for thousands of years roamed across the plains and through the valleys of the Old World. Probably the most dangerous animal likely to be encountered by man in his capacity as hunter – where the bull would unhesitatingly attack man in defence of his herd...

> There is a touching representation of the bull's courage from Cyprus in which all the other animals of the case are shown fleeting before the hunter's arrows, except for the great bull who is shown charging against the stream of the other animal in a challenge to the chariot-borne hunter and his horses ... But before the wild bull went the way of so many other noble species of which man has been the destroyer, he left behind a memory, deep in the consciousness of those who were to drive him off the planet. That memory seems likely to endure as long as, ironically, men admire the beauty and sovereign existence of these animals, which lived so majestically, when men were little more than the apes from which they had so obviously descended.
>
> *(Power of the Bull)*

Even though the drawing appears accurate enough to our eyes, to the ancient Egyptians this hieroglyph represented an abstraction formed over time as the synthesis of bovine characteristics. It does in fact sum up (and represent ideographically) the distinctive traits of the various bovine species that were to be found from remote times in the Nile Valley and adjacent areas. The oldest hieroglyphs often show significant variations on the formula, according to the species or the gender. The same careful adherence to realistic detail is even more evident in the representation of bovines in typical scenes – very common in tombs – of cattle-raising, butchering, and, in general, of animal life.

The bovines, indicated by the names k_3, $ỉh$, ng, $ỉw_3$, etc., are shown with different builds, sometimes robust and large, with short, massive legs, sometimes thinner. Even the horns vary; although frequently tall and in the shape of a lyre, they are sometimes short and rounded, and may even be lacking in either gender. In many cases, the variants can be noted in animals that bear the same name and can be considered members of the same species, but are the fruit of the cross-breedings effected by the Egyptians in order to improve the species. In the later period, and perhaps earlier, the Egyptians kept oxen as well as bulls in their herds.

The greatest distinction seems to be between ng and $ỉw_3$: the former are usually bellicose and left to roam wild, and are often the protagonists of the battles of the bulls in the typical scenes of animal life; the latter are slower and thicker, lords of the stalls and triumphant participants in the proud parades of cattle that the cattlemen liked to organise for their noble patrons. The sacred Apis bull was chosen from the ranks of the frightening ng. This particular hieroglyph shows the fighting bull, its head aggressively lowered, ready to gore (*Hieroglyphics: The Writings of Ancient Egypt*).

While Carl Beierkuhnlein, writing in *Frontiers of BioGeography* – 'Bos primigenius in Ancient Egyptian art: historical evidence for the continuity of occurrence and ecology of an extinct key species' – acknowledges that knowledge of the habitat requirements and temporal stability of populations of extinct aurochs (Bos primigenius) is surprisingly scarce.

> Reliable reports of this species, which by its domestication remains tremendously important for humans, are rare. As the species became extinct about 400 years ago and regionally disappeared much earlier, its behaviour and morphology are also under debate. Aurochs is also a crucial component of the mega-herbivore theory in nature conservation, but in fact its natural habitat and behaviour are unknown. Here, I report records of aurochs for the time period of Ancient Egypt. They are found in archaeological sites and literature, and in collections. Records of the species continue through all the periods of Ancient Egypt.
>
> (*Frontiers of BioGeography*, Vol. 7, Issue 3)

In particular, hunting scenes illustrating the merits of high-ranking persons, in their graves (mastabas) and temples, provide insights into the behaviour and ecology of the depicted game. Here, special attention is given to one outstanding hunting scene that is documented in a relief at the mortuary temple of Ramesses III at Medinet Habu. Assisted by a group of hunters, the pharaoh kills three specimens of aurochs and the whole scene is stunningly realistic. The adult bull is fleeing towards the reed belt of the River Nile, suggesting that this species' habitat was probably in large valley bottoms, where open grassland is regularly created by flooding. Endemic species of fish and game confirm that this scene took place in Lower Egypt, while the regional populations of the North-African subspecies of aurochs probably went extinct shortly after this piece of art was produced. Records of species in ancient art can be very informative in terms of ecology, especially when extinct species are depicted; in addition, the dating of old pieces of art containing biological information can be very precise, for instance when these refer to an historic personage.

It was in Egypt, however, that the bull achieves what is perhaps his most exalted incarnation, according to Michael Rice (*Power of the Bull*).

> His divinity is predicted on his identification with the king and with royal power. This becomes apparent as the idea of the kingship evolves in the Nile Valley, in the second half of the fourth millennium BC. However, the roots of the bull-cult went much deeper, much further back into time.

In other words, the belief in the bull as divine endured in Egyptian religion throughout its long existence from early Predynastic times, right up until the Ptolemaic era when it spread from Alexandria to become one of the most widespread Eastern cults in the Roman Empire.

Apis, in this ancient religion, was the sacred bull deity worshipped at Memphis in the cult of Apis that originated at least as early as the 1st Dynasty. Like other bull deities, Apis was probably at first a fertility god concerned with the propagation of grain and herds, but became associated with Ptah, the paramount deity of the Memphite area, and also with Osiris (as User-Hapi), together with Sokaris, gods of the dead and of the underworld. As Apis-Atum, he was associated with the solar cult and was often represented with the sun disc between his horns.

Much of what is known about Apis comes from Graeco-Roman writers. He was black and white and distinguished by special markings. Some ancient writers said that he was begotten by a ray of light from heaven, and others claimed that he was sired by an Apis bull. When a sacred bull died, the calf that was to be his successor was sought and installed in the *Apieion* at Memphis. His priests drew omens from his behaviour, and his oracle had a wide reputation. Upon its decease, he was buried with great pomp at Ṣaqqārah, in underground galleries known in the classical world as the *Serapeum*. It was probably in Memphis that the worship of Serapis (after the Greek form Osorapis, a combination of Osiris and Apis in the image of an eastern Greek god) arose under Ptolemy Soter.

In more modern times, however, this granodiorite sacred bull is 'a gem of a piece', says Hannah Solomon, Christie's Specialist, Head of Sale for Antiquities:

> Wonderfully carved in delicate but powerful curves, he becomes the star of any room he inhabits. The Late Period saw native

Egyptian kings return to the throne after more than a century of foreign rule. They were keen to fortify their cultural traditions in the face of foreign powers, and a new era of patronage saw naturalistic modelling of flesh and features on both human and animal sculptures pushed to unprecedented heights.

At the same time, traditional Egyptian cults flourished. While ancient Egyptians did not worship animals, zoomorphic representations exemplified qualities and characteristics that were important in society. The male bull in particular was an attractive symbol, as it had a cosmic association and generally represented strength and masculine virtue, which is why the animal had strong ties to kingship and monarchial ideology.

Between the proud horns of this bull are two symbols of its divinity – a solar disc and a uraeus cobra. These attributes reveal its identity as a sacred bull, possibly Apis, but other bull cults were also known. Apis was the sacred bull-god of the gods Ptah, Osiris, and Atum, with his cult centre located at the Egyptian Late Period capital city of Memphis. Two other closely-rated sacred bulls can be found in the Cleveland Museum of Art and the Fondation Gandur in Geneva. This sacred bull has been carved from a locally mined hard stone known as granodiorite. 'The luxuriousness of the stone, with its beautiful black, rich colour, makes a huge statement,' says Solomon. 'You want to run your hands over its surface.'

'The bull symbolised power and sexual potency in ancient Egypt, making it the perfect icon for a deity,' continues the specialist. Only one living bull at a time would be worshipped, and for it to be designated an Apis bull it would need to have split hairs on its tail, a scarab shape under its tongue, a patch of fur representing a bird of prey in flight on its shoulders, a triangular mark on its forehead, a crescent moon on its flank, and a black and white coat. Such a bull would be taken to live in the Apis sanctuary where it would be pampered as though it were a god, given a harem of cows, and worshipped daily. It was said its breath cured diseases, and its movements were translated as prophecies.

'The sculpture has a real sense of personality,' explains Solomon. 'He also exhibits wonderful movement. The waves in the mane and the brushing of the legs in the papyrus leaves give the bull this forward motion.' Interestingly, the bull's stance is not anatomically accurate, which suggests the artist strove for an idealised beauty in the time-honoured Egyptian tradition.

'For us to find such a beautiful statue, however, is only half the job,' Solomon goes on to explain. 'The other half is discovering its recent history, because it is important for antiquities to have a rich ownership history outside of Egypt.' Fortunately the discovery of this bull was published in 1959, as well as being rare and in great condition. 'People now more than ever understand the importance that ancient sculpture has played in forming the aesthetic of everyone from Giacometti to Basquiat,' Solomon explains. 'As a result, they are coming to us to find works that complement their 20th-century collections' (Christie's auction catalogue, March 2018).

Mnevis was a sacred bull deity worshipped at Heliopolis and as one of several sacred bulls in Egypt, he was most closely associated with the sun god Re-Atum. Although not attested with certainty until the Middle Kingdom, the Mnevis bull may be that which is referenced by the phrase 'bull of Heliopolis', which occurs in the *Pyramid Texts*. The Mnevis bull was either black or piebald in colour, and in sculptures and paintings he was also represented with a solar disc between his horns.

In later times, an Egyptian leaded bronze Mnevis appeared in auction in May 2021. Its provenance was as follows: 'E. B. Collection, Orion, Michigan, USA, acquired from Royal Athena in July 1987; ex-Christie's London, April 1987. On loan to Miami University Art Museum, Oxford, Ohio, USA; Ball State University Art Gallery; George Mason University; Fitchburg Art Museum, 1988 to 2016.' Catalogue details:

> Egypt, Late Period, XXVI Dynasty, 664 to 525 BCE. Finely cast via the lost wax (cire perdue) process, a bronze statue of Mnevis, the bull-headed god worshipped in Heliopolis. The sculpture is a 3/4 figure, and while lacking the right forearm/hand and legs, presents with a nice representative form that still manages to capture the god's striding pose, with what remains of one leg advanced, the left arm bent at the elbow and crossing the body, and the upper right arm extending out. Mnevis' bold visage is comprised of curved horns, ears below, a wig/headdress gracing his shoulders, and a prominent snout. He wears a kilt-like skirt, and the surface has developed a rich, dark brown patina over the ages. Size: 1.875" W x 3.25" H (4.8 cm x 8.3 cm); 5.7" H (14.5 cm) on included custom stand. Condition: Losses to both legs, left hand, right forearm and hand, and tips of both horns as shown. Minor pitting and abrasions to body, limbs, and head, with softening to some finer details. Nice earthen deposits and fantastic russet, green, and brown patina throughout. Mounted with modern brass rods through bottom of legs for display purposes. According to Plutarch, the Mnevis bull was second only to the Apis bull of Memphis in significance. Parallel to the Apis bull, worshippers believed that the Mnevis bull's movements were determined by divine will, and were utilized as an oracle. In addition, the priesthood of Mnevis claimed that Mnevis was the father of the Apis bull.

Buchis was a white bull with black markings, worshipped as a favourite incarnation of the war god, Montu, who was represented with the solar disc and two tall plumes between his horns. According to Macrobius, his hair grew in the opposite direction from that of ordinary animals and changed colour every hour. At Hermonthis (present-day Armant) in Upper Egypt, a special centre of Montu's worship, a particular bull was chosen to receive a cult status as Buchis. Upon its death, it was mummified and buried in a sarcophagus with divine honours. The mothers of these Buchis bulls received a similar cult and burial.

> Per-month (Armant) was an ancient town in Upper Egypt, near Thebes on the west bank of the Nile. It was the seat of a sun cult and was crowning place of kings. The war god Montu was worshiped there in hawk-headed human form and also in his epiphany, as the bull Buchis. Armant was probably the original home of the rulers of Thebes who reunited Egypt after the First Intermediate Period. Excavations of 1929–38 uncovered the *Bucheum* (the necropolis of the mummified Buchis bulls), cemeteries of various periods from the pre-Dynastic downward, and part of the town area, including the temple of Montu.
>
> (*Britannica*)

Much later, the cult of Serapis was promoted during the third century BC on the orders of Greek pharaoh Ptolemy I Soter of the Ptolemaic Kingdom, as a means to unify the Greeks and Egyptians in his realm. The *cultus* of Serapis was spread as a matter of deliberate policy by the Ptolemaic kings and Serapis continued to increase in popularity during the Roman Empire, often replacing Osiris as the consort of Isis in temples outside Egypt. Though Ptolemy I may have created the official cult of Serapis and endorsed him as a patron of the Ptolemaic dynasty and Alexandria, Serapis was a pre-existing syncretistic deity derived from the worship of the Egyptian Osiris and Apis, who also gained attributes from other deities, such as chthonic powers linked to the Greek Hades and Demeter, and with benevolence derived from associations with Dionysus.

Serapis was depicted as Greek in appearance but with Egyptian trappings, and combined iconography from a great many cults, signifying both abundance and resurrection. The Greeks had little respect for animal-headed figures, and so a Greek-style anthropomorphic statue was chosen as the idol, and proclaimed as the equivalent of the highly popular Apis. It was named *Userhapi* (i.e. 'Osiris-Apis'), which became Greek *Sarapis*, and was said to be Osiris in full, rather than just his *ka* (life force). There is evidence that the cult of Serapis existed before the Ptolemies came to power in Alexandria, since a temple of Serapis in Egypt is mentioned in 323 BC by both Plutarch and Arrian.

> Egyptians believed that sperm was produced in the thoracic spine, a conviction apparently based upon their understanding of the

anatomy of the bull. Egyptian texts show the close relationship felt to exist between the backbone and life, including one's ability to survive after death. The spine is shown to play a major role in after-life revivification, as reflected both in the texts and the iconography. Ankh is identified as a thoracic vertebra of an ungulate, which explains both its shape and its meaning.

(Calvin W. Schwabe, Joyce Adams and
Carleton T. Hodge, 'Egyptian Beliefs
about the Bull's Spine', 1982)

The Celestial Cow

The *Book of the Heavenly Cow* is an ancient Egyptian text dealing with the rebellion of humanity against the sun god Re, his destruction of the rebels through the goddess Hathor, the reversal of this decision and Re's mercy, followed by his ascent into the higher heavens, leaving earth in a fallen state.

According to Roland Mastaff of Tour Egypt, the first rendering of the *Book of the Heavenly Cow* was produced on the outermost of the four gilded shrines of Tutankhamun discovered in his tomb, though it was incomplete. However, we do find fairly complete versions of the book in the tombs of Seti I (KV17), Ramesses II (KV7), and Ramesses III (KV11). In each of these instances, the book is exclusively depicted in an annex off the burial chamber. We also find brief excerpts from the book in the left niche of the third corridor in the tomb of Ramesses VI, and another even shorter version on a papyrus from the Ramesside Period now in Turin. While this book does not seem to appear after the New Kingdom, it was incorporated into the *Book of the Fayoum* during the Roman Period.

Within the first part of the text in this book, a parallel to the biblical narrative of the great Flood has inspired considerable interest both within and outside of Egyptology. The heavenly cow in the tomb of Seti I was noted by early adventurers who visited the Valley of the Kings on the West Bank of Luxor (ancient Thebes) such as Henry Salt and Robert Hay. In 1876, Edouard Naville published the version of the *Book of the Heavenly Cow* found in the tomb of Seti I, translating it into French. He supplied the first translation into English in 1876. Later, in 1885, he also published the version found in the tomb of Ramesses III. Heinrich Brugsch published the first translation into German in 1881.

In 1941, Charles Maystre published the first synoptic version of the book, taking into account the text discovered in the tomb of Ramesses II (though he omitted the text from Tutankhamun). In 1983, Erik Hornung, taking into account all of the versions of the book including that found in the tomb of Ramesses III, published an improved version of the text, which included a metrical transliteration by Gerhard Fecht, which saw a second edition with four pages of supplemental material and corrections in 1991.

The *Book of the Heavenly Cow* is not a manual of spiritual instruction, or a guidebook through the Duat, as are the other funerary text of the New Kingdom. Rather, it tells a story that mixes magic spells with the exact details of the 'Divine Cow' herself. It is purely mythological in nature, and in fact, it is difficult to see how this particular book fits into the evolutionary framework of the other funerary text.

The central theme of the *Book of the Heavenly Cow* is mankind's rebellion against the elder sun god, Re, resulting in the punishment of humans by the fiery 'eye' of Re in the form of the goddess Hathor, and takes place after Re's long rule on earth. The first part places considerable emphasis on the royal role of the sun god, who bears the royal title and whose name is surrounded by a cartouche. He is specifically given rulership over both the deities and the humans. Prior to the rebellion, which required a complete re-ordering of the world, there had been a Golden Age when the various deities and humans were both under the sovereignty of the sun god. During this previous age, the sun god had not yet begun his daily course through the sky and the netherworld; hence, there was no cycle of day and night, nor was there a netherworld and death did not exist.

When mankind's rebellion took place, the sun god first consulted with the primeval deities, including Shu, Tefnut, and Geb but particularly the goddess Nun and Hathor in the Great House in Heliopolis. These gods were to come to Re in secrecy, as not to alert mankind about their meeting. Re then addressing Nu, the father of the first-born gods, told him to give heed to what men were doing, for they whom he had created were murmuring against him. And he said, 'Tell me what you would do. Consider the matter, invent a plan for me, and I will not slay them until I have heard what you shall say concerning this thing.'

Nu replied, 'You, O my son Re, are greater than the god who made You [i.e. Nu himself], you are the king of those who were created with you, your throne is established, and the fear of you is great, Let thine Eye [Hathor] attack those who blaspheme you.' And Re said, 'Lo, they have fled to the mountains for their hearts are afraid because of what they have said.'

The gods replied, 'Let thine Eye go forth and destroy those who blasphemed you, for no eye can resist thine when it goes forth in the form of Hathor.'

Afterwards, Hathor was sent to inflict her punishment. For three nights the goddess Hathor-Sekhmet waded about in the blood of men, the slaughter beginning at Hensu (Herakleopolis Magna). But the sun god took pity on those humans who were left. He saved them by causing Hathor to become drunk on blood-red beer.

Afterwards, the sun god, Re, withdrew to the sky on the back of the celestial cow who is the goddess Nut transformed; the cow is supported by

Shu, the eight Heh-gods along with the Pharaoh. This would account for the importance of the book for the king, who was the 'son' and successor of Re, and who withdraws to the sky upon his death, like Re, on the back of the heavenly cow. Now, humankind could suffer death, and so from his position in the sky, Re constructed the netherworld as their realm (third section of book). Within the netherworld, Re placed many serpents that were entrusted to the care of Geb, the earth god. He also sets the moon in the sky and appoints Thoth lord of the moon and deputy over creation. Now, through Thoth, people will know Re.

The final, or fourth part of the *Book of the Heavenly Cow* is devoted to the power of magic. It contains the theology of *ba* and explains the various deities and sacred animals that are *bas* of Hathor and Mehet-Weret, who were both thought of as the cow who birthed the sun god and placed him between her horns. Like Nut, Hathor was said to give birth to the sun god each dawn. Hathor's Egyptian name was *ḥwt-ḥrw* or *ḥwt-ḥr*, which is typically translated 'house of Horus' but can also be rendered as 'my house is the sky'.

The prehistoric peoples of the Nile region, like many early populations, revered powers of the natural world, both animate and inanimate. While some deities, like the sun god, Re, were linked with inanimate natural phenomena, most of the first clear examples of divinities were connected to animals. Falcon gods and cattle goddesses were among the earliest and may well have developed in the context of Neolithic cattle herding. Nut was also represented as a cow, for this was the form she took in order to carry the sun god, Re, on her back to the sky (*Smithsonian Magazine*).

> The most profound influences in the Egyptian collective psyche in the early periods were undoubtedly those which welled up from Africa in the south. Egypt was, supremely, an African state; its kings were African kings and its gods African gods – at least in the first 2,000 or so years of its history. The other and secondary influence came from the east; this was sporadic and whilst it was in certain details of great importance (the influence on architecture and the symbols associated with the kingship, for example) it was extraneous, not really fundamental to the formation of the historic personality.
>
> (*Power of the Bull*)

Evidence of an early experiment of the adaptation of human relationships with cattle in the region where the southern Nile Valley and the western Sahara are contiguous almost resulted in domestication at the remarkably early date of the middle of the twelfth millennium BC. At Tushka, in the southernmost part of Upper Egypt, there is evidence of men and wild cattle living in close contact and what Tushka does demonstrate is the profound penetration of the bull and its horns into the East African psyche and the deeply rooted response which it provokes. A more telling example of the 'power of the bull' could hardly be imagined and represented the first recognised Predynastic culture of Egypt.

At Hierakonpolis, notable bull cults were established from very early times and reveal it as a sacred centre, which it remained long after its political importance had declined. There were still earlier levels at Hierakonpolis which identify the city's contribution to two other significant aspects of ancient Egypt: the development of funerary architecture and, as befits a settlement founded by cattle people, of the cult of the bull itself. This place has been celebrated in the annals of Egyptology for the discovery, in 1898, of a handsome painted tomb ('Tomb 100') which is dated to the very end of the Predynastic Period. At this point, Egyptian history, and specifically Egyptian *royal* history, may be said to begin, records Michael Rice in *Egypt's Making*:

> Hierakonpolis, modern Kawm Al-Aḥmar, was the prehistoric royal residence of the kings of Upper Egypt and the most important site of the beginning of Egypt's historical period. Evidence indicates a royal presence at Hierakonpolis, then called Nekhen, which enjoyed its period of greatest importance from about 3400 BC; the town remained important into the early part of the Old Kingdom, and though it declined as a settlement, its temple to Horus of Nekhen was rebuilt in both the Middle and New Kingdoms. Three or four known tombs dating from the New Kingdom have been found here, including that of Hormose. This tomb gives evidence that the temple of Horus had been renewed by Rameses XI, who had followed the building efforts of Thutmose III five centuries earlier.

Excavations by J. E. Quibell in 1898 found monuments of early historic importance: a ceremonial slate palette of King Narmer and a decorated limestone mace-head of King Scorpion, now in the Egyptian Museum in Cairo. A large town with nearby cemeteries stretched about 2 miles along the desert margin; the late Predynastic and early dynastic kings built an oval mud-brick and stone temple and a large niched mud-brick enclosure. Later dedications included a pair of large copper statues of Pepi I and Merenre (6th Dynasty). Thutmose III completely rebuilt the archaic temple, and during the period of the New Kingdom the town of Al-Kāb (El-Kab) across the river became economically more important, although Nekhen retained its place as a religious and historic centre.

Bull and Narmer Palettes

These cosmetic palettes come in numerous shapes and sizes, and were often found in tombs or graves. They were preceded by a period of palettes called rhomboidal palettes, unadorned, and without the *cosmetic mixing circle* found on some of the later Naqada Period palettes. The Bull Palette (French: *palette célébrant une victoire*) is the fragment of a greywacke palette, carved in low relief and used, at least in principle, as a palette for the grinding of cosmetics. It is dated to Naqada III, the final two centuries of the fourth millennium, immediately preceding the Early Dynastic Period. It is in the collection of the Louvre, inventory no. E11255 (Wikipedia).

The obverse front of the Bull Palette has the top left iconography of the 'bull overpowering a warrior'. The right half is missing, with a probable second bull facing the first, as part of the upper borders, for both the left and the right. The rest of the front contains a large 'fortified walled city', and is identified in the centre with a larger lion and 'Nu' (vessel) that contains a lioness and the pot; a smaller section below contains the upper left quarter of a second fortified city. The second city is of smaller size than the identified city in the upper register.

The reverse of the palette has the same 'bull overpowering a warrior' motif; while a rope appears to encircle, or is at least part of the entire back, as one of the reverse motifs. The remaining piece of this broken cosmetic palette has possibly one of the more important motifs preserved in the palettes corpus. Five standards are shown collectively on the right of the palette, and each is an *iat* standard (hieroglyph), but notably the base of each standard transforms into a 'clenched hand', which embraces the large-diameter rope encircling the reverse side.

The five standards are:

1. A hippopotamus with open mouth
2. A hippopotamus with open mouth
3. The 'Sacred Ibis'
4. The standing Horus-Falcon
5. Symbol: 'Thunderbolt of Min' (an encircled snake on standard?)

The motifs on the sides of the palette are presumably the 'bull overpowering an enemy', the named fortified cities, war scenes, a collection of deities supporting the war scenery (on standards). That is a motif appearing on another cosmetic utensil, the well-known Narmer Palette.

Also known as the Great Hierakonpolis Palette or the Palette of Narmer, it is a significant Egyptian archaeological find, dating from about the thirty-first century BC, belonging, at least nominally, to the category of cosmetic palettes. It contains some of the earliest hieroglyphic inscriptions ever found. The tablet is thought by some to depict the unification of Upper and Lower Egypt under the king Narmer. Along with the Scorpion Macehead and the Narmer Maceheads, also found together in the main deposit at Nekhen, the Narmer Palette provides one of the earliest known depictions of an Egyptian king. On one side, the king is depicted with the bulbed White Crown of Upper (southern) Egypt, and the other side depicts the king wearing the level Red Crown of Lower (northern) Egypt, which also makes it the earliest known example of a king wearing both types of headdress. The Palette shows many of the classic conventions of ancient Egyptian art, which must already have been formalised by the time of the Palette's creation.

This material was used extensively during the Predynastic Period for creating such palettes and also was used as a source for Old Kingdom statuary. A statue of the 2nd Dynasty king, Khasekhemwy, found in the same complex as the Narmer Palette at Hierakonpolis, was also made of this material. At the bottom of the verso, a bull is seen knocking down the walls of a city while trampling on a fallen foe. Head lowered, Narmer is shown here as a stylised, two-dimensional beast who will vanquish his enemies. Bulls had an ideological connection to Egyptian kingship. 'Bull of his Mother', for example, was a common epithet given to an Egyptian king as the son of the patron cow goddess. This posture of a bovine has the meaning of 'force' in later hieroglyphics (Wikipedia).

Egyptologist Bob Brier has referred to the Narmer Palette as 'the first historical document in the world', and it is part of the permanent collection of the Egyptian Museum in Cairo. It was one of the initial exhibits which visitors were able to see when entering the museum.

Chapter Fifteen

Serpents and Scorpions

In Christian Jacq's incomparable book, *Egyptian Magic*, the author describes his encounter with a real-life magician, who came from a long line of 'native snake charmers' from Luxor. 'The earth,' he said,

> belongs to the serpents and scorpions. She is our mother, but a demanding and dangerous mother. The magician is not naïve. To understand the treasures of the earth, one must first gain the friendship of those who defend her. But that is impossible for one who is not a man of water, air and fire... but one must acknowledge that it is not within the capacity of everyone to be the brother of a snake...

Christian Jacq is an authority on traditional Egyptian religious texts and maintains that this ancient world was not the matter-of-fact, scientific world of today. It was a world so permeated with magic, which controlled every facet of life, that traces still linger in the Valley of the Nile to this day. He maintained that desiccated theory is the only result of hostility to Egyptian religion and inevitable if an Egyptologist lacks sympathy with its civilisation.

> Even in the sciences, intellectual brilliance alone can achieve nothing without sudden leaps of awareness. The greatest scientists are those who have some awareness into the mysteries of the universe and attempt to express this knowledge or understanding which matures over the years. If this is true of the pure sciences such as physics as Eisenberg, Einstein and so many others have shown, it is even more vital in Egyptology if the student is to avoid the trap of examining his subject with icy reason and historical 'detachment' alone.

During the course of his studies, like all Egyptologists, he had come across magic. He was aware that many 'scholars' have tried to weed it out of Egyptian religion as a defect inconsistent with the grandeur of the metaphysical ideas found in the great texts. But magic is stubborn. It is present everywhere in Egypt, in the turn of a story thought of as *literature*, as much as in the interiors of the tombs and on the walls of temples. In the time of the pharaohs, those who dealt with poisonous creatures were magicians who had been initiated and were privy to a knowledge, employing specific spells whose use required that they be very well qualified.

> I reminded my host of these things. He smiled. 'One must acknowledge,' he admitted, 'that indeed, perhaps, some magic is useful.' Within the bounds of oriental politeness, a genuine exchange of ideas had begun. Persuaded that my host must still know and practise the rules of ancient Egyptian magic, I compared his experience and my knowledge as an Egyptologist. Thus was born this book on the magic world of pharaonic civilisation. Between the ancient texts and the living experience there was no hiatus; which is why it is possible today to tackle a subject which previously was taboo.
>
> <div align="right">(<i>Egyptian Magic</i>)</div>

Different kinds of serpents are depicted by hieroglyphic images in addition to those given as examples in Sir Alan Gardiner's *Egyptian Grammar*, first published in 1927. A hieratic papyrus of the late period, now in the Brooklyn Museum, contains the description of thirty-eight reptiles. Each column of this *Treatise on Ophiology*, as its editor, Serge Sauneron, has called it, carried an accurate description of the physical characteristics of the horned viper, so that it could be recognised from the look of its bite and its consequence, including the prognosis. In some cases, it also includes the appropriate treatment, if such existed. It considers each serpent to be the manifestation of a god:

> In the second part of the treatise are more commonly given the recipes for treatment and antidotes against poison. Six sections are reserved for the different types of vipers the Egyptians knew and called collectively *fy*. We read in the section relative to the horned viper (*fy hr dbwy*: viper having two horns); '*His colour is similar to that of the quail; it has two horns on its forehead; the head is broad, the neck narrow, and the tail thick. If the bite's opening is ample, the face of the would swells; if the bite is small, the one bitten will become inert. but ... [he will have] fever for nine days, but will survive. It is a manifestation of Horus. One may draw the poison by making him vomit abundantly and by exorcisings...*'
>
> The supine reptile's name *d* and its female variant *dt* are documented in the *Pyramid Texts*, but the serpent's more common name is *i'rt* – the same as the erect serpent (the uraeus placed on the king's forehead). But different from this, the resting cobra does not take a place in the iconography of the divine forms of the reptile.

> The cobra is quite common in Egypt and the Egyptian *Treatise on Ophiology* gives the following description: *'As to the serpent cobra, it is the colour of sand. If it bites someone, he will feel pain in one half [of his body] where he has not been bitten and will not feel pain in the half that has been wounded. This is a pain that I will deal with. Execute all the operations that are necessary and give him numerous emetics, just [use] the knife, once he has vomited. It is a manifestation of Set. The bitten do not die.'* Professor Betro, quoting from the 'Treatise' in *Hieroglyphics* comments that the strange observations about the pain of the bite finds no comparison in modern medical texts.

The ancient Egyptians both feared and revered the snakes they encountered in their daily lives. Snakes were dangerous; a bite could be deadly. But they were also helpful, ridding the storehouses of mice and rats that fed on precious grain. We can also learn more about the snakes found in Egypt and the ways the ancient Egyptians thought about them.

For example, in the Egyptian galleries of the Michael C. Carlos Museum, we can find a rectangular coffin decorated with green hieroglyphs: the coffin of Nebetit. Look for a snake in the centre of the top row of hieroglyphs. This is an image of a horned viper. The scaly body of this desert-dwelling snake is the same colour as the stony sand in which it lives, providing excellent camouflage. Sometimes it buries itself in the sand, leaving only its head exposed.

Horned vipers move swiftly across the desert by sidewinding – throwing their bodies forward in repeated s-curve movements. The movement of the snake across the sand makes a sound like a repeating letter f. The Egyptians, close observers of the natural world, wrote the hieroglyph for the f sound in the form of the horned viper, perhaps because they heard this same sound.

The Michael C. Carlos Museum is an art museum located in Atlanta, USA, on the historic quadrangle of Emory University's main campus. One coffin in the collection, the coffin of Tanakhtnettahat or Tahat for short, is decorated with 198 different images of snakes. One detail from the side of the coffin depicts the sun god Re in his solar barque and there is an upright image of a snake right in front of him. This is Mehen, who protects the sun god as he travels nightly through the Underworld. Since the Egyptians understood that snakes could be dangerous and helpful at the same time, it makes sense that they used them to represent both Apophis, his enemy, and Mehen, his ally.

On another coffin, that of Pashedkhonsu, a long, elaborately twisting image of Mehen completely encircles Re. The name Mehen means 'the coiled one' and, during the Old Kingdom, Egyptians played a game called Mehen on a gameboard in the form of a coiled snake. The goal was to be the first to move around the image of the serpent, starting at the tail and moving to the head at the centre of the board. The rules and gameplay of Mehen are entirely unknown, except that the game was named in reference to Mehen, a snake deity.

Played from at least 3rd–6th Dynasties, although the earliest evidence for comes from the Predynastic Period (Naqada II phase, 3600–3200 BC), it is the leading contender for the accolade of 'oldest board game in the world'. The aim of the game is to get as many counters as you can around the board and back again, before they get eaten by lions! The game is for two players and each player has four counters and one lion.

> Evidence of the game of Mehen is found from the earliest period dating from approximately 3000 BC and continuing until the end of the Old Kingdom, around 2300 BC. Aside from physical boards, which mostly date to the Predynastic and Archaic periods, a Mehen board also appears in a picture in the tomb of Hesy-Ra, and its name first appears in the tomb of Rahotep. Other scenes dating to the Fifth Dynasty of Egypt and Sixth Dynasty of Egypt show people playing the game. No scenes or boards date to the Middle Kingdom of Egypt or New Kingdom of Egypt, and so it appears that the game was no longer played in Egypt after the Old Kingdom. It is, however, depicted in tombs of about 700, because the tomb decorations are copied from Old Kingdom originals. Mehen also appears to have been popular outside of Egypt as it appears alongside other boards displaying the game of *senet* at Bab 'edh Dhra and in Cyprus. In Cyprus, it sometimes appears on the opposite side of the same stone as *senet*, and those from Sotira *Kaminoudhia*, dating to approximately 2250 BC, are the oldest surviving double-sided boards known. Mehen survived in Cyprus longer than in Egypt, showing that the game was indigenized upon its adoption into the island's culture.
>
> (Wikipedia)

Snakes were a constant danger, especially to children. A small clay object called a *cippus* was used both to protect against and cure snakebites and scorpion stings. On one *cippus*, Horus-the-child stands atop two crocodiles and grasps snakes and scorpions in his hands. The main function of the Metternich Stela, for example, was for the magical healing of poisons, mostly caused by animals. Water was poured over the stela and collected to be then drunk by the person suffering from the poisonous ailment. That person would identify with the child Horus who had also suffered such tragedies. During the entire process, religious rites from the stela were recited by local priests.

On the Stela of Metternich (Metropolitan Museum of Art in New York), which is an important text worth studying for its own sake, there is what can only be described as a magical 'cartoon strip'. At the top of the stela, we see eight baboons worshipping the rising sun, whilst Thoth directs the ritual. It tells the story of the magical creation of light and the struggle against the forces of darkness, symbolically depicted in the lower bands of the stela. The central figure is that of Horus, represented as a naked child, standing on crocodiles and holding poisonous and dangerous animals in his hands. The young god fears no danger and masters the powers of evil, because he is protected by many divinities, notably by Bes, whose enormous smiling head is a pledge of safety.

According to one myth, young Horus was stung by a scorpion and cured by the god Thoth. The images and spells carved on the cippus impart the same divine healing power to others. The Egyptians believed strongly in the power of images and words. If a child was bitten or stung, family members would recite the spells incised on a cippus and give the child water that had been poured over its surface to heal the wound. *Cippi* of Horus or 'Horus on the Crocodiles' are a particular type of healing and protective statue that appeared in Egypt during the 18th Dynasty and remained in use until the Roman Period.

These magic texts, which form a considerable part of Egyptian 'literature', were written on a variety of materials: papyrus (from the time of the Middle Kingdom), *ostraca* (fragments of pottery), *stela*, statuary, and many other small objects. Contemporary scholars, accustomed to dividing things up in a rational manner, have fallen into the habit of classifying Egyptian texts as 'literary', 'religious', 'magical', etc. 'These formal distinctions do not correspond to the reality,' says Christian Jacq, in *Egyptian Magic*.

> *The Tale of the Shipwrecked Sailor* known as 'literature' is a wonderful story of magic. The *Coffin Texts* called 'funerary' constantly call on magic, in-so-much as a text written in hieroglyphs becomes effective by being so written, one could say that all Egyptian writing is magical, although one must recognize varying degrees in the validity of this principle ... There is found a kind of 'Grail' which the just find after undergoing many trials to which only knowledge of magic can provide the keys.

Many museums hold a long list of documents of varying degrees of interest – many of them unpublished, untranslated, or still inaccessible for reasons which are often obscure. These sacred writings were called *baau Ra* – the powers of the god of light. And it is not men who are the authors of the magic books, but Thoth, the master of the sacred words; Sha, the god of wisdom, and Geb, the lord of the earth. In writing they pass on to humanity the messages which they have the knowledge to use. The magician must therefore have a perfect knowledge of the divine world. The magician is not content to read: he swallows the texts, puts pieces of papyrus in a bowl, drinks the magic Word, ingests the words which hold meaning. This extraordinary rite, Christian Jacq tells us, was passed down to the guilds of the cathedral masons.

As Christian Jacq's encounter with the elderly Egyptian magician at Luxor provided the inspiration for *Egyptian Magic* (1985), so a casual meeting between a British soldier and a native snake-charmer of the Western Desert during the Second World War sowed the posthumous seeds for this book. The actual photograph from that time reveals the unnamed snake handler, whose preserved image led to an everlasting fascination with the magic of the gods of the Nile Valley many years later. According to Egyptian belief, the *ba* was everything that makes an individual unique, similar to the notion of 'personality'. In this sense, inanimate objects could also have a *ba*, a unique character that they believed would live after the body died. Could that photograph have preserved the *ba* of a long-dead snake-charmer that offered another 'gift beyond price' from his illustrious ancestors?

Scorpions in Ancient Egypt

The ancient Egyptians knew the scorpion and its toxicity, and venerated it since pre-Dynastic times. They used the scorpion as a king's name, a name of a nome (county), and a symbol to their goddess, Serqet, who protects the body and the viscera of the dead, and that accompanies them in their journey to the afterlife. They had medical prescriptions and magical spells to heal the stings and since the 5th Dynasty, the title of a 'Follower of Serket' was given to clever physicians. Scorpions are most famously depicted on the *Horus Cippus*, a talisman featuring Horus the Child holding in his hands figures of serpents, scorpions, and dangerous animals. A drawing of a scorpion with two metasomas was found in the tomb of the pharaoh Seti I (1290–1279 BC), probably the first record of this abnormality, more than 13 centuries before Pliny the Elder.

(H. K. El-Hennawy, 2011, 'Scorpions in Ancient Egypt', *Euscorpius*, no. 119: 1–12)

Serket (also known as Serqet, Selkis, and Selket) is a goddess of protection associated with the scorpion. She was worshipped widely in Lower Egypt as a great Mother Goddess in the Predynastic Period and so is among the older deities of Egypt. She is associated with healing, magic, and protection, and her name means 'She Who Causes the Throat to Breathe'. Her symbols are the scorpion, the *ankh*, and the Was Sceptre, all of which convey her benevolent aspects. In the Predynastic Period, she was the protector of the kings as evidenced by archaeological finds linking her by the name Serqet to the 'Scorpion Kings', defeated at some point around the reign of Narmer (*c.*3150 BC). During that period, she was already closely associated with protection and her worship had grown from the Delta region of Lower Egypt to the cities of Upper Egypt.

By the time of the 1st Dynasty, she was associated with the god Nun (also known as Nu), the Father of the Gods. Nun was the watery abyss from which the primordial hill (the ben-ben) rose on which Atum (Re) stood at the dawn of creation. It is unclear what role she played, if any, in the creation of the world, but evidence suggests she may have been the wife of Atum, the first son of Nun, or even the wife of Nun himself. Later, she is represented as one of the deities aboard the barge of the sun god Re, who watches out for the serpent Apophis as the boat sails through the night sky.

> She is the goddess of venomous creatures, most notably the scorpion, and is depicted as a beautiful woman, arms outstretched in a gesture of protection, with a scorpion on her head. The scorpion is purposefully shown without a stinger or claws to represent Serket's role as protector against venomous stings. Serket was eventually absorbed into the Cult of Horus where she became closely associated with death and the souls of the deceased. She was then known as 'Lady of the Beautiful Tent' which referred to the tent of the embalmers.
>
> (*World History Encyclopedia*)

There are, however, no mythological tales existing of Serket's origin as there are for most of the other deities; she is referenced as being present at the creation of the world but no mention is made of her role. She was seen as a mother goddess in the prehistoric period of Egypt and was already associated with the scorpion, which 'was a symbol of motherhood in many areas of the Near East'. She is depicted as nursing the kings of Egypt in the *Pyramid Texts*, which date to the Old Kingdom, and one of the protective spells from those texts – known as PT 1375 – reads, 'My mother is Isis, my nurse is Nephthys ... Neith is behind me, and Serket is before me.' These four goddesses would later be represented famously in Tutankhamun's tomb on the canopic chest and as gold statues protecting the gilded shrine (*The Complete Gods and Goddesses of Ancient Egypt*).

There is no evidence of temples to Serket in any region of Egypt, suggesting to some scholars that she either never had any or, more likely, that she was absorbed into the figures of other deities such as Hathor or Neith, who are equally ancient. Neith was the patron goddess of the Delta city of Zau (later known as Sais). Like Hathor, Neith was originally a fierce goddess associated with destruction who later came to be related to weaving and then to wisdom (just as Hathor was originally a blood-thirsty destroyer who became a benevolent protectress). It is possible that Serket followed this same pattern, first arising as a mother goddess with a slightly swollen womb and then coming to be associated with scorpions and venom because scorpion bites were so often fatal to Egyptian children. Scholar Geraldine Pinch writes:

> Scorpion stings were a common hazard in Ancient Egypt. The female scorpion is larger than the male and has a greater supply of poison. Representations of Selket always show the tail raised in the stinging position. Scorpion stings cause a burning pain and shortness of breath and can be fatal to young children and the elderly.
>
> *(Egyptian Mythology: A Guide to the Gods and Goddesses of Ancient Egypt)*

Transformation of Serket

In the same way that the Osiris myth changed the god Set from a protector hero-god into a villain, it also altered Serket's role. Although she continued to be seen as a protectress, her earlier attributes as mother goddess were assumed by Isis while Serket became associated with death and the afterlife. In the story of the seven scorpions, Serket is often omitted entirely, and the focus of the story is on the forgiveness of Isis and the proper way people should treat each other. After the Osiris myth had taken precedence in Egypt, Serket's role was marginalised on the earthly plane but amplified in the afterlife.

She became known as one of the guardian gods who stand watch over souls in the afterlife. Specifically, as Geraldine Pinch notes, she 'is one of the deities who guards a bend in the river on the watery route to paradise'. She was invoked at funerals for her magical abilities as it was thought she could help the dead to breathe again as they were reborn from their bodies in the afterlife.

Similarly, those on earth who preyed on the innocent or engaged in wickedness might be visited by Serket and her scorpions, who might only scare them with a mild bite, bringing shortness of breath and pain, or a stronger dose of venom leading to death. In her role as a goddess of death and the afterlife, she was also responsible for guarding the internal organs of the dead king as it was thought he would need them again once he was reborn after death. She was the protector goddess of one of the Four Sons of Horus, Qebhesenuef, who guarded the intestines in the canopic jar. Serket was the goddess of poisons and the Egyptians associated the intestines with poison, thus she was given charge over the safety and well-being of Qebhesenuef.

The most significant way in which the Osiris myth transformed Serket was to attribute her earlier manifestations of power to Isis. She remained a very popular goddess, however, and should not be considered a 'lesser goddess' as so many writers on Egyptian mythology refer to her. Although she did not have official temples in her honour, her priests and priestesses were highly sought after and valued greatly for one simple reason: they were doctors.

The clergy of the Cult of Serket were all physicians known as 'Followers of Serket'. Men and women could practise medicine and perform the Rites of Serket. According to historian Margaret Bunson, the practice of medicine was 'the science' conducted by the priests of the Per-Ankh, the House of Life, which the Egyptians termed the 'necessary art'. The House of Life wasn't necessarily a physical location, but was a concept of healing. The priests and priestesses of Serket carried the House of Life within them in their knowledge of how to heal. Bunson writes:

> Diagnostic procedures for injuries and diseases were common and extensive in Egyptian medical practice. The physicians consulted texts and made their own observations. Each physician listed the symptoms evident in a patient and then decided whether he had the skill to treat the condition. If a priest determined that a cure was possible, he reconsidered the remedies or therapeutic regimens available and proceeded accordingly. This required, naturally, a remarkable awareness of the functions of the human body. The physicians understood that the pulse was the 'speaker of the heart' and they interpreted the condition now known as angina. They were also aware of the relationship between the nervous system and voluntary movements.
> (*The Encyclopedia of Ancient Egypt*)

Not every physician in Egypt was a 'Follower of Serket' but a good many were. Serket, as goddess of healing and protector against poison and venomous stings, was naturally the patron of doctors, even those who were not directly involved in her cult. Spells invoking Serket for healing were widely used throughout Egypt. The scholar John F. Nunn notes this, writing:

> The recto of the *Chester Beatty Papyrus VII*, written in the reign of Ramesses II, contains a number of magical spells for protection

against scorpions. Most invoke various wives of Horus whom Gardiner [the Egyptologist, in 1935] suggested might be merely appellations of Serqet who is actually named in the eighth spell.

In this spell, the physician would recite the lines as though the patient were having a dialogue with the goddess or goddesses. Although she is not mentioned by name in every papyrus or inscription, her powers of healing would have been invoked no matter which aspect she was named as or what other goddesses were called upon. In her role as patron of physicians and healing goddess, she helped the people of Egypt from their birth, through their lives, and even into the afterlife.

(Ancient Egyptian Medicine)

Chapter Sixteen

Gods of War

From the primordial conflict of Horus and Set, to the well-documented battles of the New Kingdom at Megiddo and Qadesh, warfare was a recurring element in Egyptian mythology and history. Although the Egyptians may be regarded as a comparatively peaceful nation, there was a large military and bureaucratic infrastructure devoted to the expansion and maintenance of their imperial ambitions in Nubia and their near-eastern neighbours, according to the *British Museum Dictionary of Ancient Egypt*:

> The range of sources for the study of Egyptian warfare is far from complete and certain historical periods are poorly known. Overall, however, the atmosphere of army life has been well-preserved in the surviving art and texts; the very fact that the Egyptians retained their national autonomy for almost three millennia is evidence enough of their military abilities. Any act of warfare perpetrated by Egypt – whether a punitive raid on a Nubia village or a major expedition into Syria-Palestine – was therefore considered to be a legitimate restoration of the natural order of things.

In the pantheon of ancient Egyptian gods and goddesses, however, Montu was a lesser-known deity who nonetheless played a pivotal role in the mythology of this complex civilisation. As the god of war, Montu was associated with themes of violence, destruction, and divine retribution. In her article 'The Wrath of Montu: the Mythology of the Egyptian War God' for *Anthropology Review*, Claudine Casser explores the mythology surrounding this enigmatic deity and delves into his wrathful aspect as a god of war who demanded respect and loyalty from those who worshipped him. By examining how he was depicted in art and literature, as well as the rituals used to honour him, we can gain a better understanding of his significance within ancient Egyptian society.

Montu's origins can be traced back to the ancient city of Hermonthis (modern-day Armant), located in Upper Egypt. Originally a local god worshipped by the Theban people, Montu gradually gained popularity and became a more prominent figure within Egyptian religion. His association with war and victory made him an appealing deity for those military leaders and pharaohs seeking divine protection on the battlefield.

Montu appears in the *Pyramid Texts* and archaeological contexts of the Old Kingdom but his importance only rose by the 11th Dynasty, although Bisson de la Roque states that by the late 5th Dynasty, Montu was mentioned in the *Pyramid Texts* of Kings Unas, Teti, Pepi I, Merenre, and finally Pepi II. Furthermore, the *Pyramid Texts* are of great significance in declaring Montu's name, but no references are found in the *Coffin Texts*; later, his name was also found twice in the *Book of the Dead* or the *Coming Forth by Day*.

In terms of iconography, Montu was often depicted as a falcon-headed or bull-headed figure, both of which were symbols of power and strength. As a solar deity, he was also associated with the sun disc, which represented his role as a bringer of light and life, and, in some depictions, he is shown wearing a double-plumed crown or carrying weapons like the bow and arrow or the spear. This falcon-headed god of war can easily be mistaken for Horus the Elder, since he is usually represented with a headdress consisting of a sun disc and two plumes. His two consorts were the goddesses Tjenenyet and Ra'ttawy, both also associated with the Theban district.

His cult is first attested at various sites in the Theban region, and major temples, dating from the Middle Kingdom to the Roman Period, were constructed at Armant, Karnak, Medamud, and Tod.

There was a Montu priesthood attested from the time of Pepi I, with the first preserved depiction being found in the funerary temple of Pepi II at Saqqara; he is mentioned on the south wall of the antechamber of Montu and on the northern wall of the causeway. There are references to a formula, as well as Montu represented in a complete human form along with other Upper Egyptian deities. The last presence of Montu during the Old Kingdom was found in the Tomb of 'one revered as Lord of Armantî', proving the existence of a cult for the god Montu even though there is no Old Kingdom monumental evidence dating back to this era at Armant.

> The First Intermediate Period and the Middle Kingdom saw the combination of assessing him as a local deity that supported the victory of Mentuhotep but who later unfortunately fell eventually from supremacy by the 12th Dynasty. The Theban control under the re-unification extended Montu to become the official god that was similar to Re for the 5th dynasty kings and their solar temples construction. The Upper Egyptians were gratifying to Montu for the re-unification as discovered on the stela of Meru at Turin (no. 1447) mentioning Montu is giving the two lands to the sovereign, Nebhepetre, who lives forever. Also, the Metropolitan Museum of Arts has tablets 22.3187 and 128 mentioning beloved of Montu

and beloved of Montu-Re respectively. Thus, becoming the earliest suggestion mirroring Montu-Re's presence as an Upper Egyptian counterpart to the northern Re of Heliopolis. The typical form of Montu dates back to the 11th Dynasty; a falcon-headed man wearing a crown with the sun disc and two falcon feathers, as well as a double *uraei* on the forehead. The Middle Kingdom had the greatest enlargement of Montu's constructions.

(Wikipedia)

Over time, Montu's iconography evolved alongside changes in Egyptian religion and culture. For example, during the New Kingdom Period, he was sometimes depicted as part of a triad along with Amun and Mut at the Temple of Karnak in Thebes. Despite these changes, however, he remained an important symbol of power and protection throughout Egyptian history. As the god of war, Montu's identity was deeply intertwined with the concept of conflict and violence. He was often depicted as a fierce warrior, brandishing weapons like the bow and arrow, spear, and mace. In mythology, Montu was believed to lead armies into battle and grant victory to those who worshipped him.

Montu's association with specific weapons and military tactics further reinforced his role as a war deity. The bow and arrow, for example, were seen as symbols of precision and accuracy – traits that were highly valued on the battlefield. Similarly, the spear represented both offence and defence, making it an essential tool for Egyptian soldiers. In addition to his association with weaponry, Montu was also linked to military strategy and tactics. His ability to plan successful campaigns and outmanoeuvre enemies made him a valuable ally for pharaohs seeking divine guidance in times of war. Some rituals used to honour Montu involved mock battles or re-enactments of past military victories in order to appease the god and ensure future success on the battlefield.

Despite his fearsome reputation as a god of war, Montu was also associated with protection and justice. In some myths, he is depicted as a defender of Ma'at (the principle of balance or cosmic order) who punishes those who disrupt this delicate equilibrium. This duality – the ability to both wage war and maintain balance – underscores Montu's importance within the Egyptian religion as a complex deity capable of both destruction and creation. Later, during the Amarna Period, the reign of Akhenaten, Montu experienced the same fate as Amun, since both their names were chiselled out at Medamoud and other sites. Nevertheless, Tutankhamun re-opened the Montu temples at Armant, Karnak, Medamoud, and Tod. He allowed the images of Montu to be restored and presented offerings in his honour. In KV62 of Tutankhamun, a few artefacts were inscribed with the name of Montu, as a martial god. An example was the game board reading 'brave like Montu'.

Montu was not only known as a god of warfare but also for his wrathful and vengeful nature. He was often depicted as an angry deity who would punish anyone who threatened Egypt's safety or dared to cross him. One example of Montu's wrath can be found in the mythological story of his battle with the god Horus. In this tale, Horus had insulted Montu by mocking his prowess as a warrior. Enraged, Montu challenged Horus to a battle and ultimately emerged victorious, demonstrating his ferocity and power.

Montu's wrath was also directed towards enemies of Egypt. In one story, he helped defend the country against an invasion by the Nubians. According to legend, Montu appeared in the form of a giant bull and charged into battle, trampling the enemy forces underfoot. In yet another legend, Montu punished a group of rebels who had attempted to overthrow the pharaoh. Using his powers as the Egyptian god of war and destruction, he unleashed a devastating storm that destroyed their army and left their leaders begging for mercy. Montu was revered by many Egyptians as a powerful protector. His ability to channel his rage into productive action made him an important symbol of strength and resilience in times of crisis.

Devotees of Montu would often perform rituals and make offerings in order to gain his favour or appease his wrathful nature. These rituals could take many forms, from simple prayers and offerings of food to more elaborate ceremonies involving music, dance, and dramatic re-enactments of battles. One common offering made to Montu was incense, which was believed to purify the air and create a pleasing aroma that would attract the god's attention. Other offerings included flowers, fruits, and vegetables – all symbols of fertility and abundance that were believed to please the deity. In addition to these physical offerings, devotees would also perform acts of service or devotion in honour of Montu. This might involve cleaning his temple or performing tasks that were traditionally associated with warfare, such as practising archery or sword fighting.

Many temples were dedicated to Montu throughout ancient Egypt, but perhaps the most famous was the Temple at Karnak. This enormous complex featured multiple sanctuaries dedicated to different gods, including one specifically for Montu. The temple was decorated with elaborate carvings and inscriptions depicting scenes from mythological stories involving Montu and other deities. Montu is sometimes accompanied by one of his consorts in ancient scenes. Three are known, consisting of Tjenenet, Iunyt, and Rettawy. Rettawy is the female counterpart of Re, and is depicted like Hathor as a cow with a sun disc surmounting her head. Through Rettawy, Montu is connected with Horus and thus the king, for their son was Harpocrates (Horus the child). Montu's worship survived for many years, and he was eventually considered by the Greeks to be a form of their war god, Ares.

A very ancient god, Montu was originally a manifestation of the scorching effect of Re, the sun – and as such often appeared under the epithet Montu-Re. The destructiveness of this characteristic led to him gaining characteristics of a warrior, and eventually becoming a widely revered war god. The Egyptians thought that he would attack the enemies of *Ma'at* (that is, of the truth, of the cosmic order) while inspiring, at the same time, glorious warlike exploits. It is possible that Montu-Re and Amun-Re symbolised the two kingships, respectively, of Upper and Lower Egypt. When linked with Horus, Montu's epithet was 'Horus of the Strong Arm'.

Because of the association of raging bulls with strength and war, the Egyptians also believed that Montu manifested himself as a white, black-snouted bull named Buchis (hellenisation of the original Bakha: a living bull revered in Armant) – to the point that, in the Late Period, he was depicted with a bull's head too. This special sacred bull had dozens of servants and wore precious crowns and bibs. In Egyptian art, Montu was depicted as a falcon-headed or bull-headed man, with his head surmounted by the solar disc (because of his conceptual link with Re) and two feathers.

The falcon was a symbol of the sky and the bull was a symbol of strength and war. He could also wield various weapons, such as a curved sword, a spear, bow and arrow, or knives: such military iconography was widespread in the New Kingdom. He was also revered as one of the patrons of the city of Thebes and its fortresses. The sovereigns of the 11th Dynasty chose Montu as a protective and dynastic deity, inserting references to him in their own names. For example, four pharaohs of the 11th Dynasty were called *Mentuhotep*, which means 'Montu [Mentu] is satisfied'.

The cult of this military god enjoyed great prestige under the pharaohs of the 11th Dynasty, whose expansionism and military successes led to the reunification of Egypt; the end of a period of chaos known today as the First Intermediate Period, and a new era of greatness for the country. This part of Egyptian history, known as the Middle Kingdom, was a period in which Montu assumed the role of supreme god – before then having been gradually surpassed by the other Theban god Amun, destined to become the most important deity of the Egyptian pantheon. From the 11th Dynasty onward, however, Montu was considered the symbol of the pharaohs as rulers, conquerors, and winners, as well as their inspirer on the battlefield. The Egyptian armies were surmounted by the insignia of the 'four Montu' (Montu of Thebes, of Armant, of Medamud, and of El-Tod: the main cult centres of the god), all represented while trampling and piercing enemies with a spear in a classic pugnacious pose. A ceremonial battle axe, belonging to the funeral kit of Queen Ahhotep II, Great Royal Wife of the warlike pharaoh Kamose, who lived between the 17th and 18th Dynasties represents Montu as a proud winged griffin: an iconography clearly influenced by the same Syriac origin which inspired Minoan art.

Understanding the Egyptian Gods and Goddesses

Egypt's greatest general-kings called themselves 'Mighty Bull', 'Son of Montu', 'Montu is With His Strong/Right Arm' (*Montuherkhepeshef*: which was also the given name of a son of Ramesses II, one of Ramesses III, and one of Ramesses IX). Thutmose III, 'the Napoleon of Egypt', was described in ancient times as a 'Valiant Montu on the Battlefield'. An inscription from his son Amenhotep II recalls that the 18-year-old pharaoh was able to shoot arrows through copper targets while driving a war chariot, commenting that he had the skill and strength of Montu.

The latter's grandson, Amenhotep III the Magnificent, called himself 'Montu of the Rulers' in spite of his own peaceful reign. In the narrative of the Battle of Kadesh, Ramesses II the Great – who proudly called himself 'Montu of the Two Lands' – was said to have seen the enemy and 'raged at them like Montu, Lord of Thebes':

> his majesty passed the *fortress of Tjaru*, like Montu when he goes forth. Every country trembled before him, fear was in their hearts ... The goodly watch in *life, prosperity and health*, in the tent of his majesty, was on the highland south of Kadesh. When his majesty appeared like the rising of Re, he assumed the adornments of his father, Montu.
>
> (Wikipedia)

Throughout its long history of warfare, several other deities were assigned the role of 'war god' in the mythology, including:

- Anhur, god of war, not a native god
- Anuke, a goddess of war and consort of Anhur
- Apedemak, the lion god of war, sometimes shown with three heads
- Bast, cat-headed goddess associated with war, protection of Lower Egypt and the pharaoh, the sun, perfumes, ointments, and embalming
- Horus, god of the king, the sky, war, and protection
- Maahes, lion-headed god of war
- Menhit, goddess of war, 'she who massacres'
- Neith, goddess of war, hunting, and wisdom
- Pakhet, goddess of war
- Satis, deification of the floods of the Nile River and an early war, hunting, and fertility goddess
- Sekhmet, goddess of warfare, pestilence, and the desert
- Set, god of the desert and storms, associated with war
- Sobek, god of the Nile, the army, military, fertility, and crocodiles
- Sopdu, god of the scorching heat of the summer sun, associated with war
- Wepwawet, wolf god of war and death who later became associated with Anubis and the afterlife

Egyptian Military Standards

The custom of carrying military insignia is almost as old as the art of war itself. When warfare emerged from the indiscriminate tribal scrimmage into the status of an organized pursuit, and armies became large enough to be subdivided into regiments, it became customary for each component body of the host to have its own standard or ensign, raised high on a pole so that it could readily be seen in the confusion of battle. These standards, borne at the head of the regiments, served two purposes. They enabled the commander-in-chief, even in the thickest of the fight, to see at a glance where his regiments stood and how they fared, and, what was perhaps even more important, they served as a focus for the esprit de corps of the unit itself. To lose your standard, be it the eagle of a Roman legion or the colours of an English regiment, was dire disgrace, and many a commander has owed his victory to a desperate struggle to save a standard from capture at a crucial moment of the battle. Only within the last hundred years, when the increasing range and accuracy of modern weapons have rendered imperative the concealment and disguise of combatants, have military standards disappeared from the field of battle and become relegated to ceremonial parades, though even to-day the regimental colours of an army are the objects of strong sentimental attachment as the embodiments of tradition and the memorials of valorous deeds in past wars. We find this custom of bearing standards or ensigns into battle already in force in Ancient Egypt as early as the Wars of Unification in the proto-dynastic period. On votive palettes of slate deposited in the national fane at Hierakonpolis we see the ensigns of the levies composing the army of the South symbolically breaching the walls of the Northern fortresses – themselves enclosing the ensigns of their garrisons – or grasping a rope to which are bound prisoners taken in battle. On another palette depicting a lion-hunt – to a weakly armed people no sport, but a dangerous necessity akin to warfare – we actually see standards being borne by participants in the attack. Thereafter, however, the use of the standard seems to have lapsed for many centuries. Neither in the rare battle scenes of the Old Kingdom nor in those of the Middle Kingdoms are military standards depicted, while the well-known models of marching infantry from Asyiit have no ensigns at the head of their columns.

(R. O. Faulkner, *The Journal of Egyptian Archaeology*, 1 December 1941)

Chapter Seventeen

Offerings and Festivals

> Every day in every temple, specially designated persons performed a ritual focused on making offerings of food, drink, clothing and ointment, to a divine being (deity, king or blessed dead), made accessible in the form of images. Through this ritual, the Egyptians sought to maintain the fabric and process of the universe. According to their own writings, they did not worship idols – they did not consider the images themselves to be divine forces; rather, the image provided a visible and tangible form in which the offerings and service of human beings could be channelled to the divine forces.
>
> (University College London)

Communal gatherings for worship took place during festivals, and as the Egyptians set a premium on enjoying life, there were many of them throughout the year (see Chapter Eighteen). These festivals (known as heb) allowed people to experience the god intimately, give thanks for gifts that were given, and make requests for divine favours. Egyptologist Margaret Bunson writes:

> The purpose of most of the festivals was to allow the people to behold the gods with their own eyes. Particular images of the gods, sometimes carried in portable shrines, were taken out of the temple sanctuaries and carried through the streets or sailed on the Nile. Stations of the Gods were erected throughout the various cities in order to provide stages for the processions. Oracles were conducted on these festivals as the images of the deities moved in certain directions to indicate negative or positive responses to the questions posed by the faithful. These public gatherings also helped to maintain the belief structure of the culture in that everyone who attended was encouraged in the traditional understanding of how the world operated: through the will of the gods as interpreted by the priests and implemented by the king.

> There were no religious services in Egypt corresponding to worship services in the present day. The priests served the gods, not the people, and their job was to administer to the gods' daily needs, recite hymns and prayers for the souls of the dead, and engage in rituals which ensured the continued goodwill of the gods to the people. Although people would come to the temple complexes to offer sacrifices, offerings, receive various forms of aid, and make requests, they did not enter the temple to worship. Common people were allowed in the courtyard of the temple complex but not in the interiors and certainly not in the god's presence. As noted, people performed their own private rituals in communion with the gods, but collectively, their only opportunity for worship was at a festival.
>
> (*Encyclopedia of Ancient Egypt*)

Daily offering ceremonies in temples were one of the most commonly practised rituals in Egypt. The giving of food, clothing, carvings, weapons and tools was a way of honouring and caring for the gods who had created them. These daily rituals were supervised by temple priests and the offerings/oblations were brought to the temple by the local people, the most important part being the offering of 'nourishment' as a means of 'returning energy' to the god of the temple. It was later looked upon as an exchange for that which was being requested from the god in the form of dried fruits and seeds including grapes, nuts, melon seeds, dried raisins with bread, meat, and poultry, which formed part of their staple diet. Dates, beans, lentils, lettuce, onions, leeks, melons, and other gourds (e.g. figs and pomegranates) were widely used, although olives were not successfully grown until the Ptolemaic Period.

The first altars were simple cane mats or woven rushes, on which an offering of bread could be placed, giving the name *shtp* to the important rites of pacification of a god, intended to placate anger, or anxiety by making an offering. Similarly, the tall and elegant vase (*hes*), well known from scenes of cleansing and libation, could contain purifying water or water/wine to pour in libations. Fresh water was likened to the primordial waters and possessed all its regenerative and life-giving powers. The gesture of pouring water on the offering table, or on an altar, integrated the whole of the offering service, guaranteeing the same benefits.

One of the most important elements of the private tomb throughout the Pharaonic and Greco-Roman Periods was the stone offering table. This was usually placed in an accessible location such as the chapel, so that offerings could actually be brought to it by the funerary priests or relatives of the deceased. The hieroglyph representing the ancient word *hetep* (the most literal meaning of which is 'offering') consists of a depiction of that early woven mat surmounted by a loaf of bread, doubtless reflecting the most basic method of presenting an offering, according to the *British Museum Dictionary of Ancient Egypt*.

This simple visual image not only served as a metaphor for the act of offering itself but also came to be the characteristic shape of the physical surface on which offerings were placed. The upper surface of the offering table was often carved with the loaves, trussed ducks, and vessels required by the cult, so that the stone-carved images could serve as magical substitutes for the real food offerings, usually with the additional back-up of the hieroglyphic offering formula and lists of produce. Cups, grooves, or channels were also cut into the surface so that such liquids as water, beer, or wine could be poured onto the table.

Even grander were the lists of offerings on the temple walls – which were entirely separate from the menus of funeral offerings in the tombs. These reliefs reflect the basic attitudes of the ancient Egyptians to life and to the worship of their gods, which was a basic foundation of their lives. The temple was the god's home on earth: the basic food offerings presented to him or her thrice daily were equivalent in their way to the regular meals eaten by the people in daily life. From the natural phenomena of Egypt – annual Nile-flood, harvest, etc. – and the mythology of the gods, there arose occasions for special observances, special offerings to the gods, and feasting among the worshippers.

> From an early date, fixed customs must have arisen as to what constituted the appropriate regular, daily and monthly offerings to be presented to each deity, and in each temple in accord with the deity's importance and the temple's wealth ... For special festivals, depending (again) on the wealth of the temple, and on the relative importance of the feast concerned, special additional food and drink, flowers, etc., were laid on, to be offered to the gods, then enjoyed by their worshippers (in practice, principally the temple staff in each case) ... The quantities of bread, cakes, beer, wine and other relished products show how richly the Egyptians and their gods enjoyed themselves during the major festivities.
>
> (*Temple Festival Calendar of Ancient Egypt*)

The *Papyrus of Ramesses III* records that the offerings to the temple of Amun-Re for one year during this pharaoh's reign included 34 jars of incense, honey and oil; 819 jars of wine; 10,000 measures of grain; 795 bundles of vegetables; 2,064 bales of flax; 9,340 waterfowl; 28 cattle and 24 geese. Despite the mounds of food depicted in the temple reliefs, the gods themselves avoided excess – bread and water being their usual fare. The sumptuous offerings were consumed by the priests. In terms of libation, beer (*henket*) made from barley-bread and flavoured with dates, honey, and spices was the chief drink of the Egyptians, while both red and white wine (*irep*) was produced from grapes and dates, grape wine being more highly regarded in antiquity. Milk is also recorded as being a suitable offering.

> Meat was kept for special occasions and temple offerings, although cattle, sheep and goats were probably more useful for their milk than their flesh; pork was never used in temple offerings but it is believed to have formed an important part of the diet of some classes of society. Egyptian temples provided no facilities for slaughtering animals and the meat offered was already carefully butchered, the most common being that of geese and ducks. The mummified remains of different types of animals and birds have been discovered in tombs and underground chambers of temples, and this kind of mass-produced funerary relic must surely be classed as a form of animal sacrifice.
>
> (*Sacrifice to the Gods*)

There is some evidence suggesting that human sacrifice was practised during the Predynastic Period and at the beginning of the 1st Dynasty, which included retainer sacrifice, or the killing of domestic servants to bury along with their master. This practice appears to have been abandoned at the beginning of the 2nd Dynasty, the practice having survived in a more symbolic way, with statues representing servants being placed in tombs. However, the legendary custom of offering a virgin as a sacrifice to the River Nile every year to instigate a flood is 'a major historical error', according to researcher Bassam El Shamman, resulting from a mistranslation of Coptic writings.

The *hetep-di-nesw* 'a gift which the king gives' or 'offering formula' was a prayer asking for offerings to be brought to the deceased. It first appears as the principal inscription of the false door stelae in the Early Dynastic Period, which formed the focus of food offerings in early private tombs, but it continued to be used in funerary stelae throughout the Pharaonic and Graeco-Roman periods. On these stelae, the formula is often accompanied by a depiction of the deceased sitting or kneeling in front of an offering table heaped with food.

> Typically the first line of the offering formula asks for the king to make gifts to the gods Osiris or Anubis; the rest of the inscription then consists of a list of the various quantities of items of food and drink that the *ka* of the deceased requires. The inscription sometimes asks visitors to the tomb or funerary temple to recite the formula so that the necessary offerings would appear. It is

> clear from the nature of the formula that the sustenance of the *ka* of the deceased was not simply the responsibility of the surviving relatives – it was necessary for the king to intercede with the gods on his or her behalf. This illustrates the essential role played by the king as divine intermediary at the heart of each individual's funerary cult, establishing the crucial link between the fate of the individual and the festivals of Osiris. It also reflects the common practice of dividing up temple offerings and redistributing them among the funerary cults of individuals.
>
> (*British Museum Dictionary of Ancient Egypt*)

We can see from the extensive listings on temple walls that all manner of food and drink were acceptable as offerings, although many of the foods familiar to us today were unknown in ancient Egypt. Excessive consumption of alcohol was disapproved of, although both Hathor and Set were well disposed towards wine; Horus preferred a drink of grape juice and water; while Sekhmet gets roaring drunk on beer and becomes dangerous.

Some deities, however, were repulsed by certain foods and what was highly palatable to 'living' gods would be disagreeable to Otherworld deities. For example, fish was abhorrent to the gods and so the pharaoh, the priests, and the 'blessed dead' were forbidden to eat it. It did, however, form part of the diet for the common people and lesser officials. Honey was much prized as a sweetening agent but to the denizens beyond the tomb, it was bitter. The gods of the Otherworld also had a marked aversion to onions and an unidentified plant referred to as *djais*.

> The great national religious festivals, celebrated in pomp by the Pharaoh himself, were occasions of the greatest magnificence – such as the great Opet festival at Thebes, when Amon's golden image sailed in his huge gilded barque from Karnak temple to Luxor temple for ritual celebrations there, and back again. The quantities of bread, cakes, beer, wine and other relished produce show just how richly the Egyptians and their gods enjoyed themselves during the major festivals.
>
> (*Temple Festival Calendars of Ancient Egypt*)

The standard and major feasts of Osiris (and his Ennead) called for white bread, white fruit bread, biscuits, beer, wine, ordinary fowl (ducks), flowers, vegetables, fruit and milk. Since his Ennead (family) consisted of the nine gods of the Great Ennead of Heliopolis, i.e. Atum and three generations of his progeny: his children Shu and Tefnut, his grandchildren Geb and Nut, and his four great-grandchildren Osisris, Isis, Set, and Nephthys, it is safe to assume that they would partake in the offerings of the temple.

Offerings and Festivals

Daily offerings at Karnak to Amon-Re consisted of bread, beer, biscuits, and vegetable bundles; while at Elephantine, the offerings to Amon, Satis, and Anukis were supplemented with joints of roast beef. Wadjet and Nekhbet – the 'Two Ladies' worshipped by all after the Unification of Lower Egypt and Upper Egypt – and Horus were made offerings at the Amon-temple including bread, biscuits, and date-cakes, beer, geese and fowl, wine, fruit, incense, honey, vegetables, and 'all fresh herbs at his wish'.

At Abydos, at the special temple of Ramesses II, Thoth and his consort Seshat presided over the offerings of geese and ordinary fowl (ducks) to complement the bread, cake, beer, wine, milk, fruit, and vegetables. While during the Festival of Thoth, the usual offerings were supplemented by the sacrifice of a bull.

At Medinet Habu, the temple reliefs represent Amon, Mut, Khons, and *Ma'at* receiving daily offerings of 'bread, beer, bulls and desert game, wine, fruit and pure incense' with the additions of sweet white bread, beer, date-cakes, wine, geese, waterfowl, and milk. On the day of the procession of Min at the same venue, the offerings were bread and beer supplemented by geese, ordinary fowl, fruit, and vegetables. On the day of every new moon, the offerings for Amon-Re were a wide assortment of breads, cake, biscuits, beer, long-horned ox, geese, pigeons, ordinary fowl, fruit, vegetables, grapes, figs, honey, milk, flowers, and incense.

At the Festival of Hathor, the offerings included bread, white fruit bread, biscuits, beer, a bull, ordinary fowl, fruit, wine, and fresh flowers; while for the Festival of Ptah-Sokar the offerings were supplemented with gazelles, geese, goats and (rarely) pigs. At the Festival of Renenutet, the harvest goddess, there were offerings of bread and beer and also included were white fruit bread, biscuits, wine, fruit, beef, geese and ordinary fowl; and not forgetting the 'Feast of Chewing Onions' for Bastet!

Kom Ombo temple received offerings on behalf of Horus (the Greater) and Hathor, including 'bread, beer, oxen, fowl and every good thing before him'. These lists of offerings have been taken from the *Temple Festival Calendars of Ancient Egypt* and therefore give authentic details of the foods suitable for offering to the gods. The text also points out that the later Graeco-Roman calendars do not follow the Pharaonic format and, instead of the lists of supplies, they give summaries of the rituals. Presumably, the lists of supplies were kept in papyrus registers in the temple archives.

In *Temple Festival Calendars*, it is also possible to get a glimpse of the scale of the offerings being made to the gods on a daily basis as well as on the occasion of the grand festivals. The work presents Sherif el-Sabban's study for all the known available temple calendars from ancient Egypt. It starts from possible origins in the Archaic Period, and goes all the way through to the Graeco-Roman Period, covering the three greatest eras of the history of Egypt:

the Old Kingdom, the Middle Kingdom, and the New Kingdom, including a mention of the Late Period, and a summary of the Ptolemaic temple calendars.

As for these calendars being inscribed on the temple walls on a grand scale, they are, in fact, not the actual records used from day to day by the priests; they would use the current up-to-date copies on papyrus in the temple archive. What is to be found on the walls – like all other temple reliefs – is a monumental version, to be displayed before gods and men permanently. As Sherif el-Sabban explains:

> These calendars reflect the basic attitudes of the ancient Egyptians to life and to the worship of their gods as a basic foundation of their lives. The Egyptian temple was the god's home on earth; the basic food-offerings presented to him or her thrice a day were equivalent in their way to the regular meals eaten by the deity's worshippers in daily life. From the natural phenomena of Egypt – annual Nile floods, harvest, etc. – and the mythology of the gods there arose occasions for special observances, special offerings to the gods, and hence for feasting amongst their worshippers. In the cheerful nature of the ancients, major holy days took on also the character of holidays.
> (*Temple Festival Calendars of Ancient Egypt*)

From an early date, these fixed customs probably arose concerning what constituted the appropriate regular, daily and monthly offerings to be presented to each deity, and in each temple in accordance with the deity's importance and a temple's wealth. For special festivals, again depending on the wealth and importance of the feast concerned, additional provisions and flowers were offered to the gods, then enjoyed by their worshippers and the vast temple staff.

> **Opet Festival**, for example, took place in Akhet during the second month; it is the most important festival in Egyptian history and the longest celebration in the Theban festival calendar as it stretched across eleven to fifteen (or even twenty days). New Kingdom society depended on the generosity of the gods to ensure it received what it wanted or needed. Because they lacked the scientific understanding to explain specific events, the Egyptians looked upon each natural event as a sign or intervention from specific gods, willing them to maintain the natural order of the universe, or *ma'at*. In order to appease the gods, Egyptians routinely made offerings to them: through sacrifice, prayer, and festivals.
>
> Through this perceived symbiotic relationship, these celebrations of the divinity of the gods provided assurance to a historically suspicious society, allowing them to live their

> lives without fear of divine intervention. The Opet Festival re-established essential communication between the gods and ancient Egyptian society through the rebirth ceremony in the Temple of Luxor's birth-room, which initiated the Pharaoh as an intermediary for the gods by being reborn as the son of Amun-Re, 'the rebirth of the sun-god.' This rebirth promoted the fertility of the pharaoh, ensuring their right to rule was divine and consolidating their lineage.
>
> (Wikipedia)

The Opet Festival also reinforced the fertility of the harvest, which fluctuated depending on the inundation of the Nile, and was therefore celebrated in the second month of the Akhet season. It was not just the pharaoh who was active during the festival; sailors and soldiers were the most prominent non-religious groups in the event. They have been observed in the colonnade hall relief-scenes, which demonstrated that a large number of civil and military officials partook in the preparations and running of the festival. Flamboyant Egyptologist John Coleman Darnell emphasised the importance of the general population in executing the festival: 'Ramesses II listed amongst those responsible for arranging the festival: members of the civil administration, provincial governors, border-officials, heads of internal economic departments, officers of the commissariat, city-officials, and upper ranks of the priesthood.'

Those who were not actively involved in the running of the festival were 'able to observe from the riverbanks, and at least some may have had limited access to the forepart of the temple'. The festival also provided jobs for *wab* and *lector* priests, who were on three-month rotations. They recited spells and hymns among the general population on the riverbank to ensure that reverence was upheld (UCLA, *Encyclopedia of Egyptology*).

> On November 25th 2021, after a long renovation project, the Avenue of Sphinxes, which connects Karnak Temple with Luxor Temple was re-opened in a grand ceremony similar to the Opet Festival. And in the following December, the Ministry of Antiquities announced that the ceremony would be held annually. The avenue was opened to the public having concluded restoration works that took over seven decades to complete, with a march that included participants in pharaonic dress, a symphony orchestra, lighting effects, professional dancers, boats on the Nile and horse drawn carriages. Three golden pharaonic-style model boats dedicated to the ancient sun god Re, moon god Khonsu and mother goddess Mut were carried by men in sheer gold and black robes, replicas of what would have been worn for the same

festival in ancient times. The vision for this event was created by a team under the German University in Cairo, by which time the avenue was now lined with 1057 statues in total including 807 sphinx-shaped and 250 others with a ram-shaped head.

(NBC News)

Festival of Light: One of the most spectacular celebrations, during which the town or city would light oil lamps that would be left to burn throughout the night on or around the fifth day of the third month (Phamenoth) of Proyet-season. The historian Herodotus (fifth century BC) writes about such a festival at Sais, the city of Neith. He says:

> At the times when they gather together at the city of Sais for their sacrifices, on a certain night they all kindle lamps many in number in the open air round about the houses; now the lamps are saucers full of salt and oil mixed, and the wick floats by itself on the surface, and this burns during the whole night; and to the festival is given the name Lychnocaia ('Lamp-lighting'). Moreover those of the Egyptians who have not come to this solemn assembly observe the night of the festival and themselves also light lamps all of them, and this not in Sais alone are they lighted, but all over Egypt: and as to the reason why light and honour are allotted to this night, about this there is a sacred story.

(Herodotus, Histories, Book II, Chapter 62)

Wepet-Renpet Festival: 'The Opening of the Year' was the New Year's Day celebration; the festival being a kind of moveable feast as it depended on the inundation of the Nile. It celebrated the death and rebirth of Osiris, and by extension, the rejuvenation and rebirth of the land and the people. It is firmly attested to as initiating in the latter part of the Old Kingdom of Egypt and is clear evidence of the popularity of the Osiris cult at that time. Feasting and drinking were a part of this festival with the call-and-response poem known as The *Lamentations of Isis and Nephthys* being recited at the beginning to call Osiris to his feast.

Wag Festival: Dedicated to the death of Osiris and honouring the souls of the deceased on their journey in the afterlife. This festival followed the Wepet-Renpet, but its date changed according to the lunar calendar. It is one of the oldest festivals celebrated by the Egyptians and, like Wepet-Renpet, first appears in the Old Kingdom. During this festival, people would make small boats out of paper and set them toward the west on graves to indicate Osiris's death, and people would float shrines of paper on the waters of the Nile for the same reason.

Wag and Thoth Festival: A combining of the Wag Festival with the birth of the god Thoth and centred on rejuvenation and rebirth. This festival was a set date on the eighteenth day of the first month of the year. Thoth was worshipped as the god of writing, wisdom, and knowledge – among other attributes – and associated with the judgement of the dead by Osiris, thus linking the two gods. Thoth's birth and Osiris's rebirth were joined in this festival from the latter part of the Old Kingdom onwards.

Tekh Festival: 'The Feast of Drunkenness' – During an annual celebration held at the beginning of the year, a Festival of Intoxication, the Egyptians danced and played music to soothe the wildness of the goddess and drank great quantities of wine ritually to imitate the extreme drunkenness that stopped the wrath of the goddess when she almost destroyed humanity. This festival was dedicated to Hathor ('The Lady of Drunkenness') and commemorated the time when humanity was saved from destruction by beer. According to the story, Re had become weary of people's endless cruelty and nonsense and so sent Sekhmet to destroy them. She took to her task with enthusiasm, tearing people apart and drinking their blood. Re was satisfied with the destruction until the other gods pointed out to him that, if he wanted to teach people a lesson, he should stop the destruction before no one was left to learn from it. Re then ordered the goddess of beer, Tenenet, to dye a large quantity of the brew red and had it delivered to Dendera, right in Sekhmet's path of destruction. She found it and, thinking it was blood, drank it all, fell asleep, and woke up as the gentle and beneficent Hathor.

According to Egyptologist Carolyn Graves-Brown, the festival began in the Middle Kingdom, was most popular in the early New Kingdom, fell out of favour, and was then revived in Roman Egypt. She describes the central part of the festival as depicted on a 'Porch of Drunkenness' in the Temple of Mut at Karnak: 'It seems that in the Hall of Drunkenness, worshippers got drunk, slept, and then were woken by drummers to commune with the goddess Mut [who was closely linked with Hathor].' Participants would lessen their inhibitions and preconceptions through alcohol and experience the goddess intimately upon waking to the sacred drums.

In 2006, Betsy Bryan, an archaeologist with Johns Hopkins University excavating at the temple of Mut in Luxor (Thebes), presented her findings about the festival that included illustrations of the priestesses being served to excess and its adverse effects on them being ministered to by temple attendants. Participation in the festival was great, including by the priestesses and the population. Historical records exist of tens of thousands attending the festival. These findings were made in the temple of Mut because when Thebes rose to greater prominence, Mut absorbed some characteristics of Sekhmet. These temple excavations at Luxor discovered a 'porch of drunkenness' built onto the temple by the Pharaoh Hatshepsut during the height of her twenty-year reign.

Sed Festival: Usually given as the Heb-Sed Festival, this celebration honoured the king and revitalised him. It was one of the oldest feasts of ancient Egypt, celebrated by the king after thirty years of rule and repeated every three years in order to ensure he was still in harmony with the will of the gods and physically fit to rule. The festival began with a grand procession held in front of priests, nobles, and the public. The king would need to run around an enclosed space (such as the temple complex at Saqqara) in order to prove he was fit and, in later eras, would fire arrows toward the four cardinal directions as a symbol of his power over the land and his ability to bring other nations under Egypt's influence (*Britannica*).

The festival probably dates from the Predynastic Period in some form but is certainly attested to from the reign of King Den of the 1st Dynasty. The name comes from the deity Sed, an early wolf god (sometimes depicted as more of a jackal), who was originally among the most important gods, associated with the strength of the king, justice, and balance (and so linked with the goddess and concept of *Ma'at*). Sed was eventually absorbed by Wepwawet and Anubis and superseded by Osiris who, by the New Kingdom, had taken Sed's place in the festival. As with all the great festivals, the state provided the people with food and beer for the duration.

Although only supposed to be celebrated after the first thirty years of the king's reign (and every three years afterwards), the Heb-Sed was sometimes observed earlier and is often referred to as the king's jubilee. The length of a king's reign was once dated, in part, according to the observance of the Heb-Sed until it came to be understood that some kings initiated the festival earlier than the thirty-year mark if they were in poor health (and needed the gods' rejuvenation) or for other reasons.

Beer, called *hqt* by the Egyptians and *zythus* by the Greeks, was a very important Egyptian drink: it was a drink for adults and children alike. It was the staple drink of the poor (wages were sometimes paid in beer), it was a drink of the rich and wealthy, and a drink offered to the gods and placed in the tombs of the dead. Most likely, the beer was not very intoxicating – nutritious, sweet, without bubbles, and thick (the beer had to be strained with wooden syphons, used as a straw, because it was filled with impurities). Though later Greek accounts suggest that the beer was as intoxicating as the strongest wine, and it is clear that the worshippers of Bast, Sekhmet, and Hathor got drunk on beer as part of their celebrations, because of their aspects as the Eye of Re. Tenenit was another ancient goddess of beer.

Workmen at the pyramids of the Giza Plateau were given beer, thrice daily – five kinds of beer and four kinds of wine were found by archaeologists 'poking through dumps, examining skeletons, probing texts and studying remains of beer jars, and wine vats' at Giza. While in 1990, the Egyptian Exploration Society approached Scottish and Newcastle Breweries for help. This was the beginning of a partnership which, over the past five years, has considerably increased the understanding of the brewing process as it was at the time of Tutankhamun.

There is, of course, a lot of information missing, but an important question is what did the beer actually taste like? Thanks to the work done by the Egyptian Exploration Society and the Scottish and Newcastle Breweries, the ancient beer was probably 'strongly influenced by the addition of fruit or spices as flavouring'. The word *bn'* causes some problems – it is usually translated as 'date', but it may have referred to a different (or to any other) sweet-tasting additive the Egyptians used in their beer. Although the dregs from ancient beer jars do show what ingredients were used, further work is needed before the exact flavour of the different beers can be established.

In hieroglyphs, the image of the beer jug was used in words associated with beer and the importance of beer in ancient Egypt cannot be overlooked. In 1996, the *Herald-Sun* reported that Tutankhamon Ale would be based on sediment from jars found in a brewery housed in the Sun Temple of Nefertiti, and the team involved had gathered enough of the correct raw materials to produce 'just 1000 bottles of the ale'. The beer was reported to have an alcoholic content of between 5 and 6 per cent and was sold at Harrods for £50 per bottle, the proceeds going towards further research into Egyptian beer making.

From an early date, fixed customs must have arisen as to what constituted the appropriate regular daily and monthly offerings to be presented to each deity, and in each temple in accord with the deity's importance and the temple's wealth. Thus the custom arose of compiling specific documents, calendars of offerings for the gods: documents that listed the amount and variety of the regular daily and monthly offerings, and then the dates and names of the year's festivals, with lists of what extra was to be offered (and enjoyed) on those occasions (*Temple Festival Calendars of Ancient Egypt*).

Communal gatherings for worship took place during festivals, and as the Egyptians set a premium on enjoying life, there were many of them throughout the year. These festivals (known as heb) allowed people to experience the god intimately, give thanks for gifts that were given, and make requests for divine favours. In addition to these, there were many more festivals celebrated throughout the year, which were considered just as important by the ancient Egyptians. The festivals brought the past into the present, elevated the people toward the divine, and, on the simplest level, were times when the people could relax and enjoy themselves. The great number of such festivals in the Egyptian calendar is the clearest evidence of the value the culture placed on joy in life and the most common form of its collective expression (*World History Encyclopedia*).

Chapter Eighteen

Major Celebrations

The *Calendar of Ancient Egypt* was compiled from the Greek and Demotic *Magical Papyri* lodged in the British Museum; the Bibliothéque Nationale in Paris; the Staatliche Museum in Berlin; the Rijksmuseum in Leiden; and the *Sallier Papyrus IV* (no. 10184) and the *Cairo Calendar* (No. 86637) currently lodged in the British and Cairo Museums. Additional material was taken from the *Temple Festival Calendars of Ancient Egypt* by Sherif el-Sabban, while supplementary text entries for the individual gods can also be found at https://henadology.wordpress.com.

AKET-season (Inundation)

First Month: Dhwty

Day 1 (19 July): The Opening of the Year and the Feast of every god. The birth and feast of Re-Harakhte; ablution (purification) throughout the entire land in the water of the beginning of the High Nile (Inundation) which comes forth as fresh as Nun (the Chaos of Creation, or beginning). And so, all gods and goddesses are in great festivity on this day and everybody likewise. Do not navigate ships or anything that goes on the water on this day. 'Opening of the year, causing the appearance of Horus, Lord of Ombos [from Kom Ombo temple calendar]; until the second day, eating in the broad hall of Horus and Thoth; offering all good things; offering Re in his presence; appearing and resting in his temple.' At the Temple of Esna it was the Festival of the Opening of the Year for a double benefit; the Festival of Nehebkau (originally the explanation of the cause of binding of ka and ba after death), and Khnum and his Ennead. Feast of Re at Edfu. From the lowliest peasant to the mightiest of gods, everyone played a part in this important festival of celebration and feasting. The warning not to venture out onto the river was pure common sense, since the turbulent waters would be extremely hazardous for shipping. The appearance of Min on every New Moon was celebrated at Edfu.

This was the national New Year celebration which coincided with the annual inundation of the Nile and, as the land either side of the river would eventually

Major Celebrations

be flooded to a depth of several feet with black, muddy water, there was little else to do but party. The floodwaters brought about the purification of the land prior to it emerging anew (fertile) as it did from the primordial waters of Nun on the Day of Creation. Prayer or divinatory time: dawn.

Lucky and unlucky days:

The calendars generally appear to be in agreement over which days are auspicious and which are inauspicious. In some instances, a 'lucky day' may not be considered suitable for prayer or divination. Translations from the original text and god names are given in italics.

Day 2 (20 July): The feast of Shu, son of Re. It is the feast which Re made for Shu when he seized for him the Eye of Horus. If you see anything it will be good on this day. Prayer or divinatory time: noon.

Day 3 (21 July): The feast of Sekhmet which Re made for her when he pacified her. Do not do anything on this day; do not go out on any journey on this day. Prayer or divinatory time: do not observe – not a suitable day.

Day 4 (22 July): The feast of Hathor, mistress of Byblos. Do not do anything on this day. Prayer or divinatory time: dawn.

Day 5 (23 July): Feasts of Horus the Elder and Hathor. Do not do any work on the land on this day. If you see anything, it will be good on this day. Prayer or divinatory time: dawn.

Day 6 (24 July): The Feast of Mnevis, the sacred bull of Heliopolis. Sun rises in Leo. Prayer or divinatory time: do not observe – not a suitable day.

Day 7 (25 July): The Feast of Sobek, the crocodile god. The Feast of Anubis. It is a day of welcoming the river (i.e. in its state of inundation) and offering to the gods. If you see anything it will be good on this day. Prayer or divinatory time: noon.

Day 8 (26 July): Feast of every god and goddess. Do not do any work in the entire land. A public holiday. Prayer or divinatory time: throughout the day.

Day 9 (27 July): The Feast of Khumn, the ram-headed god of creation, Re and Sobek. If you see anything it will be good on this day. Do not do anything on this day. Do not walk by darkness. Prayer or divinatory time: do not observe – not a suitable day.

Day 10 (28 July): The Feast of Tefnut. Do not eat honey or sugar cane on this day. As to anyone born on this day they will die as an honoured one in old age. Do not do anything on this day. Prayer or divinatory time: throughout the day.

Day 11 (29 July): Feast of Re and Sobek. It is the day of the going forth of the great flame. (Wedjet of Buto, the fire-spitting cobra goddess whose image was incorporated in the royal crown.) Prayer or divinatory time: in the afternoon.

Day 12 (30 July): Feast of Kenty-khtay (Horus of Athribis). Feast of Satet in Elephantine. Do not eat any meat. Do not do anything on this day. Spend the day until Re sets in his horizon in meditation. Prayer or divinatory time: throughout the day.

Day 13 (31 July): Feast of Nut. Do not do anything on this day. Prayer or divinatory time: throughout the day.

Day 14 (1 August): Feast of Khonsu-Osiris. Feast of Meskhetyu (name of the constellation of Ursa Major). Feast of Ptah. If you undertake any errand, it will be accomplished immediately. Prayer or divinatory time: dawn. Khonsu-Osiris is Osiris identified with the moon so pay special attention to the lunar aspects tonight.

Day 15 (2 August): Feast of Sepa-Osiris who rules in Heliopolis. (Sepa was originally a centipede deity who prevented snakebite.) Do not eat fish. Do not start anything (new). Prayer or divinatory time: throughout the day.

Day 16 (3 August): The Coming Forth of Neith. It is favourable to do anything on this day. Prayer or divinatory time: do not observe – not a suitable day.

Day 17 (4 August): Feast of Sobek-Re. Do not eat fish on this day. Do not do anything on this day. Prayer or divinatory time: do not observe – not a suitable day.

Day 18 (5 August): Feast of Osiris. If you see anything it will be good on this day. It is the day of magnifying the Majesty of Horus more than his brother. Prayer or divinatory time: dawn and in the afternoon.

Day 19 (6 August): Feast of Thoth. A happy day in heaven in front of Re, the Great Ennead is in great festivity. Burn incense on the fire. It is the day of receiving. It is the day of going forth of Thoth. Prayer or divinatory time: dawn.

Day 20 (7 August): Feast of Hathor. Do not do any work. It is the day when the great ones are well disposed. Prayer or divinatory time: dawn.

Day 21 (8 August): Feast of Osiris. Take a holiday on this day; offer to the followers of Re on this day. It is a day to be cautious. Prayer or divinatory time: in the afternoon.

Day 22 (9 August): Creation of the world. Re calls every god and goddess, and they await his arrival. Feast of Wp-wat. Prayer or divinatory time: in the afternoon.

Day 23 (10 August): Feast of Anubis. Do not burn any incense on the fire for the god on this day. Do not listen to singing or dancing on this day. Prayer or divinatory time: dawn.

Day 24 (11 August): Feast of Osiris. The Sun's journey in the Otherworld. The Majesty of this god sails with a favourable wind peacefully. Behold, he settles down, his heart especially. As for anyone born on this day they will die as an honoured one in old age. Prayer or divinatory time: dawn.

Day 25 (12 August): The Going Forth of Sekhmet. Do not go out of your house on any road at the time of night. Prayer or divinatory time: do not observe – not a suitable day.

Day 26 (13 August): Feast of Heka, god of magic. Do not do anything on this day. It is the day of Horus fighting with Set. Prayer or divinatory time: in the afternoon.

Day 27 (14 August): Feast of Nekhbet, the vulture goddess. Peace on the part of Horus and Set. Do not kill any nhy-reptile on this day [the serpent was sacred to Set]; make a holiday. Prayer or divinatory time: throughout the day.

Day 28 (15 August): The gods are happy on this day when they see the children of Nut peaceful (Horus and Set). If you see anything, it will be good on this day. Prayer or divinatory time: throughout the day.

Day 29 (16 August): Feast of Khumn. Do not kindle fire in the house on this day. Do not burn incense; do not go out by night on this day. Prayer or divinatory time: throughout the day.

Day 30 (17 August): Feast of Osiris. If you see anything it will be good on this day. House of Re, House of Horus, House of Osiris. Prayer and divinatory time: in the afternoon.

AKET-season (Inundation)

Second Month: Phaophi

Day 1 (18 August): The Opet Festival dedicated to Amun, Mut and Khonsu at Karnak. The Marriage of Isis and Osiris. The birth and feast of Re-Harakthte. The Feast of Wedjet. Jubilation. The Great Ennead is in festivity on this day. Do not do anything on this day. A public holiday or celebration. Wedjet, the cobra goddess of Lower Egypt was bound up with the regenerative forces. Traditionally, pharaoh, or his high priest, would undergo extensive purification rituals during the two- to four-week festival. Prayer or divinatory time: dawn.

On the eastern bank of the Nile at modern Luxor is a vast enclosure containing the Great Temple of Amun; the Great Hypostyle Hall is 6,000 square metres with 134 columns built by Seti I and Ramesses II in the 19th Dynasty. Religious processions in honour of Amun, carried in state in a shrine, aboard his sacred boat, or personal confrontations between the pharaoh and his god cover every column and every inch of wall space as a testament to the piety of the royal family. The Opet Festival is one of the best-known religious festivals that took place at Thebes from the early 18th Dynasty onwards.

Occurring annually in the second month of the season of *Akhet*, and lasting for a period that varied from two to four weeks, the main event was the ritual procession of the divine images of Amun, Mut, and Khonsu from Karnak to Luxor. The Temple of Luxor was largely constructed as a suitable architectural setting for the Festival of Opet.

Day 2 (19 August): Feast of Thoth. The proceeding of the Majesty of Sais – Neith. Offer to all the gods. It is important to hear what I say to you. Prayer or divinatory time: noon.

Day 3 (20 August): Thoth is in the presence of Re in the inaccessible shrine. If you see anything, it will be good on this day. Prayer or divinatory time: do not observe – not a suitable day.

Day 4 (21 August): It is the day of the Going Forth of Anubis for the inspection of the amulet for the protection of the body of the god. Prayer or divinatory time: dawn.

Day 5 (22 August): Feast of Osiris. Do not go out of your house on this day. Do not copulate with a woman. It is the day of offering in the presences of Montu (the falcon-headed war god) on this day. Prayer or divinatory time: dawn.

Day 6 (23 August): Feast of Nekhbet. A happy day for Re in heaven, and the gods are pacified in his presence. The Ennead is making glorification in front of the Lord of the Universe. Prayer or divinatory time: do not observe – not a suitable day.

Day 7 (24 August): Feast of Horus. Do not do anything on this day. Sun rises in Virgo. Prayer or divinatory time: noon.

Day 8 (25 August): If you see anything on this day, it will be good. Favourable is to do everything on this day. Prayer or divinatory time: throughout the day.

Day 9 (26 August): Feast of Khnum. Jubilation in the heart of Re. His Ennead is in festivity, all enemies are overthrown on this day. Anyone born on this day will die at a good age. Favourable is to do everything. Prayer or divinatory time: do not observe – not a suitable day.

Major Celebrations

Day 10 (27 August): Feast of Atum. Proceeding the Majesty of Bastet... the Majesty of Re... to pay tribute to the August tree [The holy tree in Heliopolis on the leaves of which the gods' names were inscribed – symbolically the sycamore]. Favourable is to do everything. Prayer or divinatory time: throughout the day.

Day 11 (28 August): Feast of Dwmutef (one of the four sons of Horus responsible for the protection of the stomach after embalming. Shown in the form of a jackal). Everything is good on this day. Prayer or divinatory time: in the afternoon.

Day 12 (29 August): Feast of Kebeh (daughter of Anubis). Prayer or divinatory time: throughout the day.

Day 13 (30 August): Feast of Imstey (one of the four sons of Horus responsible for the protection of the liver after embalming. Shown in human form). Favourable to everything on this day. Prayer or divinatory time: throughout the day.

Day 14 (31 August): Feast of Hapy (one of the four sons of Horus responsible for the protection of the lungs after embalming. Shown in the form of a baboon; also the name of the god of the Inundation. Note that the fourth son of Horus, the hawk-headed Qebehsenuef, responsible for the intestines after embalming, is not allocated a feast day). Offer to your local gods, and pacify the spirits. Prayer or divination time: dawn.

Day 15 (1 September): Feast of Isis. Do not go out of your house at eventide. The Going Forth of the Majesty of Re at nightfall with his followers. Prayer or divinatory time: throughout the day.

Day 16 (2 September): Feast of Osiris-Onnophris. Feast of the Eye of Horus. The gods who are in his retinue are in great festivity. If you see anything on this day, it will be good. Prayer or divinatory time: do not observe – not a suitable day.

Day 17 (3 September): Give up beer and bread (i.e. fast). Burn incense to Re and the invocation offering to the spirits. It is important so that your words may be listened to by your local gods. On this goood day... favourable in everything. Prayer or divinatory time: do not observe – not a suitable day.

Day 18 (4 September): Do not do anything on this day. Prayer or divinatory time: at dawn and in the afternoon.

Day 19 (5 September): Feast of Ptah, lord of the workshop. Do everything on this day. Prayer or divinatory time: dawn.

Day 20 (6 September): Feast of Horus and Set. Do everything on this day. Prayer or divinatory time: dawn.

Day 21 (7 September): It is the day of the Going Forth of Neith in the presence of the Majesty of Atum Re-Harakhti – may he live and be prosperous. Prayer or divinatory time: in the afternoon.

Day 22 (8 September): Do not bathe on this day. Prayer or divinatory time: in the afternoon.

Day 23 (9 September): [Damaged] Prayer or divinatory time: dawn.

Day 24 (10 September): Do not go out of your house, or in any wind until Re sets. Prayer or divinatory time: dawn.

Day 25 (11 September): Do not go out on this day on any road. Prayer or divinatory time: do not observe – not a suitable day.

Day 26 (12 September): Do not order any work. Do not do any work on this day. It is the day of opening and sealing the windows of the place of Busiris (Old Kingdom temple complex at Abusir). Prayer or divinatory time: in the afternoon.

Day 27 (13 September): Do not go out. Do not give your back to any work until the sun sets. Prayer or divinatory time: throughout the day.

Day 28 (14 September): If you see anything, it will be good on this day. Prayer or divinatory time: throughout the day.

Day 29 (15 September): Anyone born on this day will die as an honourable man among his people. Prayer or divinatory time: throughout the day.

Day 30 (16 September): The land is in festivity on this day. House of Re, House of Osiris, House of Horus. Prayer or divinatory time: in the afternoon.

AKET-season (Inundation)

Third month: Athyr

Day 1 (17 September): Feast of Hathor, the Mistress of Heaven. Prayer or divinatory time: dawn.

Day 2 (18 September): Return of Wedjet from Dep. (Dep is the Predynastic name for Buto, of which Wedjet was the patron goddess.) Prayer or divinatory time: noon.

Day 3 (19 September): If you see anything it will be good on this day. Prayer or divinatory time: do not observe – not a suitable day.

Day 4 (20 September): The trembling of the earth under Nun (the god who personified the original formless ocean of Chaos). Prayer or divinatory time: dawn.

Major Celebrations

Day 5 (21 September): Do not keep fire burning in the house on this day. The turning of the year with the autumn (spring in Egypt) Equinox. In Egypt traditionally the time for planting – in the northern hemisphere, harvest and the end of summer. Prayer or divinatory time: dawn.

Day 6 (22 September): The encouragement of the gods of the Two Lands (Set and Horus). Prayer or divinatory time: do not observe – not a suitable day.

Day 7 (23 September): If you see anything it will be good on this day. Prayer or divinatory time: noon.

Day 8 (24 September): Isis goes forth unto her son, Horus. Sun rises in Libra. Prayer or divinatory time: throughout the day.

Day 9 (25 September): Do not go outside on any road from your house on this day. Do not let light fall on your face until Re is set in his horizon. It is the day of blaming the great ones ... who were in his presence. Prayer or divinatory time: do not observe – not a suitable day.

Day 10 (26 September): Great rejoicing in heaven; the crew of Re are in peace, his Ennead is cheerful (lit. 'shout loudly'). Those in the fields are working. It is the day of judgement between Horus and Set. Prayer or divinatory time: throughout the day.

Day 11 (27 September): If you see anything it will be good on this day. Prayer or divinatory time: in the afternoon.

Day 12 (28 September): Do not go to your antagonist but go to answer the neighbours (obviously a time of strife in ancient Egypt). Prayer or divinatory time: throughout the day.

Day 13 (29 September): This is the day of cutting into pieces ... This neshmet-boat of Osiris is sailing upstream to Abydos to the great town of Onnophris. Set entered the embalming booth ... to announce the god's limbs. Then they became fresh (Opening of the Mouth Ceremony). Prayer or divinatory time: throughout the day.

Day 14 (30 September): Do not do anything on this day. Prayer or divinatory time: dawn.

Day 15 (1 October): Let a man sleep with his wife on this day. Prayer or divinatory time: throughout the day.

Day 16 (2 October): The appearance of the Great Ones of the Ogduad (the Hermopolitan group of eight deities connected to the Creation myth). A happy day of infinity and eternity. Do not go out of your house on this day. Let not a man sleep with his wife. Prayer or divinatory time: do not observe – not a suitable day.

Day 17 (3 October): Landing of the Great Ones, the Upper and Lower Ones at Abydos; loud weeping and wailing by Isis and Nephthys, her sister, over Onnophris (Osiris) in Sais. The weeping and crying is heard in Abydos. Prayer or divinatory time: do not observe – not a suitable day.

Day 18 (4 October): It is the day of strife by the children of Geb … do not approach any road for making a journey on it. Prayer or divinatory time: at dawn and in the afternoon.

Day 19 (5 October): Beware the children of the storm … Let a man eat bread in his house. Do not go outside on the road on this day. Prayer or divinatory time: dawn.

Day 20 (6 October): The Going Forth of Bastet. Offer to the gods on this day. Prayer or divinatory time: dawn.

Day 21 (7 October): The Feast of Shu, son of Re. Prayer or divinatory time: in the afternoon.

Day 22 (8 October): The raising of Ma'at in order to see Re, when she is summoned by the gods in the presence of Re. Prayer or divinatory time: in the afternoon.

Day 23 (9 October): [Damaged] Prayer or divinatory time: dawn.

Day 24 (10 October): Isis goes forth, her heart being happy and Nephthys being also in jubilation when they see Onnophris (Osiris). He had given his throne to his son, Horus, in front of Re. Prayer or divinatory time: dawn.

Day 25 (11 October): If you see anything, it will be good on this day. Do not offer to the gods on this day. Prayer or divinatory time: do not observe – not a suitable day.

Day 26 (12 October): Establishing the Djed … of Atum in the heaven and land of Heliopolis reconciliation of the Two Lords and causing the land to be in peace. The whole of Egypt is given to Horus, and all the desert land to Set. Going forth of Thoth in order to judge in the presence of Re. Do not offer to the gods. Prayer or divinatory time: in the afternoon.

Day 27 (13 October): Judging of Horus and Set; stopping the fighting. Prayer or divinatory time: throughout the day.

Day 28 (14 October): The gods are in jubilation and in joy … The land is in festivity and the gods are pleased. If you see anything, it will be good. Prayer or divinatory time: throughout the day.

Day 29 (15 October): The going forth of the three noble ladies in the presence of Ptah, beautiful of face, while giving praise to Re, him who belongs to the throne of truth of the temples of the goddesses. Giving the White Crown to Horus, and the Red Crown to Set. (Usually Horus represents Lower Egypt and Set Upper Egypt, so the ascription of the Crowns may seem puzzling. But as 'all the desert land' is assigned to Set, perhaps the association of the same word, now applies to the Red Crown, and explains the previous statement.) Do not dispute with your antagonist on this day. Prayer or divinatory time: throughout the day.

Day 30 (16 October): If you see anything, it will be good on this day. Do not offer to the male gods. Do not offer to the goddesses on this day. House of Re, House of Osiris, House of Horus. Prayer or divinatory time: in the afternoon.

AKET-season (Inundation)

Fourth Month: Khoiak

Day 1 (17 October): The Great and the Small Ennead is in festivity and all those who came into being in the primordial age, their form is in every body of thine (Re). Prayer or divinatory time: dawn.

Day 2 (18 October): Gods and goddesses are in festivity; the heaven and the land are in joy. If you see anything, it will be good on this day. Prayer or divinatory time: at noon.

Day 3 (19 October): Do not do anything on this day. Prayer or divinatory time: do not observe – not a suitable day.

Day 4 (20 October): One should perform the rituals in the Temple of Sokar and in thy house on this day, with all provisions in the necropolis. (Sokar was primarily a funerary god who was later associated with both Osiris and Ptah – perhaps a day for remembering the Ancestors.) Prayer or divinatory time: dawn.

Day 5 (21 October): The Going Forth of Khentet-'abet (a goddess whose horns are prominent, i.e. Hathor, probably as the mother of Horus the Elder) in the presence of the Great Ones. Prayer or divinatory time: dawn.

Day 6 (22 October): Do not go out on this day. Prayer or divinatory time: do not observe – not a suitable day.

Day 7 (23 October): Do not eat or taste fish on this day. Prayer or divinatory time: at noon.

Day 8 (24 October): If you see anything it will be good on this day. Sun rises in Scorpio. Prayer or divinatory time: throughout the day.

Day 9 (25 October): It is the day of the action performed by Thoth. Thereupon the gods, together with Thoth caused the enemy of Set to kill himself (Apophis). Prayer or divinatory time: do not observe – not a suitable day.

Day 10 (26 October): As to anyone born on this day, he will die of old age. Prayer or divinatory time: throughout the day.

Day 11 (27 October): Feast of Osiris in Abydos. The dead are in jubilation. Prayer or divinatory time: in the afternoon.

Day 12 (28 October): Do not go out on this day on any road in the wind. It is the day of the Transformation of the Benu. Offer to the Benu in your house on this day. Prayer or divinatory time: throughout the day.

Transformation of the Benu refers to the phoenix, which personifies the everlasting sun god. The benu bird is thought to be the phoenix – the heron. Two days later, the 'Hedj-hotpe and the Tayet [both goddesses of weaving] come forth from the Temple of Benben on this day. They handed things [gifts] to Neith on this day.'

It is possible that this second festival coincides with the receding of the flood waters that symbolise the re-emergence of the land with its newly enriched soil. The goddesses of weaving also suggest that the second date is a women's festival attached to the Temple of Benben – the holy stone that symbolised the primeval Mound and was closely associated with the benu bird.

Day 13 (29 October): The Going Forth of the White One (or 'the Majesty of Heaven' – an attribute of Hathor). The Great Ennead is in festivity. Make a holiday in your house on this day. Prayer or divinatory time: throughout the day.

Day 14 (30 October): [The goddesses of weaving] come forth from the Temple of Benben on this day. They hand things to Neith on this day. Their hearts are happy. (Obviously an ancient festival and one dedicated to domestic affairs rather than commerce or business. Weaving goddesses are also associated with fate and destiny, and the intertwining of lives. Explore the strands of this special weaving, especially at a time when the festival coincides with the end of the old year in the Northern hemisphere.) Prayer or divinatory time: dawn.

Day 15 (31 October): Do nothing on this day. Prayer or divinatory time: throughout the day.

Day 16 (1 November): Feast of Sekhmet and Bast. Prayer or divinatory time: do not observe – not a suitable day.

Day 17 (2 November): Feast of Horus the Elder. Do not go out at midday on this day. Prayer or divinatory time: do not observe – not a suitable day.

Day 18 (3 November): [Damaged entry] Prayer or divinatory time: at dawn and in the afternoon.

Day 19 (4 November): Do not taste beer and bread on this day. Drink water (i.e. juice) of the grapes until Re sets. A day of fasting. Prayer or divinatory time: dawn.

Major Celebrations

Day 20 (5 November): Do not go out on any road on this day. Do not anoint thyself with ointment on this day. Do not go out of your house at midday. Prayer or divinatory time: dawn.

Day 21 (6 November): It is the day of the going forth of the mysterious Great Ones to look for the Akhet-eye. Do not go out of your house in the daytime. Prayer or divinatory time: in the afternoon.

Day 22 (7 November): If you see anything, it will be good on this day. A time for beginning the formula for the making of the spirit of Osiris (i.e. resurrection). To be repeated for the next four days. Prayer or divinatory time: in the afternoon.

Day 23 (8 November): Do not go out during night-time. Prayer or divinatory time: dawn.

Day 24 (9 November): Prayer or divinatory time: dawn.

Day 25 (10 November): Prayer or divinatory time: do not observe – not a suitable day.

Day 26 (11 November): The end of the formula for the making of the spirit of Osiris. Prayer or divinatory time: in the afternoon.

Day 27 (12 November): Feast of Thoth. Prayer or divinatory time: throughout the day.

Day 28 (13 November): If you see anything, it will be good. Do not go out at night-time on this day. Prayer or divinatory time: throughout the day.

Day 29 (14 November): Do not eat fish on this day. Do not offer it to the gods on this day. Prayer or divinatory time: throughout the day.

Day 30 (15 November): If you see anything, it will be pleasing to the heart of the gods and goddesses on this day. Offer to the gods and the assistants of the Ennead. Make an invocation to the spirits, and give food in accordance with their lust. It is the day of the pleasure of the Great Ennead. House of Re, House of Osiris, House of Horus. Prayer or divinatory time: in the afternoon.

PROYET-season (Emergence)

First Month: Tybi

Day 1 (16 November): Double the offerings and present the gifts of nhb-kaw [for the sprouting of the new crops] to the gods in the presence of Ptah in the shrines of the gods and goddesses, saviours of Re and his own followers ... and of Ptah-Sokar and Sekhmet the great, Nerfertem, Horus-Hekenu, Bastet, the great fire ... propitiating the Wedjet-eye [the cobra goddess]. It will be good ... offering before ... in nourishment. (The traditional first day of planting, i.e. spring for the ancient Egyptians.) Prayer or divinatory time: dawn.

Day 2 (17 November): Make a holiday in your house. Prayer or divinatory time: at noon.

Day 3 (18 November): Do not burn fire [i.e. incense] in the presence of Re. Prayer or divinatory time: do not observe – not a suitable day.

Day 4 (19 November): If you see anything it will be good. Anyone born on this day will die old among his people. He will spend a long life, and be well received by his father. Prayer or divinatory time: dawn.

Day 5 (20 November): It is the day of placing the flame in front of the great ones by Sekhmet who presides in the Lower Egyptian sanctuary when she was violent in her manifestations because of her detention by Ma'at, Ptah, Thoth, Heh [the personification of infinity] and Sia [the personification of the perceptive mind] and the gods on this day. Prayer or divinatory time: dawn.

Day 6 (21 November): Repeat the offerings of the victuals of him who dwells in wrt [a holy place], and return the victuals of the noble Khenti-irty [the earliest form of Osiris which shows him as a hawk with a flail] and offerings to the gods were doubled by everyone on this day. Prayer or divinatory time: do not observe – not a suitable day.

Day 7 (22 November): Do not copulate with any woman, or any person in front of the great flame [i.e. the sun – during the day] which is in your house on this day. Prayer or divinatory time: at noon.

Day 8 (23 November): If you see anything, it will be good on this day. Sun rises in Sagittarius. Prayer or divinatory time: throughout the day.

Day 9 (24 November): The gods are joyful with the offerings of Sekhmet [on this] day. Repeat the offerings. It will be pleasant to the heart of the gods and the spirits. Prayer or divinatory time: do not observe – not a suitable day.

Day 10 (25 November): Do not burn any wbd-papyrus on this day. It is the day of the Coming Forth of the flame (together with Horus from the marshes) on this day. Prayer or divinatory time: throughout the day.

Day 11 (26 November): Do not approach the flame on this day. Prayer or divinatory time: in the afternoon.

Day 12 (27 November): If you see any dog on this day, do not approach him on the day of answering every speech of Sekhmet on this day. (Possibly referring to a superstition of the time.) Prayer or divinatory time: throughout the day.

Major Celebrations

Day 13 (28 November): Prolonging life-time and making beneficent the goddess of truth [Ma'at] in the temple. Prayer or divinatory time: throughout the day.

Day 14 (29 November): Weeping of Isis and Nephthys. It is the day when they mourned Osiris in Busiris in remembrance of that which he had seen. Do not listen to singing and chanting on this day. Prayer or divinatory time: dawn.

Day 15 (30 November): If you see anything it will be good on this day. It is the day of the Going forth of Nun through the cave to the place (where the gods are) ... (in) darkness ... [Coming into the light.] Prayer or divinatory time: throughout the day.

Day 16 (1 December): The Going Forth of Shu. Prayer or divinatory time: do not observe – not a suitable day.

Day 17 (2 December): Do not wash yourself with water on this day. It is the day of the Going Forth of Nun to the place where the gods are. Those who are above and below come into existence; the land being still in darkness. Prayer or divinatory time: do not observe – not a suitable day.

Day 18 (3 December): The Going Forth of the gods to Abydos. Prayer or divinatory time: at dawn and in the afternoon.

Day 19 (4 December): The great gods are in heaven on this day and (lit. mixed with) the pestilence of the year. Prayer or divinatory time: dawn.

Day 20 (5 December): Do not do anything on this day. It is the day of the Going Forth of Bastet who protects the Two Lands and cares for him who comes in darkness. Beware of passing on land until Re sets. Prayer or divinatory time: dawn.

Day 21 (6 December): Guidance of the Two Lands by Bastet and making 'abt-offering to the followers of Re on this day. Prayer or divinatory time: in the afternoon.

Day 22 (7 December): If you see anything it will be good on this day. Prayer or divinatory time: in the afternoon.

Day 23 (8 December): Anyone born on this day will die in great old age and rich in every good thing. Prayer or divinatory time: dawn.

Day 24 (9 December): Happiness is in heaven and earth on this day. Prayer or divinatory time: dawn.

Day 25 (10 December): Do not eat milk on this day. Drink and eat honey on this day. (The prohibition of drinking milk probably means it was exclusively offered to the cow goddess – Hathor or Nut. Purification by means of milk is also referred to in other texts.) Prayer or divinatory time: do not observe – not a suitable day.

Day 26 (11 December): Do not go out in it [the day] until Re sets when offerings are diminished in Busiris. (The subject of diminishing offerings is frequently mentioned in the *Book of the Dead*.) Prayer or divinatory time: in the afternoon.

Day 27 (12 December): Great festivity on this day. Prayer or divinatory time: throughout the day.

Day 28 (13 December): Taking a solemn oath by Thoth in Ashmunein, and the Going Forth of the noble one. (The most solemn oath one can take and refers to that pledged by Horus the Elder and Set.) The land is in festivity on this day. Make a holiday in your house. Prayer or divinatory time: throughout the day.

Day 29 (14 December): Appearance in the sight of Hu [personification of the authority of a word of command]. Thoth will send his command southwards to guide the Two Lands by Bastet together with the sole mistress as Sekhmet the great, the gods being happy. If you see anything it will be good on this day. Prayer or divinatory time: throughout the day.

Day 30 (15 December): Crossing over in the presence of Nun from the Temple of Hapi, the father of the gods and the Ennead. Do not neglect them while incense is on the fire according to their lists on this day. House of Re, House of Osiris, House of Horus. Prayer or divinatory time: in the afternoon.

PROYET-season (Emergence)

Second Month: Mekhir

Day 1 (16 December): The god and goddesses are in festivity on this day (namely), in the feast of [lifting] the heaven of Re by Ptah, with his hands (he who has no equal). (The notion of the sky being lifted by Ptah rather than Shu is found in a hymn to this god, which is now in Berlin.) A holiday in the entire land. Prayer or divinatory time: dawn.

Day 2 (17 December): The day of receiving Re by the gods. The heart of the Two Lands is in festivity. Prayer or divinatory time: at noon.

Day 3 (18 December): Do not go out of your house on any road on this day. It is the day of the Going Forth of Set with his confederates to the eastern horizon, and the navigation of Ma'at to the place (where the gods are). Prayer or divinatory time: do not observe – not a suitable day.

Day 4 (19 December): Apply your heart to your local gods; propitiate your spirits. Prayer or divinatory time: dawn.

Day 5 (20 December): If you see anything, it will be good on this day. Prayer or divinatory time: dawn.

Major Celebrations

Day 6 (21 December): It is the day of putting up the djet by the Majesty of Osiris. The gods are sad with their faces turned downwards when they remember the Majesty of this god. (Refers to the resurrection of Osiris represented by the djet pillar. For ritual purposes it is highly appropriate that this day coincides with Winter Solstice in the northern hemisphere.) Prayer or divinatory time: do not observe – not a suitable day.

Day 7 (22 December): Make invocation and offering to the spirits in your house. Make offerings to the gods, and they will be accepted on this day. Sun rises in Capricorn. Prayer or divinatory time: at noon.

Day 8 (23 December): The gods and goddesses are in festivity on this day. Prayer or divinatory time: throughout the day.

Day 9 (24 December): If you see anything, it will be good on this day. Prayer or divinatory time: do not observe – not a suitable day.

Day 10 (25 December): The Going Forth of the Wedjet-eye. The raising up of the female Majesty of the sanctuary by Mnevis. Re raised up Ma'at again and again to Atum. Prayer or divinatory time: throughout the day.

Day 11 (26 December): Feast of Neith. The Going Forth of Sobek to guide her Majesty. Thou wilt see good at her hands. Prayer or divinatory time: in the afternoon.

Day 12 (27 December): If you see anything, it will be good on this day. Prayer or divinatory time: throughout the day.

Day 13 (28 December): Do not go out of your house on any road on this day. It is the day of the preceding of Sekhmet to Letopolis on this day. Prayer or divinatory time: throughout the day.

Day 14 (29 December): Do not go out on this day at the beginning (lit. in the face) of dawn. The day of the slaying of Apophis by Set. Prayer or divinatory time: dawn.

Day 15 (30 December): The gods go forth for him in heaven. Prayer or divinatory time: throughout the day.

Day 16 (31 December): Awakening of Isis by the Majesty of Re ... when the son Horus saved his father. He has beaten Set and his confederates. Prayer or divinatory time: do not observe – not a suitable day.

Day 17 (1 January): A day of keeping those things (of Osiris) which have been placed in the hands of Anubis (for safe keeping). A day for remembering 'absent friends'. Prayer or divinatory time: do not observe – not a suitable day.

Day 18 (2 January): This is the day when a search was made to retrieve the eye of Horus that had been torn out during his battle with Set. It symbolises the eternal renewal of royal divinity and Egyptian faith in the continual reintegration of universal harmony. Prayer or divinatory time: at dawn and in the afternoon.

Day 19 (3 January): Decide not to go out during daytime. It is a day of (mourning the god). (Refers to the slaying of Osiris by Set, which interrupts the harmonious cosmic flow and endangers the whole social order.) Prayer or divinatory time: dawn.

Day 20 (4 January): The proceeding of the (female) Majesty of Heaven southward to the road ... (Referring to a ritual procession of a statue of Hathor.) Prayer or divinatory time: dawn.

Day 21 (5 January): Prayer or divinatory time: in the afternoon.

Day 22 (6 January): If you see anything, it will be good on this day. Prayer or divinatory time: in the afternoon.

Day 23 (7 January): If you see anything, it will be good on this day. Prayer or divinatory time: dawn.

Day 24 (8 January): Prayer or divinatory time: dawn.

Day 25 (9 January): If you see anything, it will be good on this day. Prayer or divinatory time: do not observe – not a suitable day.

Day 26 (10 January): The Going Forth of Min from Coptos on this day. Prayer or divinatory time: in the afternoon.

Day 27 (11 January): The Feast of Sokar. Prayer or divinatory time: throughout the day.

Day 28 (12 January): The spirits are joyful, the dead are also in festivity. (A day for honouring the Ancestors and 'speaking the name of the dead in order to make them live again'.) Prayer or divinatory time: throughout the day.

Day 29 (13 January): Do not do anything on this day. (An unlucky day, marking the start of the fighting between the children of Nut and Geb. Often referred to as the 'children of disorder' because of their incessant quarrelling and the disturbances they provoked.) Prayer or divinatory time: throughout the day.

Day 30 (14 January): Do not talk with anybody (in a loud voice) on this day. House of Re, House of Osiris, House of Horus. Prayer or divinatory time: in the afternoon.

Major Celebrations

PROYET-season (Emergence)

Third Month: Phamenoth

Day 1 (15 January): It is the day (of jubilation) in heaven and earth and everybody likewise. Feast of entering into heaven and the two banks. Horus is jubilating. Feast of Horus the Elder. Prayer or divinatory time: dawn.

Day 2 (16 January): If you see anything, it will be good on this day. Prayer or divinatory time: at noon.

Day 3 (17 January): [Damaged entry] Prayer or divinatory time: do not observe – not a suitable day.

Day 4 (18 January): A Feast of Propitiation for Set. Announcement of fighting; call in Heliopolis by Set, his voice being in heaven [thunder], his voice being on earth, through great fury [storm]. Prayer or divinatory time: dawn.

Day 5 (19 January): Neith goes forth from Sais when they see (her) beauty in the night for four and a half (hours). (Possibly referring to an eclipse.) Feast of Neith. Prayer or divinatory time: dawn.

Day 6 (20 January): Jubilation of Osiris is Bursiris … Going Forth of Anubis, (his adorers) following him … he has received everybody in the hall. *Mayest thou* make the ritual. Prayer or divinatory time: do not observe – not a suitable day.

Day 7 (21 January): Do not go out of your house until Re sets. It is the day when the eye of Re called the followers, and they reached him (in) the evening. Beware of it. (Marking the day when Sekhmet punished mankind for rebelling against Re.) Sun rises in Aquarius. Prayer or divinatory time: at noon.

Day 8 (22 January): If you see anything, it will be good on this day. It is the day of making way for the gods. Khnum who presides over those who remove themselves from him. The Feast Day of Khumn, the creator god, who fashions human beings on his potter's wheel. Prayer or divinatory time: throughout the day.

Day 9 (23 January): Judgement in Heliopolis. The anniversary of the judgement of the gods between Set and Horus. Sun rises in Aquarius. Prayer or divinatory time: do not observe – not a suitable day.

Day 10 (24 January): It is the day of the coming of Thoth. They guided the very great Flame into her house of the desert of eternity (along) the way which she found among them. The celebration of Thoth bringing Sekhmet, the lion goddess, back from her self-imposed exile. Prayer or divinatory time: throughout the day.

Day 11 (25 January): As to the dead who go about in the necropolis on this day, the dead are going about in order to repel the anger of the enemy who is in the said land. A Feast of Osiris in Amenti. A day for honouring the Ancestors in the Otherworld. Prayer or divinatory time: in the afternoon.

Day 12 (26 January): Wsr [the Nile] comes from Nun on this day. Traditionally a celebration of the first appearance of the life-giving waters at the Creation. The Feast of the Nile. Prayer or divinatory time: throughout the day.

Day 13 (27 January): The coming of Thoth (with his spirits) on this day. A Feast of Thoth. Prayer or divinatory time: throughout the day.

Day 14 (28 January): Do not go out of your house (on any road) on this day. Prayer or divinatory time: dawn.

Day 15 (29 January): Rebellion in the shrine(?). Do not do any work on this day. Prayer or divinatory time: throughout the day.

Day 16 (30 January): Opening of the windows and opening of the court, and looking into the doorways of Karnak, where his place is. Do not look into the darkness on this day. Reference to the cleaning of the temple. (There is a dark, inner sanctuary of Sekhmet in the Temple of Ptah at Karnak.) Prayer or divinatory time: do not observe – not a suitable day.

Day 17 (31 January): Do not pronounce the name of Set on this day. As to him who pronounces his name without his knowledge, he will not stop from fighting in his house eternally. Set was the god of Chaos who was always at odds with his siblings. Prayer or divinatory time: do not observe – not a suitable day.

Day 18 (1 February): Feast of Nut who counts the days. Make a holiday in your house. Prayer or divinatory time: at dawn and in the afternoon.

Day 19 (2 February): Birth of Nut anew … *Do not* go out of your house; do not see the light (sw). Prayer or divinatory time: dawn.

Day 20 (3 February): Do not go out of your house on any road. Do not see the light. Prayer or divinatory time: dawn.

Day 21 (4 February): [Damaged entry] Prayer or divinatory time: in the afternoon.

Day 22 (5 February): Birth of the mysterious one (Apophis). Do not get the thought of pronouncing the names of the snakes. (Obscure meaning but some snakes were unlucky and Apophis is the serpent-god of the netherworld.) Prayer or divinatory time: in the afternoon.

Day 23 (6 February): Feast of Horus on this day of his years in his very beautiful images. Prayer or divinatory time: dawn.

Major Celebrations

Day 24 (7 February): Do not go out of your house on any road on this day. Prayer or divinatory time: dawn.

Day 25 (8 February): Do not do anything on this day. Prayer or divinatory time: do not observe – not a suitable day.

Day 26 (9 February): [Obscure meaning] Prayer or divinatory time: in the afternoon.

Day 27 (10 February): Do not do anything on this day. Prayer or divinatory time: throughout the day.

Day 28 (11 February): Feast of Osiris in Abydos. Prayer or divinatory time: throughout the day.

Day 29 (12 February): If you see anything it will be good. Prayer or divinatory time: throughout the day.

Day 30 (13 February): Feast in Busiris. The names of the doorways come into existence. House of Re, House of Osiris, House of Horus. Prayer or divinatory time: in the afternoon.

PROYET-season (Emergence)

Fourth Month: Pharmuthi

Day 1 (14 February): Great feasting in heaven. Prayer or divinatory time: dawn.

Day 2 (15 February): The Majesty of Geb proceeds to the throne of Busiris to see Anubis, who commands the council on the requirements of the day. Prayer or divinatory time: at noon.

Day 3 (16 February): Do not do anything on this day. Prayer or divinatory time: do not observe – not a suitable day.

Day 4 (17 February): If you see anything it will be good on this day. The gods and goddesses are satisfied when they see the children of Geb sitting in their places (i.e. at peace). Prayer or divinatory time: dawn.

Day 5 (18 February): Feast of Horus. Prayer or divinatory time: dawn.

Day 6 (19 February): Going Forth of the stars. Prayer or divinatory time: do not observe – not a suitable day.

Day 7 (20 February): The Going Forth of Min in festivity. The gods are jubilating. Pay attention to the incense on the fire smelling of sweet myrrh. Sun rises in Pisces. Prayer or divinatory time: at noon.

Understanding the Egyptian Gods and Goddesses

Day 8 (21 February): The Ennead is in adoration when they see this eye of Horus (the Elder) in its place. A feast day for Horus whose magnificence stretches into infinity. Prayer or divinatory time: throughout the day.

Day 9 (22 February): Do not go out at the time of darkness when Re goes into the West. If you see anything, it will be good on this day. Prayer or divinatory time: do not observe – not a suitable day.

Day 10 (23 February): Do not go out of your house on any road on this day. Prayer or divinatory time: throughout the day.

Day 11 (24 February): The gods are in the shrines of the temples. Prayer or divinatory time: in the afternoon.

Day 12 (25 February): Feast of Montu. Prayer or divinatory time: throughout the day.

Day 13 (26 February): It is the day of conducting Osiris on his ship to Abydos on this day. Prayer or divinatory time: throughout the day.

Day 14 (27 February): Do not be courageous on this day. Prayer or divinatory time: dawn.

Day 15 (28 February): A great happy day in the Eastern Horizon of heaven when instructions were given to the followers of the gods in their temples in the presence of the Great Ones in the Two Horizons. Prayer or divinatory time: throughout the day.

(The ancient calendar made no allowance for leap years.)

Day 16 (1 March): The Going Forth of Khepri. Every town is in joy. Prayer or divinatory time: do not observe – not a suitable day.

Day 17 (2 March): The Going Forth of Set, son of Nut, to disturb the Great Ones. Prayer or divinatory time: do not observe – not a suitable day.

Day 18 (3 March): Do not approach when the Majesty of Re goes forth. Do not wash yourself with water on this day. Prayer or divinatory time: at dawn and in the afternoon.

Day 19 (4 March): The Majesty of Re goes forth in his barque of heaven. If you see anything, it will be good on this day. Prayer or divinatory time: dawn.

Day 20 (5 March): Do not do any work on this day. Prayer or divinatory time: dawn.

Day 21 (6 March): Do not go out on any road on this day. Prayer or divinatory time: in the afternoon.

Day 22 (7 March): An unlucky day. Prayer or divinatory time: in the afternoon.

Major Celebrations

Day 23 (8 March): It is the day of offering victuals ... invocation offering to the spirits. Prayer or divinatory time: dawn.

Day 24 (9 March): Do not mention the name of Set in a loud voice on this day. As to anyone who mentions his name forgetfully, fighting is made in his house forever. Prayer or divinatory time: dawn.

Day 25 (10 March): Do not eat anything which comes from or on water on this day. Prayer or divinatory time: do not observe – not a suitable day.

Day 26 (11 March): [Damaged entry.] Prayer or divinatory time: in the afternoon.

Day 27 (12 March): Do not go out of your house until Re sets because the Majesty of the goddess Sekhmet is angry. Prayer or divinatory time: throughout the day.

Day 28 (13 March): If you see anything it will be good on this day. Prayer or divinatory time: throughout the day.

Day 29 (14 March): The gods are satisfied when they give adoration to Onnophris (Osiris), incense being on the fire; offer to your local gods myrrh which is pleasant on this day. Prayer or divinatory time: throughout the day.

Day 30 (15 March): Offer to Ptah-Sokar-*Osiris* ... Atum, Lord of the Two Lands ... to all the gods ... *on th*is day. House of Re, House of Osiris, House of Horus. Prayer or divinatory time: in the afternoon.

SHOMU-season (Harvest)

First Month: Pakhons

Day 1 (16 March): Feast of Horus, son of Isis and his followers on this day. Prayer or divinatory time: dawn.

Day 2 (17 March): Do not sail in any wind on this day. Prayer or divinatory time: at noon.

Day 3 (18 March): If you see anything it will be good on this day. Prayer or divinatory time: do not observe – not a suitable day.

Day 4 (19 March): Do not go out of your house on any road on this day. Follow Horus on this day. Prayer or divinatory time: dawn.

Day 5 (20 March): Feast of Ba-neb-dedet on this day. (Ba-neb-dedet was the ram god of Djet wrongly translated by Greek historians as 'the Goat of Mendes'.) Prayer or divinatory time: dawn.

Day 6 (21 March): Coming of the Great Ones from the House of Re, rejoicing on this day when they receive the Wedjet-eye, together with their followers. If you see anything, it will be good on this day. Spring Equinox (Autumn in Egypt). Sun rises in Aries. Prayer or divinatory time: do not observe – not a suitable day.

Day 7 (22 March): The crew follow Horus in the foreign land ... Every land is happy, and their heart is glad ... Prayer or divinatory time: at noon.

Day 8 (23 March): If you see anything, it will be good on this day. Prayer or divinatory time: throughout the day.

Day 9 (24 March): If you see anything, it will be good on this day. Prayer or divinatory time: do not observe – not a suitable day.

Day 10 (25 March): The proceeding of the White One of Heaven [Feast day of Osiris]. Prayer or divinatory time: throughout the day.

Day 11 (26 March): [Damaged entry.] Prayer or divinatory time: in the afternoon.

Day 12 (27 March): [Damaged entry.] Prayer or divinatory time: throughout the day.

Day 13 (28 March): [Damaged entry.] Prayer or divinatory time: throughout the day.

Day 14 (29 March): [Damaged entry.] Prayer or divinatory time: dawn.

Day 15 (30 March): Do not go out of your house until Re sets in the horizon. Prayer or divinatory time: throughout the day.

Day 16 (31 March): [Damaged entry.] Prayer or divinatory time: do not observe – not a suitable day.

Day 17 (1 April): If you see anything, it will be good on this day. Prayer or divinatory time: do not observe – not a suitable day.

Day 18 (2 April): If you see anything it will be good on this day. Prayer or divinatory time: at dawn and in the afternoon.

Day 19 (3 April): A feast day of Thoth and Ma'at. All the gods are in great festivity. Prayer or divinatory time: dawn.

Day 20 (4 April): Ma'at judges in front of the gods who became angry. The Majesty of Horus revised (over-ruled) it. Prayer or divinatory time: dawn.

Day 21 (5 April): [Obscure text.] Prayer or divinatory time: in the afternoon.

Day 22 (6 April): Anyone born on this day will die of old age. Prayer or divinatory time: in the afternoon.

Major Celebrations

Day 23 (7 April): If you see anything, it will be good on this day. Prayer or divinatory time: dawn.

Day 24 (8 April): [Damaged entry.] Prayer or divinatory time: dawn.

Day 25 (9 April): [Damaged entry.] Prayer or divinatory time: do not observe – not a suitable day.

Day 26 (10 April): If you see anything, it will be good on this day. Prayer or divinatory time: in the afternoon.

Day 27 (11 April): [Damaged entry.] Prayer or divinatory time: throughout the day.

Day 28 (12 April): [Damaged entry.] Prayer or divinatory time: throughout the day.

Day 29 (13 April): If you see anything, it will be good on this day. Prayer or divinatory time: throughout the day.

Day 30 (14 April): Feast of ... happiness. House of Re, House of Osiris, House of Horus. Prayer or divinatory time: in the afternoon.

SHOMU-season (Harvest)

Second Month: Payni

Day 1 (15 April): [Damaged entry.] Prayer or divinatory time: dawn. The lack of celebration and public feast days in the calendar continues to reflect the preoccupation with working on the land. The harvest season meant that every available pair of hands was required to gather in the crops.

Day 2 (16 April): O heart of the gods, listen well ... The crew of Re is in festivity. (Refers to the crew of the solar barque.) Prayer or divinatory time: at noon.

Day 3 (17 April): The month of the followers of Re. A day is fixed in heaven and on earth as a feast. (A time of public celebration.) Prayer or divinatory time: do not observe – not a suitable day.

Day 4 (18 April): A feast day for Geb and Nut – possibly a celebration of fruitfulness. Prayer or divinatory time: dawn.

Day 5 (19 April): If you see anything, it will be good on this day. Prayer or divinatory time: dawn.

Day 6 (20 April): A feast day for Horus who is celebrated in his guise as protector of his father Onnophris (Osiris) on this day. Prayer or divinatory time: do not observe – not a suitable day.

Day 7 (21 April): Do not go out of your house during waking time ... Re is in the horizon. It is the day of the executioners of Sekhmet counting by names. (An anniversary of the slaughtering of the human race.) Sun rises in Taurus. Prayer or divinatory time: at noon.

Day 8 (22 April): Make a holiday for Re and his followers – make a good day on this day. Prayer or divinatory time: throughout the day.

Day 9 (23 April): Make incense of sweet herbs for his (Re) followers while pleasing him on this day. Prayer or divinatory time: do not observe – not a suitable day.

Day 10 (24 April): Anyone born on this day will be noble. Prayer or divinatory time: throughout the day.

Day 11 (25 April): Do not sail in a boat on the river. It is the day of catching birds and fish by the followers of Re. (Obviously a warning not to incur the wrath of the gods.) Prayer or divinatory time: in the afternoon.

Day 12 (26 April): If you see anything, it will be good on this day. Prayer or divinatory time: throughout the day.

Day 13 (27 April): Feast of Wedjet in Dep and her followers are also in festivity when singing and chanting take place on the day of offering the incense and all kinds of sweet herbs. Prayer or divinatory time: throughout the day.

Day 14 (28 April): [Obscure entry.] Prayer or divinatory time: dawn.

Day 15 (29 April): Do not judge yourself on this day. Prayer or divinatory time: throughout the day.

Day 16 (30 April): Anyone born on this day will die a great man amongst his people. Prayer or divinatory time: do not observe – not a suitable day.

Day 17 (1 May): Do not go out on it. Do not do anything, or any work on this day. Prayer or divinatory time: do not observe – not a suitable day.

Day 18 (2 May): Do not eat meat on this day. It is the day of the Going Forth of Khenti (Osiris) of the god's house when he goes out to the august mountain (West). A day of fasting and prayer. Prayer or divinatory time: at dawn and in the afternoon.

Day 19 (3 May): The Ennead sails, they are much in the entire land. It is the judging of the Great Ones on this day. Prayer or divinatory time: dawn.

Day 20 (4 May): Do not go out in any wind on this day. Prayer or divinatory time: dawn.

Day 21 (5 May): It is the day of the living-w'rty, the children of Nut. Do not go out until daybreak. Prayer or divinatory time: in the afternoon.

Day 22 (6 May): Disturbance below and uproar of the gods of the kri-shrines on this day when Shu was complaining to Re about the Great Ones of infinity. Do not go out in it. Prayer or divinatory time: in the afternoon.

Day 23 (7 May): The crew rest when they see the enemy (Apophis) of their master (Re). (Set protected Re from the attack by Apophis in order to prevent the return to Chaos.) Prayer or divinatory time: dawn.

Day 24 (8 May): If you see anything, it will be good on this day. Prayer or divinatory time: dawn.

Day 25 (9 May): Everything and everybody is pacified. It is pleasant to the gods and Re. Prayer or divinatory time: do not observe – not a suitable day.

Day 26 (10 May): The Going Forth of Neith. She treads this day in the flood in order to look for things of Sobek (her son). Prayer or divinatory time: in the afternoon.

Day 27 (11 May): Do not do any work on this day. Prayer or divinatory time: throughout the day.

Day 28 (12 May): Purifying things and offerings in Busiris. The gods spend the day in festivity. Act in accordance with that which happens on this day. Prayer or divinatory time: throughout the day.

Day 29 (13 May): If you see anything it will be good on this day. Prayer or divinatory time: throughout the day.

Day 30 (14 May): The Going Forth of Shu with the intention of bringing back the Wedjet-eye, and appeasing Thoth on this day. House of Re, House of Osiris, House of Horus. Prayer or divinatory time: in the afternoon.

SHOMU-season (Harvest)

Third Month: Ipt-hmt

Day 1 (15 May): A great feast in the southern Heaven. Every land and everybody starts jubilating. The Mistress of Heaven (Hathor) and every land are in festivity on this day. Prayer or divinatory time: dawn.

Day 2 (16 May): Every god and every goddess spends the day in festivity in the sacred temple. Prayer or divinatory time: at noon.

Day 3 (17 May): Anger of the divine Majesty. Do not do anything on this day. Prayer or divinatory time: do not observe – not a suitable day.

Day 4 (18 May): If you see anything it will be good on this day. Prayer or divinatory time: dawn.

Day 5 (19 May): Do not go out of your house. Do not proceed on a boat. Do not do any work on this day. It is the day of the departure of the goddess to the place from whence she came. The heart of the gods is sad. Prayer or divinatory time: dawn.

Day 6 (20 May): Do not fight or make uproar in your house while every temple of the goddess is in like manner [mourning]. Prayer or divinatory time: do not observe – not a suitable day.

Day 7 (21 May): Sailing of the gods after the Majesty of the goddess ... a flame which takes place in front of everybody on this day. (All the gods depart and a consecrated flame should be allowed to burn to guide their passage.) Prayer or divinatory time: at noon.

Day 8 (22 May): Do not beat anybody. Do not strike anybody. It is the day of the massacre of the followers of the Majesty of the goddess (Sekhmet). Sun rises in Gemini. Prayer or divinatory time: throughout the day.

Day 9 (23 May): The gods are content (i.e. have returned to their respective temples) and they are happy because Re is at peace with the Akhet-eye. Every god is in festivity on this day. Prayer or divinatory time: do not observe – not a suitable day.

Day 10 (24 May): The gods who are in the shrine, their hearts are sad (at having to return). Prayer or divinatory time: throughout the day.

Day 11 (25 May): Do not perform any ritual on this day. Prayer or divinatory time: in the afternoon.

Day 12 (26 May): Holiday ... reception of Re. *His* followers are in festivity, and everybody is in festivity. Prayer or divinatory time: throughout the day.

Day 13 (27 May): The Majesty of this god proceeds sailing westwards to see the beauty of Onnophris (Osiris) on this day. Prayer or divinatory time: throughout the day.

Day 14 (28 May): Do not burn anything in your house in the way of flame with any of its glow on that day of the anger of the eye of Horus the Elder. (Traditionally all fires in the house should be extinguished for a day of fasting until sunset.) Prayer or divinatory time: dawn.

Day 15 (29 May): If you see anything, it will be good on this day. Horus hears your words in the presence of every god and every goddess on this day. You will see every good thing in your house. Prayer or divinatory time: throughout the day.

Day 16 (30 May): It is the day of the transmitting of Ma'at to the shrine by the Majesty of Re. *The gods* learnt that she was much blamed for this. (Justice is sometimes seen as blind even though it follows due process of the law.) Prayer or divinatory time: do not observe – not a suitable day.

Major Celebrations

Day 17 (31 May): [Obscure entry.] Prayer or divinatory time: do not observe – not a suitable day.

Day 18 (1 June): Do not go out of your house on any road on this day. The Going Forth of Ma'at and Re in secret on this day. Prayer or divinatory time: at dawn and in the afternoon.

Day 19 (2 June): Do not do any work on this day. Prayer or divinatory time: dawn.

Day 20 (3 June): Do not go out of your house on any road on this day. Prayer or divinatory time: dawn.

Day 21 (4 June): If you see anything, it will be good on this day. Prayer or divinatory time: in the afternoon.

Day 22 (5 June): It is the day of Sepa in Tura coming from Heliopolis. (Sepa was a centipede-god who was invoked in charms and spells against dangerous creatures. Carry a talisman with this image for protection.) Prayer or divinatory time: in the afternoon.

Day 23 (6 June): It is a day of quarrelling and reproaching. Prayer or divinatory time: dawn.

Day 24 (7 June): [Obscure entry.] Prayer or divinatory time: dawn.

Day 25 (8 June): Do not go out at midday, the great enemy [Apophis] is in the temple of Sekhmet. Prayer or divinatory time: do not observe – not a suitable day.

Day 26 (9 June): If you see anything, it will be good on this day. Prayer or divinatory time: in the afternoon.

Day 27 (10 June): Do not go out of your house on this day. Prayer or divinatory time: throughout the day.

Day 28 (11 June): Creating misery, and bringing terror into existence in conformity with the custom of what is in the year. (At this time of the year the Nile was at its lowest and this entry deals with the misery of the land when disease and pestilence were at their most dangerous.) Prayer or divinatory time: throughout the day.

Day 29 (12 June): The Feast of Mut in Shera (a lake at Karnak) on this day. It is the day of feeding the gods and her followers. Prayer or divinatory time: throughout the day.

Day 30 (13 June): If you see anything, it will be good on this day. House of Re, House of Osiris, House of Horus. Prayer or divinatory time: in the afternoon.

SHOMU-season (Harvest)

Fourth Month: Wp-rnpt

Day 1 (14 June): Transmitting offerings to those who are in heaven. Every god and goddess spend the day in the Feast of Onnophris (Osiris) on this day. Prayer or divinatory time: dawn.

Day 2 (15 June): Truth ... and all gods perform the rites as one who is in heaven (i.e. Onnophris). A feast day dedicated to Osiris as god of the dead. Prayer or divinatory time: at noon.

Day 3 (16 June): Proceeding of the Majesty of this goddess to Heliopolis of Re. A feast was made on this day. Do not go out in order to do anything on this day. (Continuing the Osirian feast days; this one is celebrated by the followers of Isis as a private affair.) Prayer or divinatory time: do not observe – not a suitable day.

Day 4 (17 June): It is the day of the precession of Sopdu [ancient god of the 20th nome of Lower Egypt] together with his followers, being in a state of youth and remaining so in the course of the day. Suggests a festival of youth. Prayer or divinatory time: dawn.

Day 5 (18 June): Min being in Akhmin [a sanctuary at Letopolis]. If you see anything, it will be good on this day. Prayer or divinatory time: dawn.

Day 6 (19 June): Transmitting the rejuvenated one (Onnophris/Osiris) and the hiding of the conspirators on this day. Do not do anything on this day. Prayer or divinatory time: do not observe – not a suitable day.

Day 7 (20 June): The dead one goes about in the necropolis and comes on earth. (A continuance of the Osirian mysteries.) Prayer or divinatory time: at noon.

Day 8 (21 June): If you see anything, it will be good on this day. Summer Solstice – the ancient New Year and the rising of Sirius. Prayer or divinatory time: throughout the day.

Day 9 (22 June): Anyone born on this day will have noble honour. Prayer or divinatory time: do not observe – not a suitable day.

Day 10 (23 June): It is the day of the entering of the eye of Re unto his horizon when he sees his beauty. Sun rises in Cancer. Prayer or divinatory time: throughout the day.

Day 11 (24 June): Causing disturbance in the presence of the followers of Re, and repelling the confederates of Set into the eastern country. (A continuance of the Osirian mysteries.) Prayer or divinatory time: in the afternoon.

Major Celebrations

Day 12 (25 June): Jubilation throughout the entire land on this day. The heart of those who are in the shrine are happy. Prayer or divinatory time: throughout the day.

Day 13 (26 June): A holiday because of the defending of the son of Osiris ... back of the portal by Set. Prayer or divinatory time: throughout the day.

Day 14 (27 June): Establishing her (Isis) seat and hail ... on the first occasion on this day. Prayer or divinatory time: dawn.

Day 15 (28 June): Do not do anything. Do not go out on any road on this day ... Going Forth of Re on it (i.e. this day) to propitiate Nun [Re's father] ... in his cavern in front of his followers and the Ennead of the mesektet-barque on this day. Prayer or divinatory time: throughout the day.

Day 16 (29 June): Give water to those who are in the Underworld ... Ennead of the West. It is pleasant to your father and mother who are in the necropolis (refers to all male and female predecessors). A day for honouring the Ancestors. Prayer or divinatory time: do not observe – not a suitable day.

Day 17 (30 June): If you see anything, it will be good on this day. Prayer or divinatory time: do not observe – not a suitable day.

Day 18 (1 July): Do not go out at the time of the morning (dawn). Prayer or divinatory time: at dawn and in the afternoon.

Day 19 (2 July): Celebrate your feast of your god. Prayer or divinatory time: dawn.

Day 20 (3 July): Do not kill a 'nkyt-reptile on this day. It is the day of the cleaning and revision of the noble ones. There is silence because of it on earth in order to propitiate the Wedjet-eye on this day. The beginning of the 'dog days' – noted from ancient times as the hottest period in the year and one of the three New Year festivals. The day is sacred to Wedjet. Prayer or divinatory time: dawn.

Day 21 (4 July): If you see anything, it will be good on this day. Prayer or divinatory time: in the afternoon.

Day 22 (5 July): The feast of Anubis who is on his mountain on this day. The children of Geb and Nut spend the day in festivity, which is a holiday after the good bath of the gods on this day. Prayer or divinatory time: in the afternoon.

Day 23 (6 July): Do not taste bread or beer on this day. A day of fasting. Prayer or divinatory time: dawn.

Day 24 (7 July): Make abt-offerings to the gods in the presence of Re. Make a holiday in your house. Prayer or divinatory time: dawn.

Day 25 (8 July): The god is established in front of the crew of Re who is happy. The sun god is currently at his highest and most powerful (i.e. dangerous). Prayer or divinatory time: do not observe – not a suitable day.

Day 26 (9 July): Do not go out at midday. The gods sail with the winds ... Do not go out of your house. Prayer or divinatory time: in the afternoon.

Day 27 (10 July): Do not do anything on this day. Prayer or divinatory time: throughout the day.

Day 28 (11 July): Feast of Min. If you see anything, it will be good on this day. Prayer or divinatory time: throughout the day.

Day 29 (12 July): Holiday in the temple of Sokar, in the estate of Ptah, and those who are in this estate are in great festivity, being healthy. Prayer or divinatory time: throughout the day.

Day 30 (13 July): Anything which comes forth on it [i.e. this day] in the estate of Ptah will be good. Anything (or offering), any rite, or anybody on this day, it is good throughout the year. Sing and offer much. Prayer or divinatory time: in the afternoon.

The Five Epagomenal or Unlucky Days

The Egyptian year was divided into twelve months of thirty days each, which means that each year was about five days short of the astronomical year. To compensate for this difference, five extra days were added to the year, called epagomenal days. Because they were not part of the normal year created by the gods, the Egyptians regarded these days as particularly ominous, and texts have survived listing exactly what may and may not be done during this period.

> The Great Ones (wrw) are born. As for the great ones ('aw) whose forms are not mysterious, beware of them. Their occasion (or deed) will not come ... They have proceeded ... the birth of Osiris, birth of Haeoeris [Horus the Elder], birth of Set, birth of Isis, birth of Nephthys. As to anyone who knows the name of the five epagomenal days, he does not hunger, he does not thirst [both conditions were feared in the underworld], Bastet [other translations mention Sekhmet] does not overpower him. He will not enter into the great law court, he will not die through an enemy of the king and will not die (or, depart) through the pestilence of the year. But he will last every day (till) death arrives, whereas no illness ill take possession of him. As to him who knows them, he will be prosperous within him, his speech is important to listen to in the presence of Re.

Major Celebrations

This point of high summer was the time of widespread disease, illness, and pestilence, which was attributed to the 'arrows of Sekhmet' and so the people would wear amulets of her image for protection. These five days that divided the old year from the new were considered unlucky since they were the birth days of the Children of Nut, who were continuously quarrelling and attempting to murder each other. The prayers were to be spoken in an attempt to pacify the divine wrath.

> Make for thyself an amulet as protection about the neck for the five epagomenal days in the name of the gods on the day and know the words to be recited over a figure of Osiris, of Horus, a figure of Set, and the female figure of Isis, the female figure of Nephthys, drawn on choice pakt-linen and placed around a man's neck ... As for him who knows the names of the five epagomenal days, he will not fall on any bad or evil things; he shall not hunger; he shall not thirst. Bastete shall not overpower him, fighting shall not overpower the birth of Osiris ... of this earth, the beneficent one who is lamented in the entire land in Egypt.

There were Festivals of Light at the New Year and on the five epagomenal days that led up to it. One these days, the birthdays of Osiris, Horus, Set, Isis, and Nephthys were celebrated and lights were placed in tombs for the dead.

> Turn back, O that enemy, death and so on when descending in the five epagomenal days. If you depart, you will not come to me for you will find Osiris, the Ruler of the West, and Thoth. Behold, that is the enemy of this land, that enemy death, and so on. May their bones be smitten. May their corpses be annihilated in the five epagomenal days. May they save me from all bad things or evil things.

First Day: The Birth of Osiris – 14 July
Second Day: The Birth of Horus – 15 July
Third Day: The Birth of Set – 16 July
Fourth Day: The Birth of Isis – 17 July
Fifth Day: The Birth of Nephthys – 18 July

Words to be said after dark when the Epagomenal Days are completed on the fifth day:

> Hail to you! O great ones according to their names, children of a goddess who have come forth from the sacred womb, lords because of their father, goddesses because of their mother, without

knowing the necropolis. Behold, may you protect me and save me. May you make me prosperous, may you make protection, may you repeat and may you protect me. I am the one who is on their list.

This is an abridged version of the *Egyptian Book of Days*, originally published in Mélusine Draco, *The Atum-Re Revival* (Axis Mundi Books, 2012).

Afterthought

Even throughout this predominantly 19th Dynasty version of the *Book of Days*, there remain scattered references to the old stellar cult, which had still not been entirely suppressed by later religious developments. Nut, 'Lady of the Starry Heavens', still protected the ancestral dead, her star-spangled body painted on the ceilings of tombs, inside coffins, and depicted in sacred writings. Set, in his own inimitable way, was still causing mayhem; while the heroic Horus (the Elder) continued to hold sway in a more subtle, earth-bound capacity. Strangely enough, these three powerful deities re-emerged at the dawning of the twentieth century as the principal players in Aleister Crowley's *Book of the Law*.

The mistake that is often made in assimilating modern magic with Egypt's ancient past, however, is that too many outside (or alien) influences are allowed to creep into the equation. Egypt's stellar cult, as much as it may have influenced *subsequent* thinking down through the centuries, was not influenced by anything other than the home-spun philosophy of the indigenous gods of the early Nile people, with all its attendant symbolism. From that very early period, the astronomer-priesthood 'not only understood astronomical science so well that they recognised the precession of the equinoxes, but also that they founded every aspect of their civilisation upon a star-orientated, religio-mystic culture derived from such knowledge' (*The Land of the Fallen Star Gods*). But let us pass the baton to George St Clair for a moment:

> The basis of the Egyptian Religion was Astronomy and the Calendar; the Divine Order in the heavens suggesting the rule for the life of man ... the men who framed this system had ceased to be savages and had attained to considerable knowledge in observational astronomy. They may have received an inheritance of custom and fancy from savage ancestors, and continued to use the language and ideas of it to some extent, but a higher revelation had come to them through the study of the stars. Hence the early

astronomers became priests, and the religion of mankind was lifted to a higher platform than that of mere animism.

(Creation Records)

We may search for evidence of Egypt's stellar cult in the writings of later civilisations, but this will always be a drastically diluted affair. One the other hand, it is unwise to view Egypt as the 'fount of all wisdom', and harbour a belief that subsequent or parallel cultures were magically or scientifically inferior. As we now realise, the social, religious, and magical elements of Egyptian life were inextricably interwoven, and therefore it is impossible to view any aspect of one without the others. But, by the time the indigenous stellar cult had been wholly integrated within the developing solar cult during the pyramid-building era, Egypt itself was on the brink of social and religious revolution. The stellar priesthood went into the shadows... but this did not necessarily mean that the cult disappeared completely, since there *is* evidence of it persisting, albeit as part of the Inner Mysteries, right up until the advent of the Ramesside family of the 12th Dynasty (Mélusine Draco, *The Atum-Re Revival*).

In *The Setian*, Billie Walker-John reveals how, hundreds of years after the end of the Pyramid Age, the Ramesside dynasty brought about a 'Setian revival' following the ascent of Seti I to the throne. The family are believed to have been descendants of a Set priest from an area where this indigenous god had long been worshipped: Seti I's birth name means 'He of the god Set' and he retained his Set-name throughout his reign. If Seti I were the only king to show Setian leanings, the Setian revival could be dismissed as wishful thinking... but this was not the case.

If his father's references to the ancient Mysteries were veiled, Ramesses II was much more up-front about his family's association with Egypt's oldest god. It was Ramesses the Great who brought Set worship out into the open and paid homage to his own ancestors who had preserved the ancient Mysteries of the Set-Horus psychopomps, as we can see from the famous statue in the Cairo Museum. It also confirms that the worship of Set was still an important and integral part of the Mysteries, which spanned over 3,000 years of continuous loyalty from an 'inner' or underground priesthood. This priesthood kept those Mysteries alive despite civil unrest, religious upheaval, invading armies, foreign rule, and the adverse publicity of having their god turned into a reviled assassin by a rival cult.

The threads of ancient Egyptian influence that have woven their way through Western civilisation are many and varied. The continuity of the religion and the revival of the Hermetic Tradition remind us of the antiquity of certain elements within Christian liturgies and beliefs, which connect Western beliefs with something much older. Gnosis, one of the chief forms of syncretism in late classical antiquity, drew on every area of culture in its day, including the

Iliad and the *Odyssey* – and continued to do so throughout its history. It was a colourful mixture of various religious elements, which lives on today in theosophy and anthroposophy.

In other words, these are coherent and consistent threads running through the story of the Egyptian Revival in Western Europe from Classical times to the present day, not to mention the revival emerging later in America. As Dr Curl points out in *The Egyptian Revival*:

> The influence was absorbed into Graeco-Roman culture and later into European civilisation as a whole. During the Renaissance the Mysteries of Hermes Trismegistus re-emerged in Gnosticism and the 'Rosicrucian Enlightenment'. And while the richness of Marian symbolism within the Roman Catholic church clearly owes much to the cult of the Egyptian goddess Isis, the Christian religion itself kept alive many other aspects of Egyptian culture.

The interest in Egyptian ideas and objects often increased after some spectacular discovery – such as the *Mensa Isiaca* (or Bembine Tablet) or the Rosetta Stone. Drawings, paintings, and a developing appreciation of antiquity brought Egyptian motifs to a wider public throughout Europe. Nevertheless, from Classical times, through the Renaissance to the eighteenth century, to the revival period after the Napoleonic campaign, the nineteenth century continued with buildings, furniture, jewellery, etc., offering thousands of variations in the style; and with travel on the increase for the Victorians, strong Egyptian elements also crept into the paintings and literature of the time. By the twentieth century, even cinemas and factories acquired the 'Nile style' veneer under the guise of Art Deco architecture – Egyptomania was here to stay.

No matter how we may think otherwise, we have to accept the fact that the splendour of Egyptian design and the simplicity of basic Egyptian architectural forms suggest something of an eternal truth and an ageless serenity. A newly discovered awareness of the persistence of Egyptian ideas in religion, art, and iconography creates fresh and enlightening perspectives. There *is* a sense of continuity from this ancient land.

As Michael Rice observes in *Egypt's Legacy*: 'to understand why Egypt exercised so profound an appeal to the imagination of men living in antiquity and why it has continued to do so over the past 4,000 years of the history of what was to become the Western world, it may be helpful to turn aside from the more ordered recital of Egypt's history.'

In his exploration of the ancient Egyptian psyche, Rice acknowledges that:

> Egypt features frequently in Carl Jung's writings, in various contexts, and that much more directly than Sigmund Freud, he

seems to have understood that there was a deep and very special stratum of experience underlying the familiar stereotype of 'Ancient Egypt'.

Jung demonstrated that the concept of the collective unconscious explains many of the less rational or otherwise inexplicable apprehensions and motivations of the human psyche at its most profound level. In the pristine society which was Egypt it is possible to see the influences of the collective unconscious at work in ways quite different from the experience of later cultures. The collective unconscious is the fountain from which the archetypes flow. The collective unconscious in Egypt is as powerful and pristine a phenomenon as the society itself.

(Egypt's Legacy)

Hopefully, by using the writings of others more experienced and scholarly than myself, it will enable more readers to understand those ancient gods of Egypt in their proper time and context. During the 2,000 years during which Egypt flourished to an extent unequalled by any other ancient society, it bequeathed to us a multitude of deities that are today instantly recognisable to anyone, with only a fleeting interest in history, anywhere in the world.

Sources and Bibliography

Taking a leaf out of Aleister Crowley's book, it is always a good move to go from each respected author to those that have been quoted in the text or bibliography:

> It established a rational consecution in my research; and as soon as I reached a certain point the curves became re-entrant, so that my knowledge acquired a comprehensiveness which could never have been so satisfactorily attained by any arbitrary curriculum. I began to understand the real relation of one subject to another…

This technique often takes us to valuable out-of-print volumes that contain material not to be found repeated *ad nauseam* on the internet and this in turn, gives our own reading and writing a sense of newness and fresh insight.

Adams, Barbara and Krzyszsztof M. Cialowicz, *Protodynastic Egypt* (Shire, 1988)
Betro, Maria Carmela, *Hieroglyphics: The Writings of Ancient Egypt* (Abbeville, 1995)
Bunson, M., *The Encyclopedia of Ancient Egypt* (Gramercy Books, 1999)
Clayton, Peter A., *Chronicles of the Pharaohs* (Thames & Hudson, 1994)
Dolnick, Edward, *The Writing of the Gods: The Race to Decode the Rosetta Stone* (Scribner, 2021)
Draco, Mélusine, *Starchild* (Ignotus Press, 2000)
Draco, Mélusine, *The Atum-Re Revival* (Axis Mundi Books, 2012)
Draco, Mélusine, *The Egyptian Book of Days* (Ignotus Press, 2001)
Draco, Mélusine, *Thrice Great Thoth* (Ignotus Press, 2021)
Draco, Mélusine, *Liber Ægyptius* (Ignotus Press, 1999)
El-Sabban, Sherif, *Temple Festival Calendars of Ancient Egypt* (Liverpool University Press, 2000)
Emery, W. B., *Archaic Egypt* (Pelican, 1985)
Faulkner, R. O., *The Ancient Egyptian Pyramid Texts* (Oxford University Press, 1969)
Coffin Texts, Vols. I–III (Arris & Philips, 1973)

Sources and Bibliography

Book of the Dead (British Museum Press, 1985)
Gardiner, Sir Alan, *Egyptian Grammar* (Griffith Institute, 1976)
Hamlyn, Paul, *Egyptian Mythology* (Hamlyn, 1965)
Jacq, Christian, *Egyptian Magic* (Arris & Philips, 1985)
Jeffereys, David G., *The Survey of Memphis: The Archaeological Report* (Egypt Exploration Society, 1985)
Lange, Kurt and Max Hirmer, *Egypt* (Phaidon, 1956)
Murray, Margaret, *Egyptian Temples* (Sampson Low, 1931)
Murray, Margaret, *The Splendour That Was Egypt* (Sidgewick & Jackson, 1963)
Meeks, Demitri and Christine Favard-Meeks, *Daily Life of the Egyptian Gods* (Murray, 1993)
Nunn, John F., *Ancient Egyptian Medicine* (British Museum Press, 2002)
Rice, Michael, *Egypt's Making* (Routledge, 1990)
Rice, Michael, *Egypt's Legacy* (Routledge, 1997)
Rice, Michael, *Power of the Bull* (Routledge, 1998)
Schwabe, Calvin W., Joyce Adams and Carleton T. Hodge, 'Egyptian Beliefs about the Bull's Spine: An Anatomical Origin for Ankh', *Anthropological Linguistics*, Vol. 24, no. 4 (1982), pp. 445–479.
Shafer, Byron E. (ed.), *Temples of Ancient Egypt* (Tauris, 2005)
Shaw, Ian (ed.), *The Oxford History of Ancient Egypt* (Oxford University Press, 2000)
Shaw, Ian and Paul Nicholson, *The British Museum Dictionary of Ancient Egypt* (British Museum Press, 1995)
St Clair, George, *Creation Records* (David Nut, 1898)
Pinch, Geraldine, *Egyptian Magic* (British Museum Press, 1994)
Pinch, Geraldine, *Egyptian Mythology: A Guide to the Gods, Goddesses, and Traditions of Ancient Egypt* (Oxford University Press, 2004)
Van Ryneveld, Maria M., *The Presence and Significance of Khepri in Egyptian Religion and Art* (University of Pretoria South Africa, 2013)
Walker-John, Billie, *The Setian* (Ignotus Press, 2003)
Wells, Ronald A., *Astronomy Before the Telescope* (British Museum Press, 1996)
Wilkinson, Richard H., *The Complete Temples of Ancient Egypt* (Thames & Hudson, 2000)
Wilkinson, Richard H., *The Complete Gods & Goddesses of Ancient Egypt* (Thames & Hudson, 2017)
Wilkinson, Toby A. H., *Early Dynastic Egypt* (Routledge, 1999)
Wilson, Hilary, *People of the Pharaohs* (Brockhampton, 1997)

Acknowledgements

Most of the books listed in the Sources and Bibliography can also be considered as 'recommended further reading', with grateful acknowledgement given to *Encyclopedia Britannica*; Wikipedia; Ian Shaw and Paul Nicholson's *The British Museum Dictionary of Ancient Egypt*; *World History Encyclopaedia*; *The Oxford History of Ancient Egypt*; *Temple Festival Calendars of Ancient Egypt* by Sherif El-Sabban at El-Minia University; Geraldine Pinch's *A Guide to the Gods, Goddesses, and Traditions of the Ancient Egyptians: A Theological Encyclopedia* (https://henadology.wordpress.com/theology/netjeru).

With a special appreciation to Paul Hamlyn's *Egyptian Mythology* (1965), based on the text translated by Delano Ames from *Mythologie Générale Larousse* (first published by Auge, Gillon, Holliere-Larousse, Moreau & Cie), which was the first serious book on Egyptology I bought myself, and which remains, in my opinion, the best title on the subject and a favourite reference source.

Also, to those both living and now departed for various and sundry extracts over the years, discussions and information that contributed in one way or another to this book, I would like to thank the following: Michael Rice, Geraldine Pinch, Abbeville Press, Dimitri and Christine Meeks, and last but certainly not least, University College London – Digital Egypt (www.ucl.ac.uk/museums-static/digitalegypt/religion/dailycult.html).